NICHO

C000066347

GUIDE TO THE

severn, avon
& birmingham

Also available:

Nicholson Guide to the Waterways

1. **Grand Union, Oxford & the South East**
3. **Birmingham & the Heart of England**
4. **Four Counties & the Welsh Canals**
5. **North West & the Pennines**
6. **Nottingham, York & the North East**
7. **River Thames & the Southern Waterways**
8. **Scotland – the Highland and Lowland Waterways**

Nicholson Inland Waterways Map of Great Britain

Published by Nicholson
An imprint of HarperCollins*Publishers*
77–85 Fulham Palace Road
Hammersmith, London W6 8JB

www.collins.co.uk
www.collinsbartholomew.com

First published by Nicholson and Ordnance Survey 1997
Reprinted 1998
New edition published by Nicholson 2000, 2003
Reprinted 2003
Copyright © HarperCollins*Publishers* Ltd 2003

This product uses map data licensed from Ordnance Survey® with the permission of the Controller of Her Majesty's Stationery Office.
© Crown copyright 1999. All rights reserved.

Ordnance Survey is a registered trade mark of Ordnance Survey, the national mapping agency of Great Britain.

The representation in this publication of a road, track or path is no evidence of the existence of a right of way.

Post Office (PO) is a trade mark of Post Office Limited in the UK and other countries.

Researched and written by David Perrott and Jonathan Mosse.
Designed by Bob Vickers.

The publishers gratefully acknowledge the assistance given by British Waterways and their staff in the preparation of this guide.

Grateful thanks is also due to the Environment Agency and members of the Inland Waterways Association, CAMRA representatives and branch members.

Photographs reproduced by kind permission of Derek Pratt Photography.

Printed in Hong Kong.

ISBN 0 00 713665 X
RJ11690 03/4/53.5

The publishers welcome comments from readers. Please address your letters to:
Nicholson Guides to the Waterways, HarperCollins Reference,
HarperCollins Publishers, Westerhill Road, Bishopbriggs, Glasgow, G64 2QT or
email nicholson@harpercollins.co.uk

Wending their quiet way through town and country, the inland navigations of Britain offer boaters, walkers and cyclists a unique insight into a fascinating, but once almost lost, world. When built this was the province of the boatmen and their families, who lived a mainly itinerant lifestyle: often colourful, to our eyes picturesque but, for them, remarkably harsh. Transporting the nation's goods during the late 1700s and early 1800s, negotiating locks, traversing aqueducts and passing through long narrow tunnels, canals were the arteries of trade during the initial part of the industrial revolution.

Then the railways came: the waterways were eclipsed in a remarkably short time by a faster and more flexible transport system, and a steady decline began. In a desperate fight for survival canal tolls were cut, crews toiled for longer hours and worked the boats with their whole family living aboard. Canal companies merged, totally uneconomic waterways were abandoned, some were modernised but it was all to no avail. Large scale commercial carrying on inland waterways had reached the finale of its short life.

At the end of World War II a few enthusiasts roamed this hidden world and harboured a vision of what it could become: a living transport museum which stretched the length and breadth of the country; a place where people could spend their leisure time and, on just a few of the wider waterways, a still modestly viable transport system.

The restoration struggle began and, from modest beginnings, Britain's inland waterways are now seen as an irreplaceable part of the fabric of the nation. Existing canals are expertly maintained while long abandoned waterways, once seen as an eyesore and a danger, are recognised for the valuable contribution they make to our quality of life, and restoration schemes are integrating them back into the network.

This series of guides offers the most comprehensive coverage of Britain's inland waterways, all clearly detailed on splendid Ordnance Survey® maps. Whether you are boating, walking, cycling or just visiting, these books will give you all the information you need.

▌CONTENTS

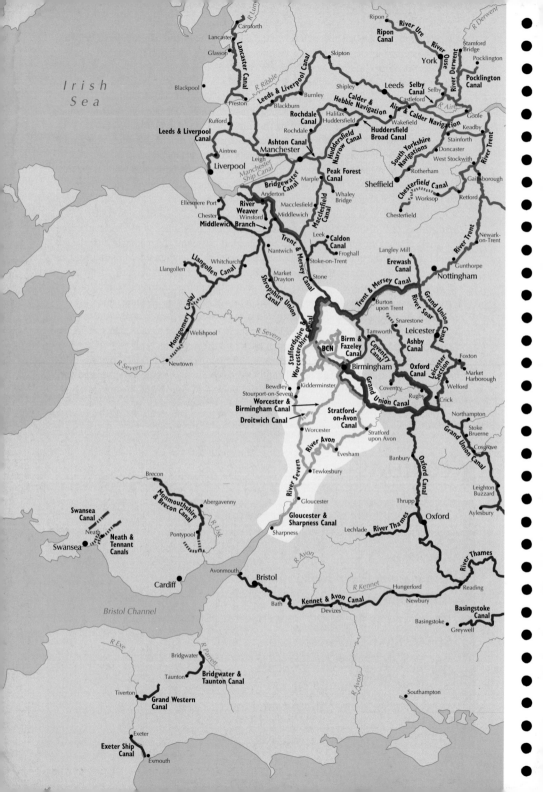

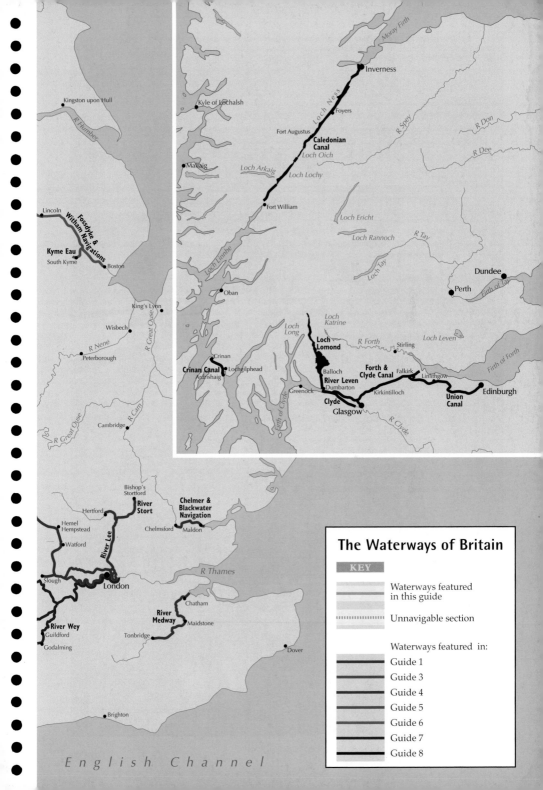

The Waterways of Britain

KEY

Waterways featured in this guide

Unnavigable section

Waterways featured in:

Guide 1
Guide 3
Guide 4
Guide 5
Guide 6
Guide 7
Guide 8

*Gloucester Docks, Gloucester & Sharpness Canal (*see page 76)

GENERAL INFORMATION FOR WATERWAYS USERS

The slogan 'Waterways For All' was coined to take account of the wide diversity of people using the inland waterways for recreation.

Today boaters, walkers, fishermen, cyclists and gongoozlers (on-lookers) throng our canals and rivers, to share in the enjoyment of a quite amazing waterway heritage. British Waterways (BW), along with other navigation authorities, is empowered to develop, maintain and control this resource in order to maximise its potential. It is to this end that a series of guides, codes, and regulations have come into existence over the years, evolving to match a burgeoning – and occasionally conflicting – demand. Set out below are key points as they relate to everyone wishing to enjoy the waterways. Please see the inside front cover for details on how to contact British Waterways.

LICENSING – BOATS

The majority of the navigations covered in this book are controlled by BW and are managed on a day-to-day basis by local Waterway Offices. Waterway Managers are detailed in the introduction to each waterway. All craft using BW waterways must be licenced and charges are based on the length of the craft. This licence covers all navigable waterways under BW's control and in a few cases includes reciprocal agreements with other waterway authorities (as indicated in the text). BW and the Environment Agency now offer an optional Gold Licence which covers unlimited navigation on the waterways of both authorities. Permits for permanent mooring on the canals are also issued by BW. For further information contact BW Customer Services. You can download licence fees and charges and an application form from the BW website.

BW and the Environment Agency operate the Boat Safety Scheme, setting technical requirements for good and safe boat-building practice. A Boat Safety Certificate or, for new boats, a Declaration of Conformity, is necessary to obtain a craft licence. For powered boats proof of insurance for Third Party Liability for a minimum of £1,000,000 is also required. Further details from BW Customer Services. Other navigational authorities relevant to this book are mentioned where appropriate.

LICENSING – CYCLISTS

Not all towpaths are open to cyclists. This is because many stretches are considered to be too rough or narrow, or because cyclists are considered to cause a risk to other users. Maps on the BW website show which stretches of towpath are open to cyclists, and local offices can supply more detailed information relevant to their area. A cycle permit is required (except on the Caledonian and Crinan Canals), and this is available free of charge (except for the Kennet & Avon Canal, where a charge is made) from BW Customer Services.

When using the towpath for cycling, you will encounter other towpath users, such as fishermen, walkers and boaters. The Waterways Code gives advice on taking care and staying safe, considering others and helping to look after the waterways.

TOWPATHS

Few, if any, artificial cuts or canals in this country are without an intact towpath accessible to the walker at least. However, on river navigations towpaths have on occasion fallen into disuse or, sometimes, been lost to erosion. Considerable efforts are being made to provide access to all towpaths, with some available to the disabled. Notes on individual waterways in this book detail the supposed status of the path, but the indication of a towpath does not necessarily imply a public right of way or mean that a right to cycle along it exists. Maps on the BW website show all towpaths on the BW network, and whether they are open to cyclists. Motorcycling and horse riding are forbidden on all towpaths.

INDIVIDUAL WATERWAY GUIDES

No national guide can cover the minutiae of individual waterways and some Waterway Managers produce guides to specific navigations under their charge. Copies of individual guides (where they are available) can be obtained from the Waterway Office detailed in the introduction. Please note that times – such as operating times of bridges and locks – do change year by year and from winter to summer.

STOPPAGES

BW works hard to programme its major engineering works into the winter period when demand for cruising is low. It publishes a *National Stoppage Programme* and *Winter Opening Hours* leaflet which is sent out to all licence holders, boatyards and hire companies. Inevitably, emergencies occur necessitating the unexpected closure of a waterway, perhaps during the peak season. You can check for stoppages on individual waterways between specific dates on the BW website. Details are also announced on lockside noticeboards and on Canalphone (*see* inside front cover).

STARTING OUT

Extensive information and advice on booking a boating holiday is available on the BW website. Please book a waterway holiday from a licenced operator – only in this way can you be sure that you have proper insurance cover, service and support during your holiday. It is illegal for private boat owners to hire out their craft. If in doubt, please contact BW Customer Services. If you are hiring a canal boat for the first time, the boatyard will brief you thoroughly. Take notes, follow their instructions and *don't be afraid to ask* if there is anything you do not understand. BW have produced a short video giving basic information on using a boat safely. Copies of the video, and the *Boater's Handbook*, are available free of charge from BW Customer Services. Sections of the *Boater's Safety Toolkit* can also be downloaded from the internet, *see* www.aina.org.uk.

GENERAL CRUISING NOTES

Most canals are saucer-shaped in section so are deepest at the middle. Few have more than 3–4ft of water and many have much less. Keep to the centre of the channel except on bends, where the deepest water is on the outside of the bend. When you meet another boat, keep to the right, slow down and aim to miss the approaching craft by a couple of yards: do not steer right over to the bank or you are likely to run aground. If you meet a loaded commercial boat keep right out of the way and be prepared to follow his instructions. Do not assume that you should pass on the right. If you meet a boat being towed from the bank, pass it on the outside. When overtaking, keep the other boat on your right side.

A large number of BW facilities – pump outs, showers, electrical hook-ups and so on – are operated by pre-paid cards, obtainable from BW regional offices; local waterways offices (*see* introductions to individual navigations); lock keepers and some boatyards within the region. Cards are available in £5, £6, £10 and £15 denominations. Please note that if you are a weekend visitor, you should purchase cards in advance.

Speed

There is a general speed limit of 4 mph on most BW canals. This is not just an arbitrary limit: there is no need to go any faster and in many cases it is impossible to cruise even at this speed: if the wash is breaking against the bank or causing large waves, slow down.

Slow down also when passing moored craft, engineering works and anglers; when there is a lot of floating rubbish on the water (and try to drift over obvious obstructions in neutral); when approaching blind corners, narrow bridges and junctions.

Mooring

Generally speaking you may moor where you wish on BW property, as long as there is sufficient depth of water, and you are *not causing an obstruction*. Your boat should carry metal mooring stakes, and these should be driven firmly into the ground with a mallet if there are no mooring rings. Do not stretch mooring lines across the towpath. Always consider the security of your boat when there is no one aboard. On tideways and commercial waterways it is advisable to moor only at recognised sites, and allow for any rise or fall of the tide.

Bridges

On narrow canals slow down and aim to miss one side (usually the towpath side) by about 9 inches. *Keep everyone inboard when passing under bridges*, and take special care with moveable structures – the crew member operating the bridge should be strong enough and heavy enough to hold it steady as the boat passes through.

Tunnels

Make sure the tunnel is clear before you enter, and use your headlight. Follow any instructions given on notice boards by the entrance.

Fuel

Hire craft usually carry fuel sufficient for the rental period.

Water

It is advisable to top up daily.

Lavatories

Hire craft usually have pump out toilets. Have these emptied *before* things become critical. Keep the receipt and your boatyard will usually reimburse you for this expense.

Boatyards

Hire fleets are usually turned around on a Saturday, making this a bad time to call in for services. Remember that moorings at popular destinations fill quickly during the summer months, so do not assume there will be room for your boat. Always ask.

LOCKS AND THEIR USE

A lock is a simple and ingenious device for transporting your craft from one water level to another. When both sets of gates are closed it may

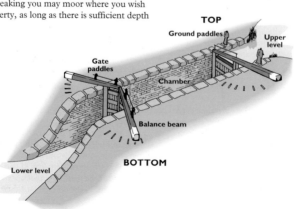

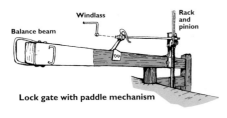

Lock gate with paddle mechanism

Labels: Windlass, Rack and pinion, Balance beam

be filled or emptied using gate or ground paddles at the top or bottom of the lock. These are operated with a windlass.

General tips

- Make safety your prime concern. *Keep a close eye on young children.*
- Always take your time, and do not leap about.
- Never open the paddles at one end without ensuring those at the other end are closed.
- Never drop the paddles – always wind them down.
- Keep to the landward side of the balance beam when opening and closing gates.
- *Never* leave your windlass slotted onto the paddle spindle – it will be dangerous should anything slip.
- Keep your boat away from the top and bottom gates to prevent it getting caught on the gate or the lock cill.
- Be wary of fierce *top gate* paddles, especially in wide locks. Operate them slowly, and close them if there is *any* adverse effect.
- Always follow the navigation authority's instructions, where these are given on notices or by their staff.

PLANNING A CRUISE

Many a canal holiday has been spoiled by trying to go too far too fast. Go slowly, don't be too ambitious, and enjoy the experience. Note that mileages indicated on the maps are for guidance only.

A *rough* calculation of time taken to cover the ground is the lock-miles system:

Add the number of *miles* to the number of *locks* on your proposed journey, and divide the resulting figure by three. This will give you a guide to the number of *hours* it will take. But don't forget your service stops (water, shopping, pump out), and allow plenty of time to visit that special pub!

TIDAL WATERWAYS

The typical steel narrow boat found on the inland waterways system has all the seagoing characteristics of a bathtub, which renders it totally unsuitable for all-weather cruising on tidal estuaries. However, the more adventurous will inevitably wish to add additional 'ring cruises' to the more predictable circuits within the calm havens of inland Britain. Passage is possible in most estuaries if careful consideration is given to the key factors of weather conditions, tides, crew experience, the condition of the boat and its equipment and, perhaps of overriding importance, the need to take expert advice.

In many cases it will be prudent to employ the skilled services of a local pilot. Within the text, where inland navigations connect with a tidal waterway, details are given of sources of both advice and pilotage. It is also advisable to inform your insurance company of your intention to navigate on tidal waterways as they may very well have special requirements or wish to levy an additional premium. This guide is to the inland waterways of Britain and therefore recognizes that tideways – and especially estuaries – require a different approach and many additional skills. We therefore do not hesitate to draw the boater's attention to the appropriate source material.

GENERAL

Most inland navigations are managed by BW or the Environment Agency, but there are several other navigation authorities responsible for smaller stretches of canals and rivers. For details of these, contact the Association of Inland Navigation Authorities at www.aina.org.uk or BW Customer Services. The boater, conditioned perhaps by the uniformity of our national road network, should be sensitive to the need to observe different codes and operating practices. Similarly it is important to be aware that some waterways are only available for navigation today solely because of the care and dedication of a particular restoration body, often using volunteer labour and usually taking several decades to complete the project. This is the reason that, in cruising the national waterways network, additional licence charges are sometimes incurred. The introduction to each waterway gives its background history, details of recent restoration (where relevant) and also lists the operating authority.

BW is a public corporation, responsible to the Department of Environment, Food and Rural Affairs and, as subscribers to the Citizen's Charter, they are linked with an ombudsman. BW has a comprehensive complaints procedure and a free explanatory leaflet is available from Customer Services. Problems and complaints should be addressed to the local Waterway Manager in the first instance – the telephone number is listed in the introduction to individual waterways.

The Inland Waterways Association campaigns for the 'conservation, use, maintenance, restoration and development of the inland waterways', through branches all over the country. For more information contact them at PO Box 114, Rickmansworth, WD3 1ZY, telephone 01923 711114, fax 01923 897000, email iwa@waterways.org.uk or visit their website at www.waterways.org.uk.

BRITISH WATERWAYS EMERGENCY HELPLINE

Emergency help is available from BW outside normal office hours on weekdays and throughout weekends via British Waterways' Emergency Helpline (*see* inside front cover). You should give details of the problem and your location.

Fladbury Mill (see *page 19*)

▌RIVER AVON

MAXIMUM DIMENSIONS

Length: 70'
Beam: 13' 6" (reducing on Upper Avon)
Draught
– Lower Avon: 4'
– Upper Avon: 3'
Headroom
– Lower Avon: 10' (at normal river levels)
– Upper Avon: 8' (at normal river levels)

Lower Avon Navigation Trust
(Tewkesbury to Evesham Lock tail)
Mill Wharf, Mill Lane, Wyre Piddle,
Pershore, Worcs. WR10 2JF
01386 552517; claire.lant@netway.co.uk

Upper Avon Navigation Trust
(Evesham Lock tail to Alveston Sluice)
Bridge 63, Harvington, Evesham, Worcs.
WR11 5NR.
01386 870526
The Upper Avon/Lower Avon boundary is
the tail of Evesham Lock and Weir.

MILEAGE
Avon Lock, TEWKESBURY to:
Pershore Lock: 14$\frac{1}{2}$ miles
Evesham Lock: 25$\frac{3}{4}$ miles
Bidford Bridge: 32$\frac{1}{4}$ miles
Tramway Bridge, STRATFORD: 42$\frac{1}{4}$ miles
Alveston Sluice: 45$\frac{1}{2}$ miles
Locks: 17

Rising at Welford on the Leicestershire and Northampton boundary and joining the River Severn at Tewkesbury, the River Avon was first made navigable to Stratford by William Sandys of Fladbury during the period 1635-9, with authority to extend eventually to Warwick, Coventry and beyond.

In 1717 the ownership of the river was split into the Upper and Lower Avon, the dividing line being the tail of Evesham Weir. Following several changes in ownership, the upper river was purchased by the OWW Railway in 1856. By refusing tolls they avoided the obligation to maintain the river and as a result within ten years it was in a ruinous state. By 1875 all traffic on the Upper Avon had ceased.

Although deteriorating gradually, the Lower Avon did remain navigable to Pershore until it was bought, for £1500, by C.D. Barwell OBE in 1950. At this time the Lower Avon Navigation Trust was formed and restoration began, with navigation being restored to the Bridge Inn, Offenham by June 1964. In July of that year, the southern section of the Stratford-on-Avon Canal from Kingswood Junction to Stratford was also re-opened, making the restoration of the Upper Avon the next logical step. But with no right of access to the river, a non-effective navigation authority, all but three of the weirs collapsed and the locks in complete ruin, it seemed an all but impossible task.

The Upper Avon Navigation Trust was formed in 1965 and in 1969, under the leadership of David Hutchings MBE, work began. An appeal was made to raise £375,000 and eventually over a third of this sum was given by one anonymous donor. Despite enormous difficulties, the upper river was officially opened by HM Queen Elizabeth the Queen Mother on 1 June 1974. A truly magnificent achievement for private initiative and volunteer labour.

CRUISING ON THE AVON

This is a river navigation, and as such can present problems to those more accustomed to the still waters of the canals. On the Lower Avon just 36 hours of summer rain can put sufficient fresh water into the river to make passage difficult – the pull upstream of the weirs increases, cross-currents below the weirs become fierce and the water piles up as it rushes through narrow bridge-holes. However an efficient warning system now operates and floods have been handled without serious incident for many years. *See* page 13 for general navigational details.

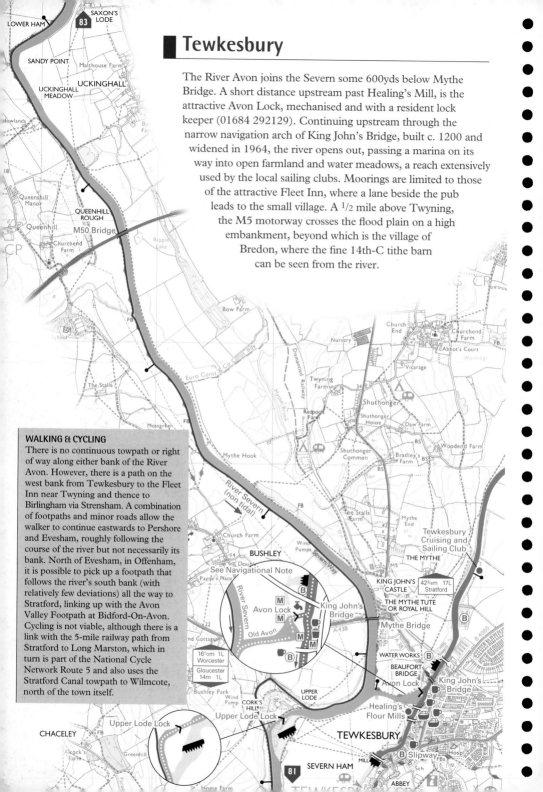

Tewkesbury

The River Avon joins the Severn some 600yds below Mythe Bridge. A short distance upstream past Healing's Mill, is the attractive Avon Lock, mechanised and with a resident lock keeper (01684 292129). Continuing upstream through the narrow navigation arch of King John's Bridge, built c. 1200 and widened in 1964, the river opens out, passing a marina on its way into open farmland and water meadows, a reach extensively used by the local sailing clubs. Moorings are limited to those of the attractive Fleet Inn, where a lane beside the pub leads to the small village. A $1/2$ mile above Twyning, the M5 motorway crosses the flood plain on a high embankment, beyond which is the village of Bredon, where the fine 14th-C tithe barn can be seen from the river.

WALKING & CYCLING

There is no continuous towpath or right of way along either bank of the River Avon. However, there is a path on the west bank from Tewkesbury to the Fleet Inn near Twyning and thence to Birlingham via Strensham. A combination of footpaths and minor roads allow the walker to continue eastwards to Pershore and Evesham, roughly following the course of the river but not necessarily its bank. North of Evesham, in Offenham, it is possible to pick up a footpath that follows the river's south bank (with relatively few deviations) all the way to Stratford, linking up with the Avon Valley Footpath at Bidford-On-Avon. Cycling is not viable, although there is a link with the 5-mile railway path from Stratford to Long Marston, which in turn is part of the National Cycle Network Route 5 and also uses the Stratford Canal towpath to Wilmcote, north of the town itself.

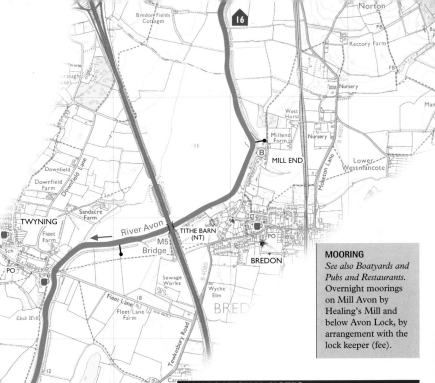

16

MOORING

See also Boatyards and Pubs and Restaurants. Overnight moorings on Mill Avon by Healing's Mill and below Avon Lock, by arrangement with the lock keeper (fee).

BOAT TRIPS

Pride of Avon sails from Riverside Walk, Tewkesbury on private charter trips and evening supper cruises. Telephone (01684) 275906 or visit www.telstarcruisers. co.uk for further details.

Telstar Cruisers Riverside Walk, Tewkesbury (01684 294088; www. telstarcruisers.co.uk) hire open launches, day boats and 27' cruisers *by the hour or day.* They also operate the Kingfisher Ferry from Tewkesbury to the Riverside pub at Twyning *Easter–Sep.* Charge.

NAVIGATIONAL NOTES

1 The River Avon is a unique navigation in terms of both its nature and the structures thereon. In spring and autumn water levels can fluctuate dramatically while the locks, weirs and bridges are, in most cases, the product of history, painstaking restoration, ingenuity and continuing loving care. The Lower Avon Navigation Trust is self-funding and can ill-afford to put right damage that results from carelessness or ignorance. To this end they publish *Gateway to the Avon*: an essential, detailed guide to the responsible use of the waterway (*see* address on page 11).

2 Craft entering the Avon from the Severn should be wary of a shallow spit projecting south west from the north bank at the junction of the two rivers. When approaching from upstream on the Severn, do not cut the corner but steer close to the south side of the junction. Craft leaving the Avon and wishing to proceed upstream on the Severn should not turn north until Mythe Bridge can be seen in its entirety.

3 The Avon Lock is operated by a resident lock keeper – do not disturb him outside his usual operating times, which are as for Evesham Lock on page 23. When entering the Avon from the lock, and when passing through the navigation arch of King John's Bridge, visibility is restricted, and great care should be taken.

Boatyards

Ⓑ **Tewkesbury Marina** Bredon Road, Tewkesbury (01684 293737; www.tewkesbury-marina.co.uk). 🚽 🚰 ⚓ P D E Pump out, gas, overnight mooring, long-term mooring, winter storage, gantry, chandlery, books and maps, boat sales, toilets, showers, solid fuel.

● **Tewkesbury**

Glos. All services. A historic town at the junction of the rivers Avon and Severn, with many attractive and ancient buildings to see, chief among these being, of course, the abbey. One of the more unusual aspects of Tewkesbury is the great number of tiny alleys leading off the main street that is the backbone of the town. These alleys yield tempting views of discreet cottages, gardens, back walls and private yards. One of these – Baptist Chapel Court – leads to the old chapel, built around 1655. This tiny, simple building and its little burial ground reflect well the modest aspirations of the minority Baptist movement. There are many other buildings of great interest throughout Tewkesbury, chiefly of the half-timbered variety, with overhanging gables. Some have curious names like House of the Nodding Gables and Ancient Grudge. There is also a liberal scattering of historic pubs, notably the Hop Pole Inn (associated with Dickens' *Pickwick Papers*) and the Bell hotel, an Elizabethan building which was Abel Fletcher's home in the book *John Halifax, Gentleman.*

Tewkesbury Abbey This superb building is cathedral-like in proportions and is generally reckoned to be one of the finest Norman churches in the country. It is contemporary with Gloucester Cathedral, and has the same type of vast cylindrical arches the length of the nave. This massive scale is repeated throughout the building: the beautifully decorated central tower, 46ft square and over 130ft high, is the largest Norman tower in existence. The recessed arch that frames the mighty west window is over 60ft high. The abbey's interior is no less splendid than the exterior, and contains interesting monuments, notably the Despencer and Beauchamp tombs. The abbey, which was completed c.1120, was part of a Benedictine monastery until this was threatened with dissolution by King Henry VIII in 1539. The townspeople bought the Abbey – for £453 – to save it from demolition, and it became the town's parish church. *Open all year Sun 07.30–19.00: summer, Mon–Sat 07.30–18.00; winter Mon–Sat 07.30–17.30 (16.30 on winter Sat).* The Abbey Shop (01684 276655), situated within the Abbey, sells all manner of gifts and souvenirs and is *open 09.30–17.00. Daily* guided tours of the abbey and on *summer Sun* some parties are taken up the tower. For further details contact Visitors Officer on (01684) 850959 or visit www.tewkesburyabbey.org.uk.

The Abbey Cottages Church Street. The most unusual buildings in Tewkesbury must surely be the row of medieval shops near the abbey. These 25 cottages were rescued from dereliction and threatened demolition when it was realised that they are unique in this country. As built, in about 1450, they were made of wattle and daub in a heavy timber framework. The ground floor consisted of trodden earth, the windows had no glass, and there was no chimney in the roof – the smoke from the fireplace escaped through a hole under the eaves. The shutters covering the big window facing the street folded down to form a shop counter. One of the houses has been restored to this original state and may be visited; the others have been modified to provide pleasantly discreet modern houses. This restoration won a Civic Trust award.

Abbey Gatehouse Church Street, Tewkesbury. Another worthy building, rescued by the Landmark Trust and given a new lease of life as holiday accommodation. For details of how to become a temporary gate keeper, telephone (01628) 825925/825920 or visit www.landmarktrust.co.uk.

Cascades Leisure Pool Tewkesbury (01684 293740). The usual mix of water-based fun.

Croft Farm Leisure and Water Park, Bredon's Hardwick, Tewkesbury (01684 772321). Follow track and footpath south east from the bank opposite Twyning. Canoe, windsurfing and sailing facility offering tuition and hire of craft, wetsuits and buoyancy aids. *Open Mar–Oct, daily 09.00–18.00 (or later); Nov–Feb weekends only.* Fishing and a wide variety of birdlife. Clubhouse and shop. Charge.

John Moore Countryside Museum 41 Church Street, Tewkesbury (01684 297174). Established in the memory of a local conservationist, the museum features a wide range of indigenous animals and birds, hand tools, wildlife sculptures, temporary exhibitions and live animal days. Set in a delightful 15th-C timber-framed merchant's cottage and garden. Shop. *Open Apr–Oct, Tue–Sat and B Hols 10.00–13.00 and 14.00–17.00.* Charge. Not suitable for wheelchair users.

30 & 32 St Mary's Lane Tewkesbury. Rare survivors of framework knitters' cottages from a previous era of prosperity within the town. Stocking makers worked at home at frames lit by the long, airy windows on the first floor. The quality of the construction of these houses suggests that the living was a decent one. These represent another rescue on the part of the Landmark Trust and a means by which the visitor can linger longer in the town. Details as per Abbey Gatehouse.

Roses Theatre Sun Street, Tewkesbury (01684 295074/290734; arts@rosestheatre.org). Lively focus for the arts in Tewkesbury offering a mix of music, theatre, cinema and workshops for all ages and tastes.

Tewkesbury Museum Barton Street (01684 295027). A small museum in a delightfully irregular timber-framed house. Displays of local history, costumes and furniture. Also a large model of the Battle of Tewkesbury. *Open Easter–early Oct, daily 10.00–13.00 and 13.30–16.30 (Sun and B Hols 13.30–15.30).* Charge.

Barton Fair takes place in Tewkesbury *9–10 Oct every year,* except when that date falls on a Sunday. A hop fair and one of the oldest in the country, it used to be held at the monastery gate.

Battle of Tewkesbury 4 May 1471 The penultimate battle in the Wars of the Roses, fought to the south of the town, where the Lancastrians, under Queen Margaret's commanders Somerset, Wenlock and Devonshire were defeated by Edward IV's Yorkists under Edward, Gloucester and Hastings.

Tourist Information Centre 64 Barton Street, Tewkesbury (01684 295027; www. visitcotswoldsandsevernvale.gov.uk). *Open Mon–Sat 09.00–17.00 all year; Sun and B Hols 10.00–16.00 Easter–Oct.*

● **Twyning**
Glos. PO, tel.

● **Bredon**
Worcs PO, tel. A substantial and attractive village with many fine timbered buildings. Close to the river is a 14th-C tithe barn (NT, *open Apr–Oct,* charge), 124ft long and once one of the best preserved in the country, where grain – paid as taxes to the church – was stored. Severely damaged by fire, it has now been rebuilt. The Church of St Giles has a vaulted Norman porch, and dates from c.1180 – it was mentioned by John Masefield in 'All the land from Ludlow Town to Bredon Church's spire'. Bredon Hill, which dominates the river for several miles, rises to 961ft some 3 miles to the north east – it is said that eight or more counties can be seen from its summit on a fine day. On the southern slope is an 18th-C castellated folly, Bell's Castle, and on the top is a 2nd-C BC hill fort containing Parson's Folly, a prominent tower built in the late 18th C. The hill was celebrated in A. E. Housman's *A Shropshire Lad.*

Pubs and Restaurants

There are many pubs and hotels in Tewkesbury, including:

✇ ✗ **The Bell** 52 Church Street, Tewkesbury (01684 293293). 12th-C inn opposite the abbey, complete with 500-year-old wall carvings, serving real ale. Bar snacks and a full restaurant menu (V) available *all day, every day.* Children welcome *until 20.30;* dogs welcome in bar and lounge area only. Garden. B & B.

✇ **The Berkeley Arms** 8 Church Street, Tewkesbury (01684 293034, kemp@ berkeleyarms.freeserve.co.uk). 17th-C pub, free from machines, offering a warm welcome, good beer and good food (V) *L and E (not Thur or Wed E in winter).* Children must be over 14 if not eating. Dogs welcome in front bar. Regular *Sat* music nights. Traditional pub games. B & B. *Open all day.*

✇ **The Olde Black Bear** High Street, Tewkesbury (01684 292202). In existence since 1308 and said to be the oldest inn in Gloucestershire. Real ale and bar meals (V) served in a dining area that was once stables *L and E, daily.* Family room and riverside garden. Moorings. *Open all day.*

✇ **The White Bear** Bredon Road, Tewkesbury (01684 296614). An excellent selection of real ales dispensed in a basic single-bar pub. Real draught cider and traditional pub games. Children welcome and children's games available. Garden. *Open all day.*

✇ **The Royal Hop Pole Hotel** On the Mill Avon, near Abbey Mill (01684 293236). Restaurant *E and Sun L.* Bar meals (V) *L and E, daily.* Rotating guest ales. Children's menu. Mooring by arrangement. B & B.

✇ **The Fleet Inn** Fleet Lane, Twyning (01684 274310). Busy, friendly pub dispensing real ale together with food (V) *all day until 21.30* in both bar and restaurant (booking advisable). Children welcome. Riverside with gardens. Overnight mooring for patrons. Live music *Fri and Sat.*

✇ **The Village Inn** Twyning Green (01684 293500). Real ales and food (V) available *L and E, daily (except L Mon and Tue all year, and Sun E in winter).* Children welcome. Garden.

✇ **The Cross Keys Inn** Bredon's Hardwick (01684 772626). Follow track and footpath south east on bank opposite Twyning. Real ale served in a friendly one-roomed village local. Bar snacks *(not Sun).* Garden and children's play area.

✇ **The Royal Oak Inn** Main Road, Bredon (01684 772393; royaloak@btopenworld.com). A traditional old coaching inn serving real ale. Bar meals (V) available *L and E (not Sun and Mon E).* Children welcome. Patio. Traditional pub games. B & B.

✇ **The Fox & Hounds** Bredon (01684 772377). Thatched 15th-C inn dispensing real ale. Restaurant and bar meals (V) available *L and E, daily.* Children welcome. Garden.

Eckington

The river is wide to Strensham Lock and is used extensively by the unusually named Severn Sailing Club. Below the lock a pipe bridge carries the Coventry Water Main over the navigation, and beyond this the weir spills into the river, creating a very strong cross current when there is fresh water in the river. The river now starts to meander around Eckington village, passing under a railway bridge carrying the main Exeter to Newcastle-upon-Tyne line before reaching Eckington Bridge, a many-arched and irregular 16th-C structure still in good condition. Above the bridge, the river meanders beside the ever-present Bredon Hill, turning a full 180 degrees at the Swan's Neck. Nafford Lock adjoins the wilderness of Nafford Island, a nature reserve, and a path leads from here to Birlingham, 1 mile to the north west. The swing bridge across the lock must be left closed on leaving. The path over the sluice leads to Eckington, Woollas Hall and Great Comberton but, alas, there are no moorings by the lock, the next being those at Comberton Quay. The village of Nafford was obliterated some 300 years ago by a landslide on Bredon Hill. There is little to see from the river until Pershore.

● **Strensham**
Worcs. Birthplace of Samuel Butler (1612–80), verse satirist and secretary to Judge Thomas Jeffrey, who lived in the 16th-C house by the well-sited Church of St Philip and St James, which has a painted gallery and two fine brasses of the Russells, once the Lords of the Manor. The key is kept at the farm.

● **Eckington**
Worcs. PO, tel, stores, butcher. A dormitory village of little interest except for Holy Trinity Church, which dates from the 12th C, and three pubs. Walk from Strensham Lock or Eckington Bridge.

Woollas Hall A mile south of Nafford Lock. Elizabethan manor house with a three-storey porch, now divided into flats. Beyond the hall a track climbs to the summit of Bredon Hill.

Great Comberton
Worcs. Tel. One of the timeless small villages which surround Bredon Hill – Little Comberton, Bricklehampton and especially Elmley Castle, with its half-timbered cottages and Church of St Mary containing fine 17th-C monuments, are worth visiting.

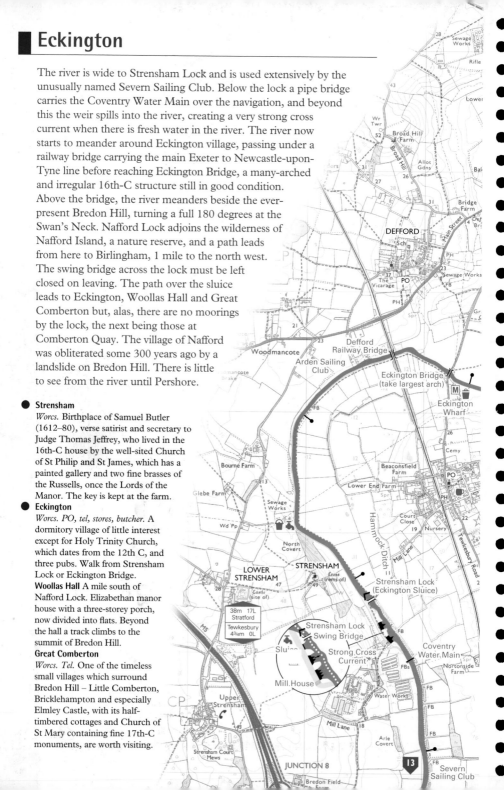

JUNCTION 8

13

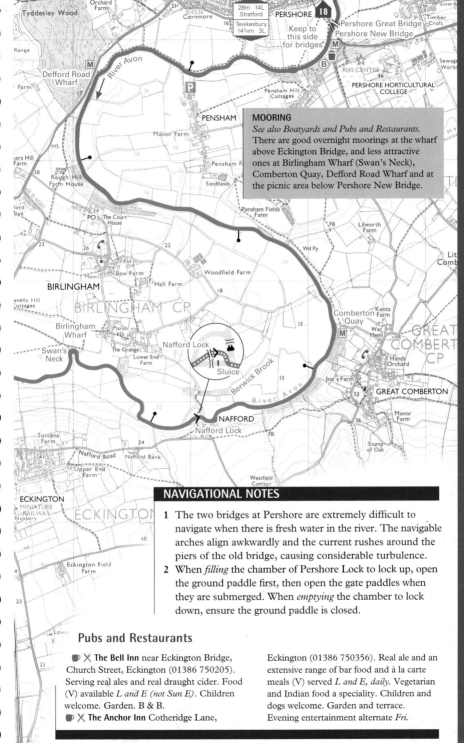

MOORING

See also Boatyards and Pubs and Restaurants. There are good overnight moorings at the wharf above Eckington Bridge, and less attractive ones at Birlingham Wharf (Swan's Neck), Comberton Quay, Defford Road Wharf and at the picnic area below Pershore New Bridge.

NAVIGATIONAL NOTES

1 The two bridges at Pershore are extremely difficult to navigate when there is fresh water in the river. The navigable arches align awkwardly and the current rushes around the piers of the old bridge, causing considerable turbulence.

2 When *filling* the chamber of Pershore Lock to lock up, open the ground paddle first, then open the gate paddles when they are submerged. When *emptying* the chamber to lock down, ensure the ground paddle is closed.

Pubs and Restaurants

The Bell Inn near Eckington Bridge, Church Street, Eckington (01386 750205). Serving real ales and real draught cider. Food (V) available *L and E (not Sun E)*. Children welcome. Garden. B & B.

The Anchor Inn Cotheridge Lane, Eckington (01386 750356). Real ale and an extensive range of bar food and à la carte meals (V) served *L and E, daily*. Vegetarian and Indian food a speciality. Children and dogs welcome. Garden and terrace. Evening entertainment alternate *Fri*.

Wyre Piddle

The reach between the locks at Pershore and Wyre Piddle is the shortest on the navigation, being just 1 mile. Wyre Mill, called by the traveller Charles Showell 'the ugliest, of which the Avon is ashamed', is now a sailing and social club. The lock is diamond-shaped, the last of its kind on the river. Approaching from downstream the weir creates a strong cross current, especially after prolonged rain. Pump out facilities are available in the weir stream above the lock. Wyre Piddle (the Piddle Brook runs behind the village) spreads around the outside of a wide bend, with gardens down to the river, and the Anchor Inn provides a useful mooring for patrons. The villages then skirt the flood plain of the Avon, and there is little to see except for the wild life – those interested in herons

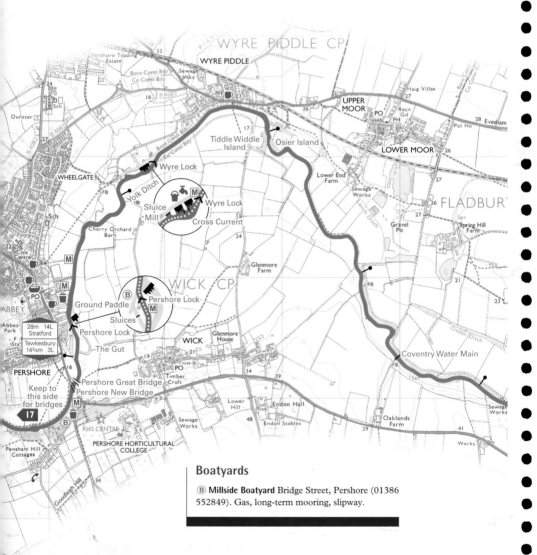

Boatyards

Ⓑ **Millside Boatyard** Bridge Street, Pershore (01386 552849). Gas, long-term mooring, slipway.

will be particularly pleased. Beyond the Coventry Water Main Bridge the village of Cropthorne sits on higher ground to the south east. Below Jubilee Bridge are the remains of the last flash lock on the river, dismantled in 1961. The approach channel below Fladbury Lock is extremely narrow and steep sided, with restricted vision. The lock walls narrow towards the base and this should be borne in mind when two craft lock down together. The beautiful Fladbury Mill overlooks the weir – it was in use as recently as 1930, and ferry wires, *difficult to see from upstream*, stretch across the weir stream. On the north side, beyond the railway bridge carrying the main London to Worcester line, is Evesham golf course. Above Craycombe Turn are extensive woodlands, while to the south lie the inevitable water meadows, with few buildings or roads near the river. There is another handsome mill at Chadbury Lock, which was restored in 1952–3, the first major project carried out by the Lower Avon Navigation Trust, who were helped by the Royal Engineers.

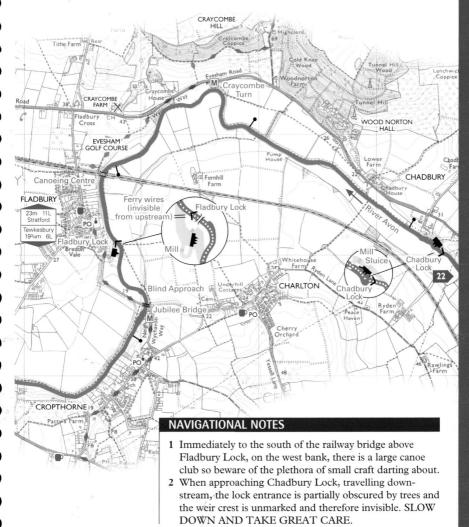

NAVIGATIONAL NOTES

1 Immediately to the south of the railway bridge above Fladbury Lock, on the west bank, there is a large canoe club so beware of the plethora of small craft darting about.

2 When approaching Chadbury Lock, travelling downstream, the lock entrance is partially obscured by trees and the weir crest is unmarked and therefore invisible. SLOW DOWN AND TAKE GREAT CARE.

NAVIGATIONAL NOTES

1 All the locks on the river are wide locks, and those on the Upper Avon once demonstrated considerable ingenuity in the recycling of gates and paddle gear from other canals and rivers – as a consequence some of the locks were difficult to operate, and required a good deal of physical strength. Since 1995 all locks have new gear and have been re-gated.

2 Those accustomed to the cosy informality and go as you please atmosphere of the narrow canals will find more restrictions on the river. There is no continuous towpath and, therefore, no right to land and moor as one pleases. Many villages are sited back from the river, away from the floods, and the scenery is generally that of quiet water meadows with prolific bird life.

3 The Lower and Upper Navigation Trusts are charities relying, in some instances, on volunteers. Boat crews can help them to keep down their costs by observing their rules and requests. They should also be acquainted with the relevant by-laws, and ensure that their craft is equipped with such items as an anchor made off to a chain and warp, a bow fender and so on.

4 Remember that sailing clubs operate on the river and on meeting a sailing boat maintain a fixed speed and a steady course on the right-hand side of the channel. Maximum speed (over the bed of the river) – 6 mph downstream and 4 mph upstream.

5 Watch out for anglers, and slow down.

6 Keep off private land and well away from weirs. Slow down when approaching locks or blind corners – especially through bridges.

7 Moor only at recognised sites, moor economically, and be prepared to breast up (moor side-by-side) where this does not obstruct traffic. Moorings – marked [M] on the maps – can be limited at the height of the season.

MOORING

See also Pubs and Restaurants. The recreation ground moorings above Pershore Lock are convenient for the town, and thus very popular. There are also limited moorings below the lock and at the picnic area downstream of the new bridge. There are overnight moorings in the weir stream at Wyre Lock and at Craycombe Turn. Moorings are also available below Jubilee Bridge upon payment of a fee to the landowner living at Riverdale, on the east bank.

● **Pershore**

Worcs. All services and swimming baths by the river. A busy market town with many well-kept Georgian buildings, set among fruit farms and market gardens. The fine 6-arched 14th-C bridge over the Avon no longer carries traffic – a 3-arched structure built in 1928 now takes the load. The abbey, now the Parish Church of Holy Cross, was built on the site of a wooden building erected in AD689 by King Oswald. This was replaced in AD983 by a new building commissioned by Ethelwold, and again by a later Norman building, finally consecrated in 1239. In 1288 a fire destroyed part of the Abbey (and a large part of the town) resulting in much rebuilding before the dissolution in 1539. Restoration was by Scott 1862–5. Of the original Norman building, the nave, crossing and transepts survive. The Church of St

Andrew, very close by, is now a community centre. Perrott House in Bridge Street was built in 1760 by George Perrott, when he purchased the Lower Avon Navigation.

● **Wyre Piddle**

Worcs. Stores (at garage). A main road village with no public mooring. The church has a Norman chancel arch and font, and an Early English bellcote.

● **Cropthorne**

Worcs. An attractive village of thatch and timbers on the Spring blossom route. Much local fruit and vegetable produce is sold from small roadside stalls in this area.

● **Charlton**

Worcs. Stores.

● **Fladbury**

Worcs. Stores, garage. A picturesque village of half-timbered houses and cottages around a square, once the home of William Sandys, who began making the Avon navigable in 1636. The Church of St John Baptist has a fine 14th-C rib-vaulted porch and contains some fine brasses to John Throckmorton and his wife. About 1 mile to the north east is Craycombe House, built c.1791 by George Byfield for George Perrott and later restored by the author Francis Brett Young, who lived here from 1932 until he went to South Africa after World War II.

Craycombe Farm Old Worcester Road, Fladbury (01386 860732). Just north of Fladbury and Evesham golf course. Country shop selling fresh fruit and vegetables, local ciders and perries, traditional country wines and home-made cakes and preserves. Craft workshops. Gift shop. *Open daily all year.*

Wyre Piddle Micro-Brewery High Grove Farm, Pinvin, Pershore (01905 841853). North west of the Anchor Inn. Well known for its 'Piddle in the Hole' ale (amongst others of a less risqué parentage) this brewery uses the traditional English full mash system comprising hot liquor tank, mash tun, copper and three fermenting vessels. If you don't wish to purchase your ale by the barrel then take a container of your choice. *Open 07.00–16.00 Mon–Fri.*

Wood Norton Above the north bank below Chadbury Lock. Once the seat of the Duc d'Aumale and later the Duc d'Orleans, pretender to the throne of France, it now houses an engineering school run by the BBC, who have built some incongruous modern buildings to accompany the mansion.

Pubs and Restaurants

The Queen Elizabeth West Side, Main Street, Elmley Castle (01386 710209). Named after its famous visitor of 1575. Real ale, pub games and open fires. No children. Garden and camping.

The Miller's Arms Bridge Street, Pershore (01386 553864). Bustling pub patronised by the town's younger clientele, dispensing real ale. Food (V) *L, also E in summer.* Garden. *Monthly* folk nights.

The Angel Inn Pershore (01386 552046). Real ale and bar meals (V) served *L and E, daily.* Children welcome. Riverside garden and moorings by arrangement. B & B.

The Brandy Cask Pub and Brewery 25 Bridge Street, Pershore (01386 552602). Opposite Pershore Lock. Pershore's only free house – totally machine-free. Serving real ale together with bar and à la carte restaurant meals. Children welcome in award winning riverside garden in summer; likewise dogs. Open fires in the winter. Annual beer festival *Aug B Hol.* and *regular* live music. Mooring by arrangement.

The Star Inn Bridge Street, Pershore (01386 552704; info@thestarinnpershore.co.uk). Real ales in Pershore's oldest hostelry. Bar snacks and restaurant meals (V) available *L and E (restaurant closed Oct–Easter and Sun in summer).* Well-behaved children and dogs welcome. Riverside garden. Mooring by arrangement. B & B.

The Anchor Inn Wyre Piddle (01386 552799). A good selection of real ale served in a 17th-C pub. Home-made bar snacks and restaurant meals (V) available *L and E, daily.* Fish a speciality. Children welcome, as are dogs on a lead. Large riverside garden and the only mooring for the village.

The New Inn Main Road, Cropthorne (01386 860347). Real ales and an enticing selection of home-made food (V) using home-grown produce, served *L and E daily.* Children and dogs (in bars only) welcome. Large garden with children's play area.

The Anchor Fladbury (01386 860391; www.anchorinn.ukf.net). Overlooking the village green, this pub serves real ale together with inexpensive bar meals (V) *L and E (not Sun E or all day Mon).* Sunday lunches, steaks and home-made specials. Children welcome; dogs only on outside patio. Darts, crib and pool. *Monthly* musical entertainment.

The Gardener's Arms The Strand, Charlton (01386 860388). Real ales and meals (V) available *L and E (except Sun E or all day Mon).* Children welcome if eating. Garden.

Craycombe Farm Old Worcester Road, Fladbury (01386 860732). Just north of Fladbury and Evesham golf course. Home-made local food (V) for *breakfast, L and E (E by request).* Snacks and delicious cakes and puddings. Wines and bottled beers. Parties catered for.

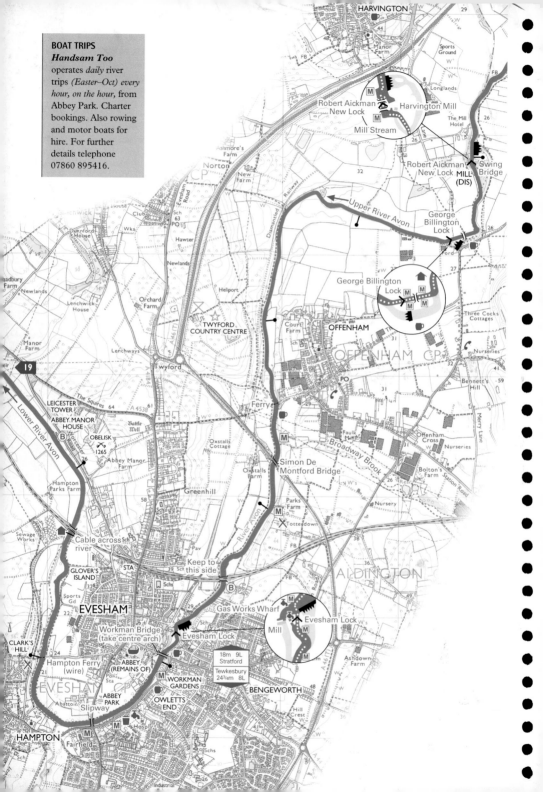

BOAT TRIPS
Handsam Too operates *daily* river trips *(Easter–Oct) every hour, on the hour,* from Abbey Park. Charter bookings. Also rowing and motor boats for hire. For further details telephone 07860 895416.

Evesham

Beyond Chadbury Lock, the river passes the Abbey Manor House and a boatyard, before passing through Evesham in a wide loop. There is a free, self-operated pump out on the west bank, immediately upstream of the railway bridge. Care should be taken approaching Hampton Ferry, where a wire stretches across the river – this will be lowered when the ferry man hears three long blasts of your hooter. Above the ferry to the west is Clarke's Hill, where the monks of Evesham once grew vines. Beyond the A435 road bridge the Abbey Public Park opens out to the north, with riverside gardens giving way to the borough and Trust moorings and Workman Gardens to the east, below the handsome Workman Bridge, built in 1856. After passing through the centre arch of the bridge, you will see the lock to the left past the old mill stream. This marks the boundary between the Lower and Upper Navigation. There is a resident lock keeper here (01386 446511), who lives in an unusual triangular house built in 1972 to span the chamber of an old sluice. He has a small shop and sells Lower Avon Navigation Trust licences. Lock open *Easter–Apr 09.00–18.00; May–Aug 09.00–20.00; Sep–Oct 09.00–1800; Nov–Easter – during this period the lock keeper may be absent but the lock is set for manual operation and crews of licensed boats may use it at any time.* There may be some slight variation in these times and dates, from year to year (*the lock keeper's lunch break extends from 13.00–14.00; last locking 12.45*). Hours may be extended, for a fee, by prior booking. Craft should keep well away from the weir above the lock, passing close to the boatyard on the opposite bank. The river is then once again in open country, entering the Vale of Evesham, a major fruit and vegetable growing area. George Billington Lock is the first of the new Upper Avon locks, built in the winter of 1969. The unusual flood-proof lock keeper's hut, the Offenham light, is a more recent addition. The new lock cut joins the river at right angles, and care should be exercised when rejoining the main course. Robert Aickman New Lock soon follows, overlooked by Harvington Mill and a newly constructed dry dock, disused since the turn of the century. The steep ridge of Cleeve Hill closes from the south to a virtual cliff at the water's edge below Cleeve Prior.

Boatyards

Ⓑ **Sankey Marine** Worcester Road, Evesham (01386 442338; hazel.hanlon@lineone.net). Below the Abbey Manor House. 🛠 D Gas, overnight mooring, long-term mooring, winter storage, slipway, chandlery, boat sales, engine repairs, crane, hull blasting and painting, toilets, showers. Restaurant and bar at *weekends*.

Ⓑ **Wyre Leisure Marine** 38 Waterside, Evesham (01386 860063/07831 434279). 🛠 E Gas, overnight mooring, long-term mooring, hoist, slipway, boat sales, boat servicing and repairs, winter storage, engine repairs (including outboards), DIY facilities,

hull blasting and blacking, boat transport. *Emergency call out.*

Ⓑ **Evesham Marina** Kings Road, Evesham (01386 48906; eveshammarina@hotmail.com). 🛠 D Pump out, gas, narrowboat hire, overnight mooring, long-term mooring, winter storage, slipway, crane (30 ton), boat sales, engine repairs, covered and heated wet dock, DIY facilities, books and maps.

Ⓑ **Heritage Boatbuilders** Kings Road, Evesham (01386 48882; www.heritageboatbuilders.co.uk). Located in Evesham Marina. Boat builders constructing a wide range of narrow and wide-beam boats for British and Continental waters.

THE LEAM LINK

For the past 25 years the Upper Avon Navigation Trust (UANT) has administered, financed, maintained and developed the river for the considerable benefit of the local community. It is, arguably, the most popular section of the Avon ring – made up of almost equal lengths of canal and river – and its charms and facilities are well documented in the *UANT Guide* (a copy of which can be obtained from their address on page 11).

To further enhance the value of the Upper Avon for its wide diversity of users, UANT have now published a proposal to construct a navigable link connecting the Grand Union Canal and the River Leam, between Leamington and Warwick. This scheme displays great sensitivity in its enhancement of a wide range of wildlife habitats, whilst at the same time providing increased leisure opportunities to walkers, fishermen, boaters and cyclists alike. The proposal makes imaginative use of natural features and materials to open up a water-way, not only as a potential link between existing river and canal systems but, just as importantly, as a series of environmentally-rich, managed and secure sites attracting wildlife to the River Leam.

The proposed structures – in the form of locks (four in total), islands, dams and bypass channels – are designed to create adjoining wetlands which will be complemented by a series of silt banks, reeds and sedges, hardwood copses and hedge planting. Thus birds, fish and mammals, either low in numbers or non-existent at present, will be attracted back to an area which the inevitable urban growth has gradually depleted.

In the initial phase of work, the plan is to connect the Grand Union Canal, east of Leamington Spa, with the River Leam via two locks. A further two locks along the river will be constructed to maintain navigable levels before the Leam meets the River Avon north of Warwick. This would, in turn, enable pleasure craft to access these two historic towns, providing attractive moorings. Longer term plans could encompass a scheme to improve the Upper Avon as a navigation between Warwick and Stratford-upon-Avon, thereby opening up a further wide range of leisure possibilities.

Abbey Manor House 1 mile above Chadbury Lock, on the north bank, c.1840. An obelisk in the grounds overlooks the site of the Battle of Evesham, 4 August 1265, when Simon de Montfort and his rebel barons were defeated by the Royalists under Prince Edward, resulting in some 4000 deaths. Another memorial, the Leicester Tower, built c.1840, is visible in the woodland.

● **Hampton**
Worcs. PO.

● **Evesham**
Worcs. All services including laundrette. A town which owes the major part of its prosperity to the fruit and vegetable growing in the Vale of Evesham – in the spring a mass of blossom, and in the autumn rich in local produce. All that remains of the once-important Benedictine abbey, founded in AD714 by Bishop Egwin and dissolved by Henry VIII in 1539, is the fine tim-bered gatehouse, a detached bell tower (1533) and a few ruins. Close by there are elegant Georgian buildings and half-timbered houses, Booth Hall (late 15th-C) being a fine example.

Close to the bell tower are two notable churches – St Lawrence (16th-C) and All Saints (12th-C). There is an annual regatta on *Spring Bank Holiday.*

Almonry Museum Abbey Gate, Evesham (01386 446944; tic@almonry.ndo.co.uk). 14th-C building, once the home of the Almoner at Evesham Abbey, it now houses artefacts, exhibitions and information detailing events from the rich history of the area. A superb example of Early English architecture with its warren of rooms. Attractive and peaceful garden. *Opening as per the Tourist Information Centre. Last admission 16.30.* Charge.

Arts Centre Victoria Avenue, Evesham (01386 45567). 300-seat theatre presenting music, drama, dance, etc during school term-time. Telephone (01386) 48883 for box office which is only open during events.

Evesham Country Park Twyford, Evesham (01386 41661; www.eveshamcountrypark. co.uk). Shopping and Garden Centre incorporating the Vale Wildlife Centre. Also restaurant and Visitor Centre. *Open Mon–Sat*

09.00–18.00 (17.30 winter) and Sun 10.30–16.30.

Evesham River Festival *Held annually over the second weekend in Jul.* Further details from the Tourist Information Centre.

Tourist Information Centre The Almonry Museum, Abbey Gate, Evesham (01386 446944; www.evesham.uk.com). *Open Mon–Sat 10.00–17.00 and Sun 14.00–17.00. Closed Sun Nov–Jan and over Xmas and New Year.* Guided walks around the town start from here *Easter–Sep, Tue and Sun 14.00.* Free.

● **Offenham**
Worcs. PO, tel, stores. Twelve centuries ago this was the headquarters of Offa, King of Mercia; today it is one of the few English villages to possess a maypole. The village has grown considerably, and of the original Church of St Mary and St Milburga only the tower remains.

● **Middle Littleton**
Worcs. Walk east from the Fish & Anchor Inn to see the tithe barn (NT, *open Apr–Oct,* charge) thought to have been built by John de Ombersley, Abbot of Evesham from 1367 to 1377. Nearby is the 17th-C manor house and St Nicholas's Church.

● **Harvington**
Worcs. PO, tel, stores. A typical half-timbered, black and white Worcestershire village.

MOORING
See also Boatyards and Pubs and Restaurants. Upstream of Abbey Bridge the waterside moorings on the right bank, provided by the Trust, are free as are the extensive borough moorings by Workman Gardens. Weir Meadow Caravan Park (01386 442417), between Workman Bridge and the lock, has overnight moorings (by prior arrangement) with full facilities for craft *up to 24ft long* above Evesham Lock (fee). There are free overnight moorings at George Billington Lock and Robert Aickman New Lock.

Pubs and Restaurants

✕ � **Raphaels** Hampton Ferry, Boat Lane, Evesham (01386 45460; www.hamptonferry.com). Licensed riverside café serving food (V) *08.00–23.00 daily during the season.* Breakfasts and bread puddings a speciality. Children welcome, as are dogs in riverside garden. Moorings.

▣ ✕ **The Northwick Arms Hotel** Waterside, Evesham (01386 40322; enquiries@ northwickarmshotel.co.uk). Intimate restaurant serving a wide-ranging à la carte and table d'hôte cuisine *E, daily.* Also Flacons Bar serving real ale together with food (V) *L and E, daily.* Children welcome. Garden. Moorings opposite, by arrangement. B & B.

▣ **The Green Dragon** Oat Street (off High Street), Evesham (01386 446337). Own-brew town-centre pub which serves real ale. Bar meals (V) *L and E (not Sun).* Children welcome if eating. Traditional pub games. Garden. Brewery tours by arrangement.

▣ **The Trumpet Inn** Merstow Green (off High Street), Evesham (01386 446227). A good selection of real ale dispensed in a welcoming pub serving bar meals (V) *L daily,* together with restaurant meals *E, Tue–Sat. Sunday* roasts. Children welcome. No-smoking room. Large garden and outside patio seating.

✕ � **Khayam Indian Restaurant** 13 Vine Street, Evesham (01386 47227). A worthwhile, Asian culinary experience *open daily, all year including B Hols.* Food available *L and E until midnight.* Takeaway service.

▣ ✕ **The Bridge Inn** Offenham (01386 446565). Riverside pub that also operates the local ferry. Real ale. Food (V) available *L and E, daily.* Children welcome. Riverside seating. Moorings.

▣ ✕ **The Fish & Anchor Inn** George Billington Lock, Offenham (01386 41094). Real ale in a spacious riverside pub. Restaurant and bar food available *L and E, daily.* Children welcome. Gardens and moorings. Gas can be purchased close by.

▣ ✕ **The Golden Cross** Harvington (01789 772420). Smart, comfortable modernised pub offering good value bar food *L and E, daily.* Restaurant open *E and Sun L.* As many as six guest real ales. Children welcome. Garden.

Bidford-on-Avon

The river now heads north away from Marcliff Hill, entering Warwickshire and approaching Bidford-on-Avon with its splendid old bridge. There is a new supermarket in the village. Proceeding upstream, craft should follow the narrower right-hand channel below Bidford Grange – there were once two mills and a lock here, but now nothing remains. Beyond is the new Pilgrim Lock, built in the winter of 1970. The navigation flows through attractive meadowland, and pleasant orchards announce the village of Welford-on-Avon and W.A. Cadbury Lock, completed in July 1971. The river meanders round the village, passing a fine Victorian house inappropriately adorned with a modern chimney, before the multi-arched Binton Bridges and the Four Alls pub are reached. Weston-on-Avon lies to the south on a very attractive stretch of deep water with many trees lining the banks.

Pubs and Restaurants

The Frog and Bulrush High Street, Bidford-on-Avon (01789 772369). Welcoming pub, responsible for funding the new public moorings at the bottom of its riverside gardens. Real ale. Food (V) is available *L and E* in both the restaurant and bar, *daily* (booking advisable for the restaurant, especially at *weekends*). Pub games. *Open all day in summer.*

The Cottage of Content Barton (01789 772279). Picturesque 15th-C pub, with a riverside garden and children's play area, dispensing real ales and bar and restaurant meals (V) *L and E, daily*. Dogs welcome in garden only. Karaoke *Sat*. Campsite.

The Four Alls Binton Bridges (01789 750228). Smart riverside pub and restaurant with a garden, serving a selection of real ale. Food (V) available *L and E, daily*. Children catered for. Camping and children's play area. Darts and dominoes. Overnight mooring by arrangement. (A similarly named pub, the Five Alls, is situated in Chepstow.).

The Bell Binton Road, Welford-on-Avon (01789 750353). Comfortable 17th-C beamed pub in the village centre with an attractive garden. Real ale together with an interesting and varied range of home-made food (V) available *L*

and *E, daily*. Children welcome. Attractive garden.

The Shakespeare Inn Chapel Street, Welford-on-Avon (01789 750443). Popular, friendly local dispensing real ale and bar meals (V) served *L and E*. Children's menu. Large garden.

NAVIGATIONAL NOTES

1 The downstream approach to IWA Lock can be shallow, particularly when turning into the lock cut.
2 The navigational channel under Bidford Bridge is through the southern-most arch.
3 On the sharp bend, west of Binton Bridges, the channel is in the centre of the river and not to the outside.

● **Cleeve Prior**
Worcs. PO, stores.
● **Bidford-on-Avon**
Warwicks. PO, stores, chemist, bank, off-licence, laundrette. The irregularly-arched bridge was built in 1482 by the monks of Alcester, near the site of a Roman ford which was finally removed in 1970. The village has an excellent delicatessen and bakery, selling a tempting array of home-made pies, which is to be found not far from the bridge.
● **Barton**
Warwicks. PO.
● **Welford-on-Avon**
Warwicks. PO, tel, stores, butcher, garage.

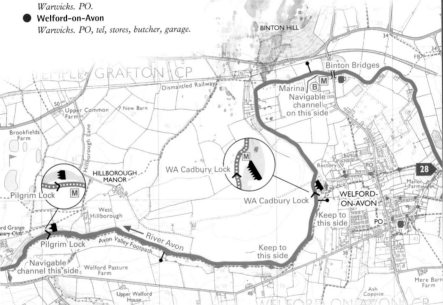

MOORING
See also Pubs and Restaurants. Overnight moorings are available, for a fee, at Abbots Salford Caravan Site (unfortunately on the opposite bank to Cleeve Prior), and at IWA Lock (free). The free public moorings at Bidford are very good, but limited in number. There is a single mooring available at Bell Court on the town side, and more at Bidford Boats, both for a fee. The Frog and Bulrush pub also has public moorings. Upstream, at Barton, there are free overnight moorings in the lock cut. There are also free overnight moorings at Pilgrim Lock, W.A. Cadbury Lock, Welford (no access to village), and below Binton Bridges (access to Welford) for a fee.

Boatyards

ⓑ **Bidford Boats** Riverside House, 4 The Pleck, Bidford-on-Avon (01789 773205; www.bidfordboats.co.uk). 🚿 🔧 Pump out, narrowboat hire, overnight mooring, long-term mooring, winter storage, 30ft slipway, boat sales and repairs, engine repairs and servicing, boat fitting out, DIY facilities.

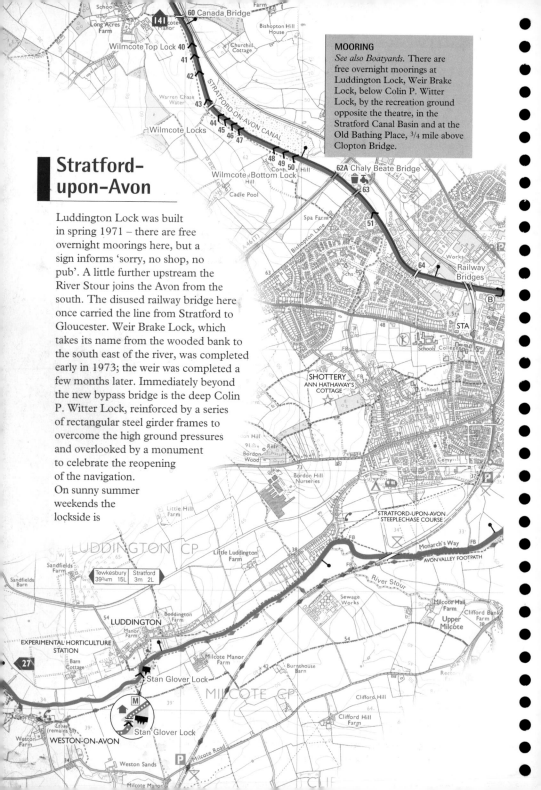

Stratford-upon-Avon

MOORING
See also Boatyards. There are
free overnight moorings at
Luddington Lock, Weir Brake
Lock, below Colin P. Witter
Lock, by the recreation ground
opposite the theatre, in the
Stratford Canal Basin and at the
Old Bathing Place, 3/4 mile above
Clopton Bridge.

Luddington Lock was built
in spring 1971 – there are free
overnight moorings here, but a
sign informs 'sorry, no shop, no
pub'. A little further upstream the
River Stour joins the Avon from the
south. The disused railway bridge here
once carried the line from Stratford to
Gloucester. Weir Brake Lock, which
takes its name from the wooded bank to
the south east of the river, was completed
early in 1973; the weir was completed a
few months later. Immediately beyond
the new bypass bridge is the deep Colin
P. Witter Lock, reinforced by a series
of rectangular steel girder frames to
overcome the high ground pressures
and overlooked by a monument
to celebrate the reopening
of the navigation.
On sunny summer
weekends the
lockside is

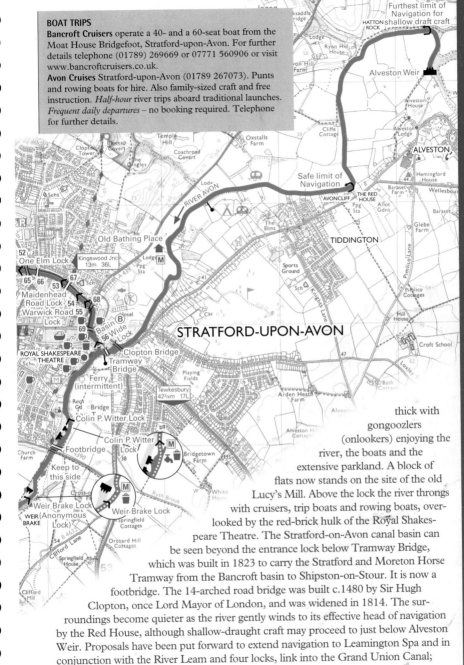

thick with gongoozlers (onlookers) enjoying the river, the boats and the extensive parkland. A block of flats now stands on the site of the old Lucy's Mill. Above the lock the river throngs with cruisers, trip boats and rowing boats, overlooked by the red-brick hulk of the Royal Shakespeare Theatre. The Stratford-on-Avon canal basin can be seen beyond the entrance lock below Tramway Bridge, which was built in 1823 to carry the Stratford and Moreton Horse Tramway from the Bancroft basin to Shipston-on-Stour. It is now a footbridge. The 14-arched road bridge was built c.1480 by Sir Hugh Clopton, once Lord Mayor of London, and was widened in 1814. The surroundings become quieter as the river gently winds to its effective head of navigation by the Red House, although shallow-draught craft may proceed to just below Alveston Weir. Proposals have been put forward to extend navigation to Leamington Spa and in conjunction with the River Leam and four locks, link into the Grand Union Canal; thereby completing the country's first, significant, wide-beam ring (*see* page 24).

NAVIGATIONAL NOTES

When approaching Weir Brake Lock coming downstream, keep to the south east side of the river and look out for the lock cut on your left.

● **Luddington**

Warwicks. It is thought that Shakespeare may have been married here, in a church now replaced by a more recent building.

● **Stratford-upon-Avon**

Warwicks. All services. Tourism has been established for a very long time in Stratford. It was in 1789 that the first big celebrations in William Shakespeare's honour were organised by the actor David Garrick. They are now held annually on St George's Day (23 April), which is believed to have been Shakespeare's birthday. An annual Mop Fair on 12 October reminds the visitor that Stratford was already well-established as a market town long before Shakespeare's time. Indeed the first grant for a weekly market was given by King John in 1196. Today, Stratford is well used to the constant flow of charabancs and tourists, ancient charm vying with the expected commercialism that usually mars popular places like this. There are wide streets of endless low, timbered buildings that house dignified hotels and antique shops; plenty of these are also private houses. On the river, hired punts and rowing boats jostle each other while people picnic in the open parkland on the banks. The Royal Shakespeare Theatre, opened in 1932, is a splendid institution on an enviable site beside the Avon, but the aesthetic appeal of its massive industrial style is limited. It was designed by Elizabeth Scott to replace an earlier theatre, destroyed by fire in 1926. More in keeping with the historic Shakespearian tradition is the delightful Swan Theatre, risen phoenix-like from the ashes of the original building, thanks to the exceptional generosity of a single benefactor – for a long time anonymous. Attached to the main building, this theatre has a simple charm echoing the 16th-C Globe Playhouse and, in most part, presenting plays written by contemporaries of Shakespeare.

Shakespeare Birthplace Trust Stratford-upon-Avon (01789 204016; www.shakespeare.org.uk). This Trust was founded in 1847 to look after the five buildings most closely associated with Shakespeare; four of these are in Stratford (listed below) and the other is Mary Arden's Cottage at Wilmcote (*see page 140*). Admission charge to each building. *The summer season is mid Mar–mid Oct. An all-inclusive ticket is available covering either the in-town properties, or all five Shakespeare Houses.*

Shakespeare's Birthplace Henley Street. An early 16th-C half-timbered building containing books, manuscripts and exhibits associated with Shakespeare and rooms furnished in period style. Gardens. Next door is the Shakespeare Exhibition. *Open late Mar–May and Sep–Oct, Mon–Sat 10.00–17.00, Sun 13.00–17.00; Jun–Aug Mon–Sat 09.00–17.00, Sun 09.30–17.00; Jan–late Mar and Nov–Dec Mon–Sat 10.00–16.00, Sun 10.30–16.00. Closed Xmas.*

Hall's Croft Old Town. A Tudor house complete with period furniture – the home of Shakespeare's daughter Susanna and her husband Dr John Hall, and . . .

New Place Chapel Street. The foundations of Shakespeare's last home set in a replica of an Elizabethan garden. *Open late Mar–May and Sep–Oct, Mon–Sat 11.00–17.00, Sun 11.00–17.00; Jun–Aug Mon–Sat 09.30–17.00, Sun 10.00–17.00; Jan–late Mar and Nov–Dec Mon–Sat 11.00–16.00, Sun 12.00–16.00. Closed Xmas.*

Anne Hathaway's Cottage Shottery, 1 mile west of Stratford (01789 292100). Dating from the 15th C this fine thatched farmhouse was once the home of Anne Hathaway before she married William Shakespeare in 1582. Her family, yeoman farmers, remained in occupation until 1892, when the cottage was purchased by the Shakespeare Birthplace Trust. The rooms retain their original features. The cottage was badly damaged by fire in 1969, but has since been completely restored. It has a mature, typically English garden, and long queues of visitors in the summer. *Open late Mar–May and Sep–Oct, Mon–Sat 10.00–17.00, Sun 13.00–17.00; Jun–Aug Mon–Sat 09.00–17.00, Sun 09.30–17.00; Jan–late Mar and Nov–Dec Mon–Sat 10.00–16.00, Sun 10.30–16.00. Closed Xmas.*

Royal Shakespeare Theatre (Tickets 01789 403403; www.stratford.co.uk/rsc/home). The home of the Royal Shakespeare Company, which produces Shakespeare plays to a very high standard *Apr–Dec every year.* The building is a large, chunky red-brick affair, designed by Elizabeth Scott and completed in 1932. Radical at the time, it now appears quite dated. The first theatre in Stratford was a temporary octagon built for Garrick's festival in 1769. A permanent theatre was not erected until 1827, with a library and art gallery being added in 1881. These buildings survive, and are connected to the present theatre by a bridge.

The Ragdoll Shop 11 Chapel Street (01789 404111). An ideal place for those with young children, who will enjoy playing with the toys and speaking on the tots telephones. Toys and books for sale. They also work with British Waterways to produce water safety information for children. *Open Mon–Sat 09.30–17.30, Sun 12.00–16.00.*

Stratford-upon-Avon Butterfly Farm Tramway Walk, Swan's Nest Lane (01789 299288; www.butterflyfarm.co.uk). Just south of the Tramway Bridge. Rainforest growth, fish pools and waterfalls, hundreds of butterflies and fascinating insects. For the not-so-squeamish there is Arachnoland, where you can view deadly insects (in perfect safety). Adventure playground, gift shop and refreshments. *Open 10.00–18.00 (dusk in winter).* Charge.

Cox's Yard Bridgefoot, Stratford-upon-Avon (01789 404600; www.coxsyard.co.uk). Home of the Stratford Tales: a time travel journey to meet characters, hear legends and witness events from bygone centuries. A chance to decipher local dialect, explore the workings of the Stratford Canal and view the town today through the camera obscura. *Open daily 09.00–23.00. Free. However the various areas within the Yard do keep* different opening times and Stratford Tales makes *a charge*. Full disabled access. Charge.

Holy Trinity Church Attractively situated among trees overlooking Colin P. Witter lock on the River Avon. It is mainly of the 15th C but the spire was rebuilt in 1763. Interesting misericords depict amusing scenes, and fine monuments include one of William Shakespeare who is buried in the chancel. His tomb bears a curse against anyone who dares to disturb it.

Shire Horse Centre Clifford Road, Stratford-upon-Avon (01789 415274/266276). Approximately 1¹/₂ miles out of the town or ¹/₂ mile south of Weir Brake lock. There is an infrequent, daily bus service from Stratford-upon-Avon. Rare breeds and small animals; shire horses at work and in the stable; owls and falcons; nature trail; picnic areas; walks; wagon rides; gift shop, snack bar and licensed restaurant. *Open Sat–Wed 10.00–17.00 and daily during school holidays.* Charge. Full disabled access.

Tourist Information Centre Bridgefoot, Stratford-upon-Avon (01789 293127; stratfordtic@shakespeare-country.co.uk). A mine of information, and lots of guide books and souvenirs for sale.

● **Tiddington**
Warwicks. PO, tel.

Boatyards

There are trip boats and many rowing and motor boats for hire in Stratford-upon-Avon.

Ⓑ **Stratford Marina** Clopton Bridge, Stratford-upon-Avon (01789 778358). ⚓ Pump out, gas, day-hire craft, overnight mooring, slipway, chandlery.

Pubs and Restaurants

There are numerous restaurants, snack bars, fast-food outlets and pubs in Stratford-upon-Avon.

🍺 ✕ **The Thistle** Waterside (01789 294949; stratford.uponavon@thistle.co.uk). Opposite the theatre. Convenient for a visit to the theatre and close to the moorings in Bancroft Basin, this establishment serves real ales together with bar snacks and restaurant meals (V) *L and E, daily*. Children welcome. Garden.

🍺 **The Old Tramway Inn** 91 Shipston Road (01789 297593). Real ales in a recently refurbished pub, with a large garden. Meals (V) are served *L and E (not Sun E or Mon)*. Children welcome.

🍺 **The Pen & Parchment** Bridgefoot, Stratford-upon-Avon (01789 297697). By bridge 69, at the entrance to the basin. This is a pleasant beamy pub in a listed building, where you can enjoy real ale in peace, without piped music. Good selection of Belgium beers. Wide range of food (V), including Balti and trout and tuna steaks is available *L and E*. There are outside seats surrounded by tubs of flowers, where you can watch the tourist sightseeing buses depart. Quiz *weekly* and music *monthly*.

🍺 ✕ **The Slug & Lettuce** Guild Street (01789 299700). Friendly and cheerful pub serving real ale and food (V) *all day, every day*. Garden and roof terrace. Changing ownership as we go to press.

🍺 **The Queen's Head** Ely Street (01789 204914). Real ale dispensed in a boistrous town centre pub which takes a serious interest in the small independent brewer. Food *L*, and real cider. Outside seating in *summer* and log fires in *winter*.

🍺 **The Ferry Inn** Ferry Lane, Alveston (01789 269883). Real ale together with bar snacks and an à la carte restaurant menu (V) served *L and E (not Sun E or Mon L, except Mon B Hols)*. Continental and English cuisine. Children welcome. Patio seating.

🍺 **Jester at Cox's Yard** Bridgefoot (01789 404600; www.coxsyard.co.uk). Pub; micro-brewery; restaurant; teashop and art gallery, this 'total leisure experience' offers food *all day, every day,* together with a selection of real ales brewed on site. Children welcome, outside seating area. Non-smoking area. Regular live music events including jazz *Sun*. Disabled access. *Open all day*.

WALKING & CYCLING
The Stratford Greenway is a linear country park, almost five miles long, following the old Honeybourne Railway Line and providing a traffic-free walking and cycling route, together with two picnic sites. It starts immediately to the south of Colin P. Witter Lock, finishing in Long Marston and interlinks with other riverside footpaths which can be used to form a number of circular walks. *See also* Walking & Cycling on page 145 and visit Country Parks Information Service at www.warwickshire.gov.uk.

BIRMINGHAM CANAL NAVIGATIONS (BCN) – MAIN LINE

MAXIMUM DIMENSIONS
Length: 70'
Beam: 6' 10"
Headroom: 6' 6"

MANAGER
0121 506 1300
enquiries.tipton@britishwaterways.co.uk

MILEAGES
Birmingham Canal new main line
BIRMINGHAM Gas Street to:
SMETHWICK JUNCTION (old main line):
$2^7/8$ miles
BROMFORD JUNCTION: $4^7/8$ miles
PUDDING GREEN JUNCTION
(Wednesbury Old Canal): $5^5/8$ miles
TIPTON FACTORY JUNCTION
(old main line): $8^3/4$ miles
DEEPFIELDS JUNCTION
(Wednesbury Oak loop): 10 miles
(Bradley Workshops: $2^1/4$ miles)
HORSELEY FIELDS JUNCTION
(Wyrley & Essington Canal): 13 miles
Wolverhampton Top Lock: $13^1/2$ miles
ALDERSLEY JUNCTION
(Staffordshire & Worcestershire Canal):
$15^1/8$ miles
Locks: 24

Birmingham Canal old main line
SMETHWICK JUNCTION to:
SPON LANE JUNCTION: $1^1/2$ miles
OLDBURY JUNCTION
(Titford Canal, 6 locks): $2^1/2$ miles
BRADESHALL JUNCTION
(Gower Branch, 3 locks): $3^1/2$ miles
Aqueduct over Netherton Tunnel Branch:
$4^3/8$ miles
TIPTON JUNCTION (Dudley Canal):
$5^1/2$ miles
FACTORY JUNCTION (new main line):
6 miles
Locks: 9

Netherton Tunnel Branch
WINDMILL END JUNCTION to:
DUDLEY PORT JUNCTION: $2^7/8$ miles
No locks

Wednesbury Old Canal
PUDDING GREEN JUNCTION to:
RYDER'S GREEN JUNCTION: $5/8$ mile
No locks

Walsall Canal
RYDER'S GREEN JUNCTION to:
Ryder's Green Bottom Lock: $1/4$ mile
DOEBANK JUNCTION: $1^3/8$ miles
WALSALL JUNCTION: $6^7/8$ miles
Locks: 8

Walsall Branch Canal
WALSALL JUNCTION to:
BIRCHILLS JUNCTION (Wyrley &
Essington Canal): $7/8$ mile
Locks: 8

Wyrley & Essington Canal
HORSELEY FIELDS JUNCTION to:
SNEYD JUNCTION: $6^1/4$ miles
BIRCHILLS JUNCTION (Walsall Branch
Canal): 8 miles
PELSALL JUNCTION (Cannock Extension):
$12^7/8$ miles
Norton Canes Docks: $1^1/2$ miles
CATSHILL JUNCTION: $15^3/8$ miles
OGLEY JUNCTION (Anglesey Branch):
$16^3/8$ miles
Anglesey Basin and Chasewater: $1^1/2$ miles
No locks

Daw End Branch
CATSHILL JUNCTION to:
LONGWOOD JUNCTION (Rushall Top
Lock): $5^1/4$ miles
No locks

Rushall Canal
LONGWOOD JUNCTION to:
RUSHALL JUNCTION: $2^3/4$ miles
Locks: 9

Tame Valley Canal
DOEBANK JUNCTION to:
RUSHALL JUNCTION: $3^1/2$ miles
Perry Barr Top Lock: $5^1/2$ miles
SALFORD JUNCTION: $8^1/2$ miles
Locks: 13

Currently a British Waterways T-shaped anti-
vandal key is needed for Wolverhampton
Locks. Other lock flights on the BCN are
under review for similar treatment.

The Birmingham Canal Company was authorised in 1768 to build a canal from
Aldersley on the Staffordshire & Worcestershire Canal to Birmingham. With James
Brindley as engineer the work proceeded quickly. The first section, from Birmingham
to the Wednesbury collieries, was opened in November 1769, and the whole $22^1/2$-mile

route was completed in 1772. It was a winding, contour canal, with 12 locks taking it over Smethwick, and another 20 (later 21) taking it down through Wolverhampton to Aldersley Junction. As the route of the canal was through an area of mineral wealth and developing industry, its success was immediate. Pressure of traffic caused the summit level at Smethwick to be lowered in the 1790s (thus cutting out six locks – three on either side of the summit), and during the same period branches began to reach out towards Walsall via the Ryder's Green Locks, and towards Fazeley. Out of this very profitable and ambitious first main line there grew the Birmingham Canal Navigations, more commonly abbreviated to BCN.

As traffic continued to increase so did the wealth of the BCN. The pressures of trade made the main line at Smethwick very congested and brought grave problems of water supply. Steam pumping engines were installed in several places to recirculate the water, and the company appointed Thomas Telford to shorten Brindley's old main line. Between 1825 and 1838 he engineered a new main line between Deepfields and Birmingham, using massive cuttings and embankments to maintain a continuous level. These improvements not only increased the amount of available waterway (the old line remaining in use), but also shortened the route from Birmingham to Wolverhampton by 7 miles.

Railway control of the BCN meant an expansion of the use of the system, and a large number of interchange basins were built to promote outside trade by means of rail traffic. This was of course quite contrary to the usual effect of railway competition upon canals. Trade continued to grow in relation to industrial development and by the end of the 19th C it was topping $8^1/2$ million tons per annum. A large proportion of this trade was local, being dependent upon the needs and output of Black Country industry. After the turn of the century this reliance on local trade started the gradual decline of the system as deposits of raw materials became exhausted. Factories bought from further afield and developed along the railways and roads away from the canals. Yet as late as 1950 there were over a million tons of trade and the system continued in operation until the end of the coal trade in 1967 (although there was some further traffic for the Birmingham Salvage Department), a pattern quite different from canals as a whole. Nowadays there is no recognisable commercial traffic – a dramatic contrast to the roaring traffic on the newer Birmingham motorways.

As trade declined, so parts of the system fell out of use and were abandoned. In its heyday in 1865, the BCN comprised over 160 miles of canal. Today just over 100 miles remain. However, all the surviving canals of the BCN are of great interest; excellent for leisure cruising, walking and cycling, they represent a most vivid example of living history and will reward exploration – one of the most important monuments to the Industrial Revolution.

Much has been done in recent years in landscaping waste land (as at the south end of Dudley Tunnel), dredging old basins (such as at the top of the Wolverhampton 21) and restoring disused buildings (such as the Pump House at Smethwick). The Birmingham Canal Partnership (British Waterways, Birmingham City Council, Groundwork Birmingham and various other departments and partners including European funds) is implementing a programme of improvements, having recognised the unique recreational potential of the canal system and its value as an area of retreat for the harassed city dweller and as a new area of exploration for the canal traveller.

Birmingham Canal Navigations – Main Line Introduction

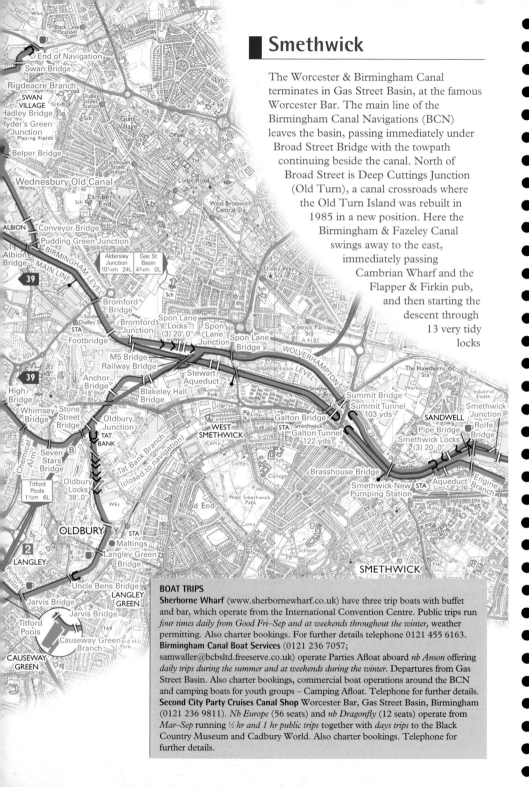

Smethwick

The Worcester & Birmingham Canal terminates in Gas Street Basin, at the famous Worcester Bar. The main line of the Birmingham Canal Navigations (BCN) leaves the basin, passing immediately under Broad Street Bridge with the towpath continuing beside the canal. North of Broad Street is Deep Cuttings Junction (Old Turn), a canal crossroads where the Old Turn Island was rebuilt in 1985 in a new position. Here the Birmingham & Fazeley Canal swings away to the east, immediately passing Cambrian Wharf and the Flapper & Firkin pub, and then starting the descent through 13 very tidy locks

BOAT TRIPS

Sherborne Wharf (www.sherbornewharf.co.uk) have three trip boats with buffet and bar, which operate from the International Convention Centre. Public trips run *four times daily from Good Fri–Sep and at weekends throughout the winter*, weather permitting. Also charter bookings. For further details telephone 0121 455 6163. **Birmingham Canal Boat Services** (0121 236 7057; samwaller@bcbsltd.freeserve.co.uk) operate Parties Afloat aboard nb *Anson* offering *daily trips during the summer and at weekends during the winter*. Departures from Gas Street Basin. Also charter bookings, commercial boat operations around the BCN and camping boats for youth groups – Camping Afloat. Telephone for further details. **Second City Party Cruises Canal Shop** Worcester Bar, Gas Street Basin, Birmingham (0121 236 9811). Nb *Europe* (56 seats) and nb *Dragonfly* (12 seats) operate from *Mar–Sep* running *½ hr and 1 hr public trips* together with *days trips* to the Black Country Museum and Cadbury World. Also charter bookings. Telephone for further details.

to Aston Junction (*see* page 58). The main line turns west at Farmer's Bridge, while the short Oozell's Street loop goes to the south, quickly disappearing behind old warehouses. This loop, which now houses a boatyard and moorings, and the others further along, are surviving parts of Brindley's original contour canal, now known as the Birmingham Canal Old Main Line. The delays caused by this prompted the Birmingham Canal Company to commission Telford to build a straighter line, the Birmingham Canal New Main Line. This was constructed between 1823 and 1838, and when completed reduced Brindley's old 22^1/2-mile canal to 15 miles. The Oozell's Street loop reappears from the south, and then, after two bridges, the Icknield Port loop leaves to the south. This loop acts as a feeder from Rotton Park Reservoir and rejoins after ^{1}/4 mile at another canal crossroads – the Winson Green or Soho loop, which leaves the main line opposite the Icknield Port loop. This last loop is the longest of the three, running in a gentle arc for over a mile before rejoining the main line again. It is also the only loop to have a towpath throughout its length. At its eastern end is Hockley Port, formerly railway-owned but now used for residential moorings. There are houseboats, a community hall, dry docks and workshops. The main line continues towards Smethwick Junction. Here there is a choice of routes: Brindley's old main line swings to the right, while Telford's new main line continues straight ahead – the old line is the more interesting of the two. The two routes run side by side, but the old line climbs to a higher level via the three Smethwick Locks. Here there were two flights of locks side by side. Beyond the junction, Telford's new line enters a steep-sided cutting. This 40ft-deep cutting enabled Telford to avoid the changes in level of the old line and thus speed the flow of traffic. The two routes continue their parallel courses, the one overlooking the other, until the lower line passes under the Telford Aqueduct. This elegant single span cast iron struc-ture carries the Engine Branch, a short feeder canal that leaves the old line, crosses the new line and then turns back to the south for a short distance. This arm is named after the first Boulton & Watt steam pumping engine to be bought by the Birmingham Canal Company.

This continued to feed the old summit level for 120 years. It was then moved to Ocker Hill for preservation and demonstrations, until the 1950s, when it was finally retired. The sides of the cutting are richly covered with wild flowers and blackberry bushes, and the seclusion of the whole area has turned it into an unofficial nature reserve. The old pumping station at Brasshouse Lane has been restored after years of disuse as part of the new Galton Valley Canal Park development. A Tangyes Engine has been installed to replace the original. The New Main Line continues through natural wilderness to Galton Tunnel. Telford's Galton Bridge crosses the cutting in one magnificent 150ft cast iron span. This bridge is preserved as an ancient monument. The old and the new Birmingham canal lines continue their parallel course, and soon the pleasant semi-rural isolation of the cutting ends, to be replaced by a complex meeting of three types of transport system. The M5 motorway swings in from the east, carried high above the canal on slender concrete pillars; the railway stays close beside Telford's new line; and the canals enter a series of junctions that seem to anticipate modern motorway practice. The new line leaves the cutting and continues in a straight line through industrial surroundings. It passes under Stewart Aqueduct and then reaches Bromford Junction. Here a canal sliproad links the old and the new lines via the three Spon Lane Locks, joining the new at an angle from the east. Note the unusual split bridge at Spon Lane top lock, which was rebuilt in 1986. The old line swings south west following the 473ft contour parallel to the M5, crossing the new line on Stewart Aqueduct. Thus canal crosses canal on a flyover. Spon Lane Locks, the linking sliproad, survive unchanged from Brindley's day and are among the oldest in the country. The old and the new lines now follow separate courses. The old line continues below the motorway to Oldbury Locks Junction. Here the short Titford Canal climbs away to the south via the six Oldbury Locks; this canal serves as a feeder from Titford Pools to Rotton Park Reservoir. After the junction the old line swings round to the north west and continues on a parallel course to the new line once again. After Bromford Junction the new line continues its straight course towards Wolverhampton. At Pudding Green Junction the main line goes straight on; the Wednesbury Old Canal forks right to join the Walsall Canal, which in turn joins the Tame Valley Canal at Doebank Junction.

WALKING & CYCLING

Much of Birmingham's 100-mile network of canals offers excellent opportunities for walkers and cyclists, and provides the chance to explore a side of the city well away from the obvious tourist attractions and close to the area's industrial roots. From a more formal approach, Birmingham is a crossroads for the National Cycle Network with Route 5 approaching from Kings Norton via Worcester & Birmingham Canal. Route 81 follows the Birmingham Level Main Line from the city to Wolverhampton, to eventually head into Mid Wales. Several excellent routes lead out from the city centre along traffic-free or contraflow cycle lanes. Further details are contained in *CycleCity's Birmingham Cycling Map – City Centre and Suburbs* and is available from Sustrans (0117 929 0888; www.sustrans.org.uk). Charge.

NAVIGATIONAL NOTES

Since the Titford Canal is the highest level on the BCN, it is advisable to telephone the BW Waterway Office (0121 506 1300) to check that there is adequate water before you visit the canal. You will need a water conservation key for Oldbury Locks in order to access this canal.

The Titford Canal

Built in 1837 as part of the original Birmingham Canal scheme, acting as a feeder to Spon Lane, the Titford Canal served Causeway Green. This must have been a very busy canal in its heyday, with many branches, wharves and tramways connecting it to the surrounding mines and engineering works. Today it survives in shortened form and has the distinction of being the highest navigable part of the BCN, with a summit level above Oldbury Locks of 511ft. The locks are sometimes referred to as the Crow – a branch which left the canal above the third lock and served the alkali and phosphorus works of a local industrialist and benefactor Jim Crow. The last surviving recirculatory pumphouse can be seen by the top lock. It is hoped that BW, in partnership with the local Canal Society, can raise funds for its restoration. The waterway now terminates at the wide expanse of water of Titford Pools

Tourist Information Centre *see* page 59.

Boatyards

Ⓑ **Sherborne Wharf** Sherborne Street Wharf, Birmingham (0121 455 6163; www.sherbornewharf.co.uk). On the Oozell's Street Loop. 🚿 🎁 ♿ D E Pump out, gas, day-hire boats, overnight mooring, long-term mooring, wet docks, winter storage, chandlery, boat repairs, engine sales and repairs, books, maps and gifts, DIY facilities, electrical hook-up, solid fuel, toilets, showers, laundrette, large supermarket nearby. *Emergency call out.*

Pubs and Restaurants

In a large city such as Birmingham there are many fine pubs and restaurants. As a result of the recent development of the area adjoining the canal, between Gas Street Basin and Cambrian Wharf, there are now approaching two dozen eating and drinking establishments. This choice is further expanded by walking south along Broad Street, from Broad Street Bridge, at Gas Street Basin. However beyond the canalside the enterprising boater (walker and cyclist) might like to seek out some of the City's more diverse hostelries:

🍺 **The Flapper & Firkin** Cambrian Wharf, Kingston Row (0121 236 2421). Real ale in a student-type pub, together with food (V) available *L and E*. Children welcome *until 19.00*. Outside terrace seating by the basin. Light music *most evenings. Open all day.*

🍺 **The Figure of Eight** 236-239 Broad Street (0121 633 0917). Sensibly priced real ale in a pub handy for Gas Street Basin. Food (V) available *all day, every day*. Outside seating and no smoking area. Disabled access. *Open all day.*

🍺 **The Fiddle & Bone** 4 Sheepcote Street, Ladywood (0121 200 2223; www.fiddle-bone.co.uk). Once an old school house, this two-storey canalside pub, with a strong musical theme, now dispenses real ales and an excellent range of food (V) *L and E (not Sun E)*. Patio seating. Disabled access. Mooring. *Open all day.*

🍺 **The Anchor** 308 Bradford Street (0121 622 4516). Edwardian pub tucked away behind the Digbeth coach station. Food (V) available *daily (until 18.00)* together with real ales, German and Belgian draught beers and real cider. Also an excellent range of bottled beers from far and wide. Outside seating. *Open all day.*

🍺 **The Woodman** 106 Albert Street, Digbeth (0121 643 1959). Friendly and very popular traditional pub that has survived the city's wholesale rebuilding programme. Real ales and food (V) available *L and E*.

🍺 **The Gunmaker's Arms** Bath Street (0121 236 1201). Comfortable, two-roomed pub serving real ales and food (V) *L and E, Mon–Fri*. Outside seating. *Closed Sun E.*

🍺 **Darwins** 57 Grosvenor Street, Five Ways (0121 643 6064). Near Tesco's. Traditional two-roomed city pub, with a wide ranging clientele, dispensing real ales together with food *L and E, daily*. Children welcome *until 21.00*. Skittles, darts and pool. *Tue evening* entertainment.

🍺 **The Black Eagle** 16 Factory Road, Hockley (0121 523 4008). North of Hockley Port. Real ales and food (V) available *L and E (not Sun E)*. Children welcome. Outside seating. Booking advisable for meals.

🍺 **The Olde Windmill** 84 Dudley Road, Winson Green (0121 455 6907). East of Lee Bridge, opposite the hospital. Real ales served in a compact, traditional old pub. Food available *L, daily*. Children welcome *until 16.00*. Beer garden and pub games. *Fortnightly Sat* musical entertainment. *Open all day.*

🍺 **The Finings & Firkin** 91 Station Road, Langley (0121 544 6467). A range of real ales dispensed in the old HP&D brewery tap. Friendly, welcoming atmosphere. Meals and bar snacks (V) available *L and E (until 20.00), daily*. Pub games, regular *weekday* quiz and *weekend* music. *Open all day.*

🍺 **The New Navigation** 156 Titford Road, Langley (0121 552 2525). Beside Jarvis Bridge. Canalside pub with a wide ranging clientele, serving food *L and E*. Children and dogs welcome. Outside seating. Mooring. *Weekend* quiz and musical entertainment.

🍺 **The Whiteheath Tavern** 400 Birchfield Lane, Whiteheath (0121 552 3603). Just west of Titford Pools, near M5 junction 2. Real ale in a pub close to Titford Pools. Children welcome at lunchtime. Traditional pub games.

Dudley

At Bradeshall Junction the Gower Branch links the two lines, descending to the lower level of the new line through three locks. To the south west of Tipton Junction is the branch leading to the Black Country Museum and the Dudley Tunnel. This branch connects with the Dudley Canal, the Stourbridge Canal, and thus with the Staffordshire & Worcestershire Canal. The old line turns north at the junction, rejoining the new line at Factory Junction. At Albion Junction the Gower Branch turns south to join the old line at Bradeshall. At Dudley Port Junction the Netherton Tunnel Branch joins the main line. The Netherton Tunnel Branch goes through the tunnel to Windmill End Junction; from here boats can either turn south down the old Dudley Canal to Hawne Basin, or west towards the Stourbridge Canal, and thus to the Staffordshire & Worcestershire Canal. North of Dudley Port the new line crosses a main road on the Ryland Aqueduct. Continuing its elevated course the new line reaches Tipton, where there are moorings with shops close by, and a small basin. The new line climbs the three Factory Locks and immediately reaches Factory Junction, where the old line comes in from the south.

Pubs and Restaurants

The Old Court House Lower Church Lane, Tipton (0121 520 2865). North east of Dudley Port Station. Real ales and food (V) available *L and E, daily* in a pub that used to be the holding cells for the police station across the road. Children and dogs welcome. Outside seating. Live bands *Tue* and karaoke *Fri.*

The Bottle & Glass Inn Black Country Living Museum, Tipton Road, Dudley (0121 557 9643). Real ale in a wonderful old pub, moved to the site. Cheese and onion cobs available *all day. Open 10.00–16.00.* More substantial refreshment available in the adjoining Stables Restaurant and 1930s fish & chip shop.

The Port 'N' Ale 178 Horsley Heath, Tipton (0121 532 2805). North east of Dudley Port railway station. One of the rare, genuine free houses left dispensing an excellent range of real ales and two traditional ciders. Children's room, outside seating and traditional pub games.

The Rising Sun 116 Horsley Road, Tipton (0121 530 9780). North of Dudley Port railway station. Real ale and a friendly welcome make this pub worth the walk. Also real cider. Food served *E (not Sun).* Open fires in winter and traditional pub games. Camping.

The Barge & Barrel Factory Road, Tipton (0121 520 6962). A recently refurbished pub in a wine bar setting, serving real ale, and inexpensive bar meals (V) *L.* Children welcome. Karaoke *Thur and Sun,* DJ *Fri and Sat.*

The Boat Inn Coseley (01902 492993). Friendly, canalside pub serving real ales. Snacks and basket meals (V) available *L and E.* Children welcome. Garden seating and traditional pub games. Karaoke *Wed and Sat evenings.* Barbecue facilities available for patrons use.

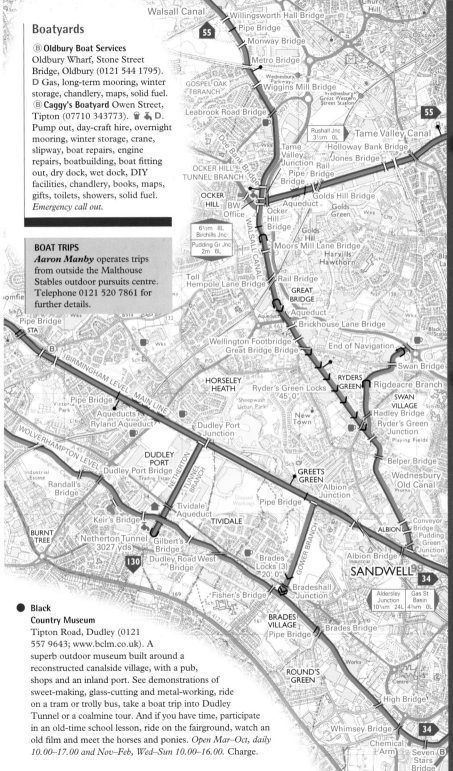

Boatyards

Ⓑ **Oldbury Boat Services** Oldbury Wharf, Stone Street Bridge, Oldbury (0121 544 1795). D Gas, long-term mooring, winter storage, chandlery, maps, solid fuel.

Ⓑ **Caggy's Boatyard** Owen Street, Tipton (07710 343773). 🚽 ♨ D. Pump out, day-craft hire, overnight mooring, winter storage, crane, slipway, boat repairs, engine repairs, boatbuilding, boat fitting out, dry dock, wet dock, DIY facilities, chandlery, books, maps, gifts, toilets, showers, solid fuel. *Emergency call out.*

BOAT TRIPS

Aaron Manby operates trips from outside the Malthouse Stables outdoor pursuits centre. Telephone 0121 520 7861 for further details.

● **Black Country Museum** Tipton Road, Dudley (0121 557 9643; www.bclm.co.uk). A superb outdoor museum built around a reconstructed canalside village, with a pub, shops and an inland port. See demonstrations of sweet-making, glass-cutting and metal-working, ride on a tram or trolly bus, take a boat trip into Dudley Tunnel or a coalmine tour. And if you have time, participate in an old-time school lesson, ride on the fairground, watch an old film and meet the horses and ponies. *Open Mar–Oct, daily 10.00–17.00 and Nov–Feb, Wed–Sun 10.00–16.00.* Charge.

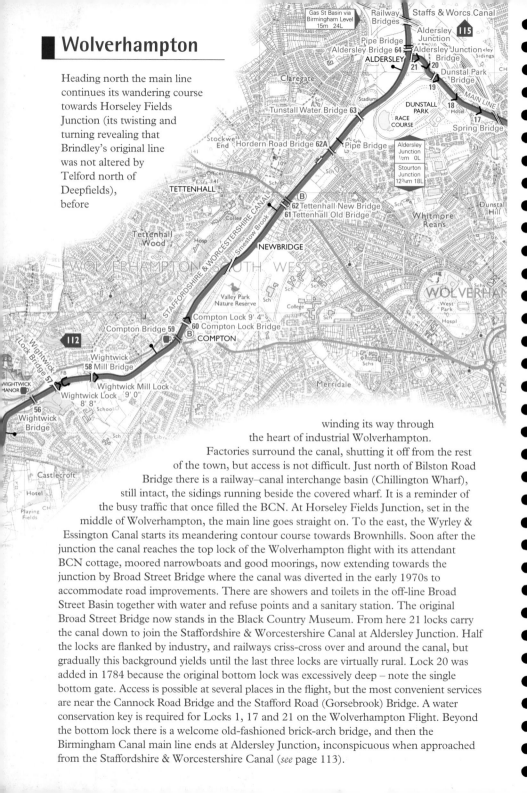

Wolverhampton

Heading north the main line continues its wandering course towards Horseley Fields Junction (its twisting and turning revealing that Brindley's original line was not altered by Telford north of Deepfields), before

winding its way through the heart of industrial Wolverhampton. Factories surround the canal, shutting it off from the rest of the town, but access is not difficult. Just north of Bilston Road Bridge there is a railway–canal interchange basin (Chillington Wharf), still intact, the sidings running beside the covered wharf. It is a reminder of the busy traffic that once filled the BCN. At Horseley Fields Junction, set in the middle of Wolverhampton, the main line goes straight on. To the east, the Wyrley & Essington Canal starts its meandering contour course towards Brownhills. Soon after the junction the canal reaches the top lock of the Wolverhampton flight with its attendant BCN cottage, moored narrowboats and good moorings, now extending towards the junction by Broad Street Bridge where the canal was diverted in the early 1970s to accommodate road improvements. There are showers and toilets in the off-line Broad Street Basin together with water and refuse points and a sanitary station. The original Broad Street Bridge now stands in the Black Country Museum. From here 21 locks carry the canal down to join the Staffordshire & Worcestershire Canal at Aldersley Junction. Half the locks are flanked by industry, and railways criss-cross over and around the canal, but gradually this background yields until the last three locks are virtually rural. Lock 20 was added in 1784 because the original bottom lock was excessively deep – note the single bottom gate. Access is possible at several places in the flight, but the most convenient services are near the Cannock Road Bridge and the Stafford Road (Gorsebrook) Bridge. A water conservation key is required for Locks 1, 17 and 21 on the Wolverhampton Flight. Beyond the bottom lock there is a welcome old-fashioned brick-arch bridge, and then the Birmingham Canal main line ends at Aldersley Junction, inconspicuous when approached from the Staffordshire & Worcestershire Canal (see page 113).

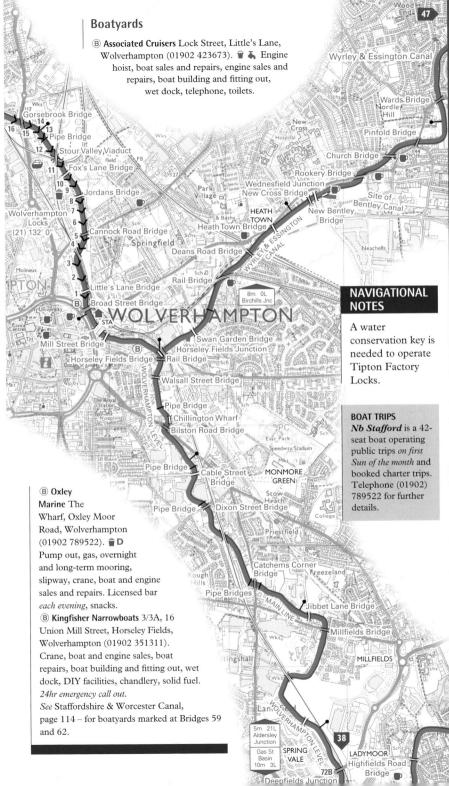

Boatyards

Ⓑ **Associated Cruisers** Lock Street, Little's Lane, Wolverhampton (01902 423673). Engine hoist, boat sales and repairs, engine sales and repairs, boat building and fitting out, wet dock, telephone, toilets.

NAVIGATIONAL NOTES

A water conservation key is needed to operate Tipton Factory Locks.

BOAT TRIPS

Nb Stafford is a 42-seat boat operating public trips *on first Sun of the month* and booked charter trips. Telephone (01902) 789522 for further details.

Ⓑ **Oxley Marine** The Wharf, Oxley Moor Road, Wolverhampton (01902 789522). D Pump out, gas, overnight and long-term mooring, slipway, crane, boat and engine sales and repairs. Licensed bar *each evening*, snacks.

Ⓑ **Kingfisher Narrowboats** 3/3A, 16 Union Mill Street, Horseley Fields, Wolverhampton (01902 351311). Crane, boat and engine sales, boat repairs, boat building and fitting out, wet dock, DIY facilities, chandlery, solid fuel. *24hr emergency call out.*

See Staffordshire & Worcester Canal, page 114 – for boatyards marked at Bridges 59 and 62.

Map labels:

Wyrley & Essington Canal · Wood End · Wards Bridge · Nordley Hill · Wyrley & Essington Canal · Pinfold Bridge · Church Bridge · Rookery Bridge · Wednesfield Junction · New Cross Bridge · Site of Bentley Canal · New Bentley Bridge · Neachells · HEATH TOWN · Heath Town Bridge · Deans Road Bridge · WYRLEY & ESSINGTON CANAL · 8m 0L Birchills Jnc · Gorsebrook Bridge · Pipe Bridge · Stour Valley Viaduct · Fox's Lane Bridge · Jordans Bridge · Wolverhampton Locks (21) 132' 0" · Cannock Road Bridge · Springfield · Molineux · Rail Bridge · Little's Lane Bridge · Broad Street Bridge · WOLVERHAMPTON · University · Civic Centre · STA · Mill Street Bridge · Horseley Fields Bridge · Swan Garden Bridge · Horseley Fields Junction · Rail Bridge · Walsall Street Bridge · Pipe Bridge · Chillington Wharf · Bilston Road Bridge · WOLVERHAMPTON LEVEL · Pipe Bridge · Cable Street Bridge · MONMORE GREEN · East Park · Speedway Stadium · Stow Heath · Pipe Bridge · Dixon Street Bridge · College · Priestfield · Catchems Corner Bridge · Freezeland · Rough Hills · Pipe Bridges · MAIN LINE · Jibbet Lane Bridge · Millfields Bridge · MILLFIELDS · Lanesfield · WOLVERHAMPTON LEVEL · 5m 21L Aldersley Junction · Gas St Basin 10m 3L · SPRING VALE · 38 · LADYMOOR · Highfields Road Bridge · 72B · Deepfields Junction

Pubs and Restaurants

In a town such as Wolverhampton there are many pubs to choose from. Below are a selection for the enterprising to seek out:

🍺 **The Feathers** Molineux Street, Wolverhampton (01902 426924). By the football ground. Small friendly local renowned for its garden. Real ale, and food *L Mon–Fri*. Children welcome. Pub games. Karaoke *Sat. Open all day Mon–Sat*.

🍺 **The Clarendon** Chapel Ash, Wolverhampton (01902 420587). A41, just to the west of the town centre. Refurbished, somewhat to its detriment, this pub offers real ale and food *L Mon–Fri*. Also breakfasts *08.00–L*. Children's room. Outside seating. *Open all day.*

🍺 **The Combermere Arms** 90 Chapel Ash, Wolverhampton (01902 421880). Real ale served in a terraced house look-alike: both cosy and intimate. Open fires and garden. Food *L Mon–Fri*. Children welcome. Disabled access.

🍺 **The Great Western** Sun Street, Wolverhampton (01902 351090. Real ale, railway memorabilia and good local cooking *L (not Sun)*. Children welcome at lunchtime if eating, dogs welcome in the evening. Garden and traditional pub games.

🍺 **Posada** 48 Lichfield Street, Wolverhampton (01902 711304). Grade ll listed building with its striking tiled frontage. A good range of real ales and snacks *L Mon–Fri* (together with tea and coffee) are always available. *Open all day except Sun.*

🍺 **The Tap & Spile** 35 Princes Street, Wolverhampton (01902 713319). An open bar and two snugs in a city centre pub dispensing an excellent range of real ales and home-made food (V) *L Mon–Fri*. Also real cider and traditional pub games. Disabled access. *Open all day, every day.*

Birmingham New Main Line at Winson Green (see page 35)

Brownhills

The Wyrley & Essington Canal meanders quietly through suburbs, passing a useful general store at Little Bloxwich Bridge and a post office by Teece's Bridge. At Pelsall Junction, amidst the flat grassy expanse of Pelsall Wood, the Cannock Extension Canal leaves to the north. This waterway was built between 1858 and 1863 and once connected with the Staffordshire & Worcestershire Canal. The old basins just before the present terminus used to serve the Brownhills Colliery. It is wholly rural until the boatyards are reached, and is well worth the short diversion – indeed there is a pub 50yds from the terminus. The section to the north of Watling Street was closed in 1963 due to subsidence. It was apparently quite a spectacular length, with massive embankments and vast brick overflow weirs. About 70 boats were left for scrap when it was abandoned. The main line continues on its eccentric course through fields, factories and houses until it approaches the wharf at Brownhills, now a tidy public area with a large super-market, market place and shops within easy reach. The Daw End Branch begins south of Catshill Junction – it was built in 1803 to carry lime from the workings around Daw End and Hay Head – and although constructed originally as a contour canal following the 473ft line, mining and subsidence have frequently left it in a very high, exposed position. This is immediately apparent when approaching Walsall Wood Bridge, a good stop for *shops and a post office*. The Anglesey Branch, which heads off east at Catshill Junction, last carried coal from the Cannock Mines in 1967, so those who make this worthwhile diversion may be surprised to find that the route is extremely rural, with open country to the north. An elegant cast iron bridge spans Ogley Junction, where the main line of the Wyrley & Essington once descended through locks to join the Coventry Canal at Huddlesford Junction; the route, abandoned in 1954, is now the subject of an energetic restoration campaign. What was once just a feeder from Chasewater now passes through sandy heathland to terminate at Anglesey Basin, a wide expanse where there are still the remains of loading chutes to be seen. Note the fine overflow weir, and the octagonal valve house high up on the dam. Chasewater Park is just a short walk from here.

Pelsall North Common Walsall Countryside Services (0121 360 9464). Originally rough grazing, much of the common was consumed by a great ironworks between 1832 and 1888, which employed 100 people from Pelsall village. Eventually iron prices fell, and the company went into liquidation, with the works being demolished in the late 1920s. A large machine, known as 'the cracker', was used to break up the mounds of foundry waste, and this gave the common its local nickname 'the cracker'. This machine was disposed of shortly after World War II. The common covers 137 acres, 92 of which, north of the canal, are designated a local nature reserve. There are areas of valuable lowland heath, pools containing mallard, snipe and mute swans, and many lime-loving plants in the west. Bright green and blue emperor dragonflies can be seen near the canal in summer.

Chasewater Built as a canal feeder reservoir, and so efficient was it that at one time its owners, the Wyrley & Essington Canal Company, sold its water to other companies. Just after building, in 1799, the dam collapsed, pouring a torrent of water across Watling Street and into the River Tame at Tamworth. Meadows were left strewn with gravel, and some livestock was drowned, but luckily little other damage was caused. The dam was rebuilt, faced with stone, and has remained stoically intact ever since. Note the fine octagonal valve house, built in the same style as the once common BCN toll houses.

Chasewater Country Park (01543 452302). A 700-acre park where there is rich bird life, fishing and nature trails to enjoy. Sailing and power boating on the reservoir are for clubs only, but you can, of course, always watch. *Open daily.*

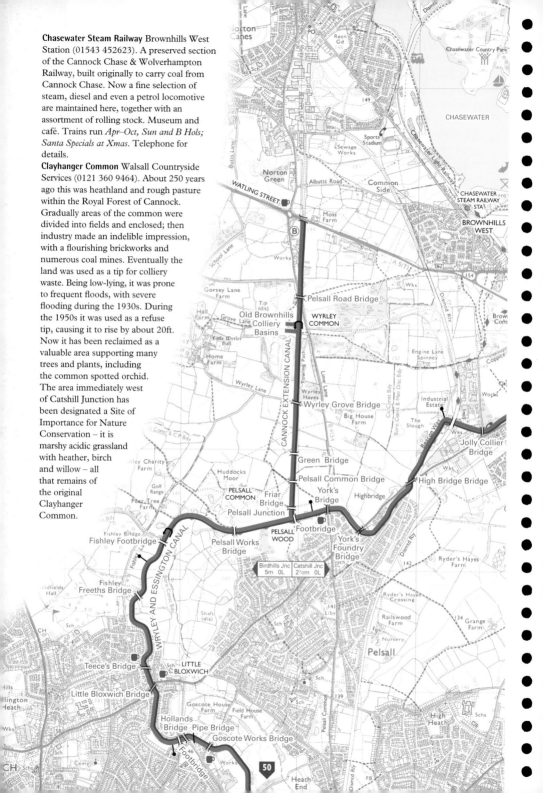

Chasewater Steam Railway Brownhills West Station (01543 452623). A preserved section of the Cannock Chase & Wolverhampton Railway, built originally to carry coal from Cannock Chase. Now a fine selection of steam, diesel and even a petrol locomotive are maintained here, together with an assortment of rolling stock. Museum and café. Trains run *Apr–Oct, Sun and B Hols; Santa Specials at Xmas.* Telephone for details.

Clayhanger Common Walsall Countryside Services (0121 360 9464). About 250 years ago this was heathland and rough pasture within the Royal Forest of Cannock. Gradually areas of the common were divided into fields and enclosed; then industry made an indelible impression, with a flourishing brickworks and numerous coal mines. Eventually the land was used as a tip for colliery waste. Being low-lying, it was prone to frequent floods, with severe flooding during the 1930s. During the 1950s it was used as a refuse tip, causing it to rise by about 20ft. Now it has been reclaimed as a valuable area supporting many trees and plants, including the common spotted orchid. The area immediately west of Catshill Junction has been designated a Site of Importance for Nature Conservation – it is marshy acidic grassland with heather, birch and willow – all that remains of the original Clayhanger Common.

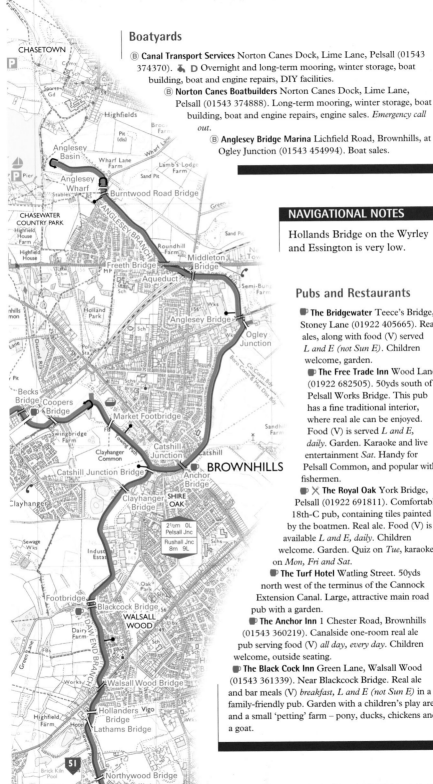

Boatyards

Ⓑ **Canal Transport Services** Norton Canes Dock, Lime Lane, Pelsall (01543 374370). ⚓ D Overnight and long-term mooring, winter storage, boat building, boat and engine repairs, DIY facilities.

Ⓑ **Norton Canes Boatbuilders** Norton Canes Dock, Lime Lane, Pelsall (01543 374888). Long-term mooring, winter storage, boat building, boat and engine repairs, engine sales. *Emergency call out.*

Ⓑ **Anglesey Bridge Marina** Lichfield Road, Brownhills, at Ogley Junction (01543 454994). Boat sales.

NAVIGATIONAL NOTES

Hollands Bridge on the Wyrley and Essington is very low.

Pubs and Restaurants

🍺 **The Bridgewater** Teece's Bridge, Stoney Lane (01922 405665). Real ales, along with food (V) served *L and E (not Sun E)*. Children welcome, garden.

🍺 **The Free Trade Inn** Wood Lane (01922 682505). 50yds south of Pelsall Works Bridge. This pub has a fine traditional interior, where real ale can be enjoyed. Food (V) is served *L and E, daily*. Garden. Karaoke and live entertainment *Sat*. Handy for Pelsall Common, and popular with fishermen.

🍺 ✕ **The Royal Oak** York Bridge, Pelsall (01922 691811). Comfortable 18th-C pub, containing tiles painted by the boatmen. Real ale. Food (V) is available *L and E, daily*. Children welcome. Garden. Quiz on *Tue*, karaoke on *Mon, Fri and Sat*.

🍺 **The Turf Hotel** Watling Street. 50yds north west of the terminus of the Cannock Extension Canal. Large, attractive main road pub with a garden.

🍺 **The Anchor Inn** 1 Chester Road, Brownhills (01543 360219). Canalside one-room real ale pub serving food (V) *all day, every day*. Children welcome, outside seating.

🍺 **The Black Cock Inn** Green Lane, Walsall Wood (01543 361339). Near Blackcock Bridge. Real ale and bar meals (V) *breakfast, L and E (not Sun E)* in a family-friendly pub. Garden with a children's play area and a small 'petting' farm – pony, ducks, chickens and a goat.

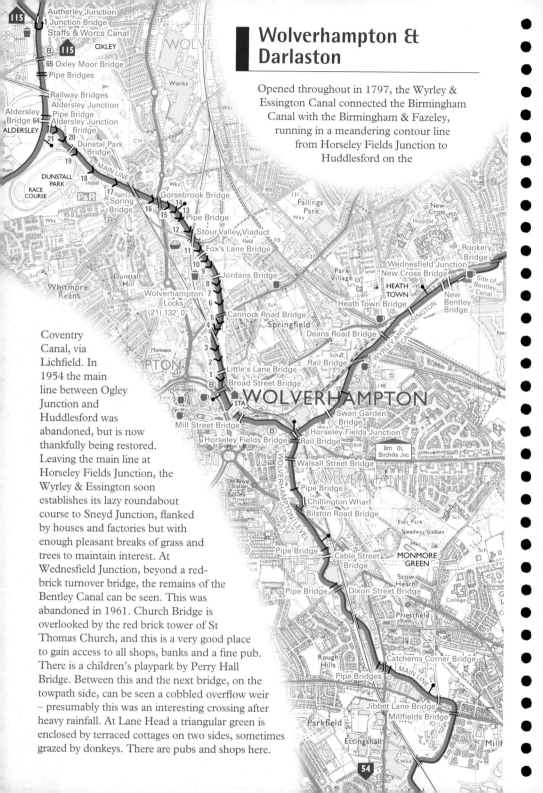

Wolverhampton & Darlaston

Opened throughout in 1797, the Wyrley & Essington Canal connected the Birmingham Canal with the Birmingham & Fazeley, running in a meandering contour line from Horseley Fields Junction to Huddlesford on the Coventry Canal, via Lichfield. In 1954 the main line between Ogley Junction and Huddlesford was abandoned, but is now thankfully being restored. Leaving the main line at Horseley Fields Junction, the Wyrley & Essington soon establishes its lazy roundabout course to Sneyd Junction, flanked by houses and factories but with enough pleasant breaks of grass and trees to maintain interest. At Wednesfield Junction, beyond a red-brick turnover bridge, the remains of the Bentley Canal can be seen. This was abandoned in 1961. Church Bridge is overlooked by the red brick tower of St Thomas Church, and this is a very good place to gain access to all shops, banks and a fine pub. There is a children's playpark by Perry Hall Bridge. Between this and the next bridge, on the towpath side, can be seen a cobbled overflow weir – presumably this was an interesting crossing after heavy rainfall. At Lane Head a triangular green is enclosed by terraced cottages on two sides, sometimes grazed by donkeys. There are pubs and shops here.

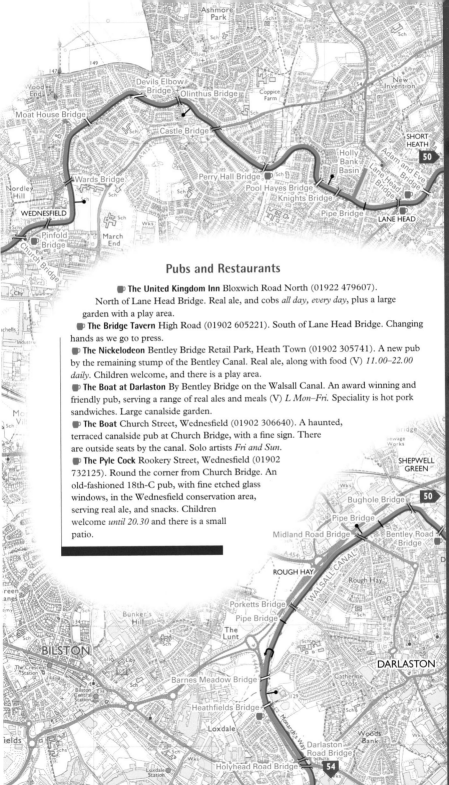

Pubs and Restaurants

The United Kingdom Inn Bloxwich Road North (01922 479607). North of Lane Head Bridge. Real ale, and cobs *all day, every day*, plus a large garden with a play area.

The Bridge Tavern High Road (01902 605221). South of Lane Head Bridge. Changing hands as we go to press.

The Nickelodeon Bentley Bridge Retail Park, Heath Town (01902 305741). A new pub by the remaining stump of the Bentley Canal. Real ale, along with food (V) *11.00–22.00 daily*. Children welcome, and there is a play area.

The Boat at Darlaston By Bentley Bridge on the Walsall Canal. An award winning and friendly pub, serving a range of real ales and meals (V) *L Mon–Fri*. Speciality is hot pork sandwiches. Large canalside garden.

The Boat Church Street, Wednesfield (01902 306640). A haunted, terraced canalside pub at Church Bridge, with a fine sign. There are outside seats by the canal. Solo artists *Fri and Sun*.

The Pyle Cock Rookery Street, Wednesfield (01902 732125). Round the corner from Church Bridge. An old-fashioned 18th-C pub, with fine etched glass windows, in the Wednesfield conservation area, serving real ale, and snacks. Children welcome *until 20.30* and there is a small patio.

Walsall

Beyond Foresters Bridge and the railway viaduct the Anson Branch used to fork off
north east – this once connected with the Bentley Canal, which in turn joined the
Wyrley & Essington. Now the Walsall Canal is up on an embankment, crossing James
Bridge Aqueduct (dated 1797), very exposed but with fine views over distant housing,
a car breaker's yard and a cemetery. The M6 motorway zooms overhead. There is a
pub at Pagetts Bridge, but access is difficult. At Walsall Junction the Town Arm
branches off below the locks, and it is worth the short diversion to visit the fine new
pub and the art gallery. The town centre, for shops and banks, is a short walk straight
on from here. Walsall Locks climb away north, enclosed by tall buildings – note
especially Albion Flour Mill, dated 1849, with its covered loading bay, at lock 7.
Once again traditional paddle gear and big wooden balance beams contribute to the
enjoyment of the flight, while at the top lock there is a museum in the old Boatman's
Rest, opposite Thomas's Wharf. Note also the toll office and BCN house no. 206 here.
A pub and a shop are close by. The canal then makes for Birchills Junction, passing the
old brick arch of Raybolds Bridge on the way.

BOAT TRIPS
Nb Wharf is a 42-seater boat which operates from Walsall Town Wharf *during the summer season.*
Trips daily during school holidays, plus every Sat and alternate Suns at 12.00, 12.30, 13.00, with longer
trips at 13.30. Telephone 0121 568 7929 for details.

Goscote

The Wyrley & Essington Canal continues its eccentric course around Rough Wood to
join the M6 motorway for a short way, but this is thankfully soon left well behind as
Edwards Bridge is approached. At Sneyd Junction the main line turns sharp right
under the bridge. Ahead, beyond the derelict lock, the old Wyrley Branch once linked
with coal workings and the Essington Branch, at 533ft above sea level the highest point
reached on the BCN. It was never successfully operated due to water supply problems.
Beyond the wharf buildings and crane the canal makes its journey through Leamore to
Birchills Junction, where the Walsall Canal leaves to the south, and the Wyrley &
Essington continues, passing factories and car parks. These soon give way to neat rows
of suburban houses, and then finally the canal is in open country.

Daw End Branch

Continuing south, the Daw End Branch of the Wyrley & Essington now finds itself
high up on an embankment with very deep clay pits either side, some now partially
flooded and landscaped, some still being worked. These dramatic surroundings give
way to factories and sports grounds, which in turn are followed by a surprisingly rural
area which is to last until Walsall's smarter suburbs are reached. There is a remarkable
stone cottage and red-brick arch at Brawn's Bridge; these red-brick arches then appear
regularly, enhancing the canal's remote quality. At Longwood Junction the main line of
the Daw End Branch used to continue to Hay Head – this is now abandoned and
forms part of a nature reserve *(see below)*. Longwood Boat Club have their moorings at
the junction, and their club house is in an old canal building next to BCN house no. 93
at the top lock. With pretty gardens, the whole makes for a charming canal scene.

Longwood Junction

Leaving Longwood the character of the route south changes to that of a straight modern canal, revealing that the traveller is now on the Rushall Canal; this was built in 1847 to connect the Daw End Branch with the Tame Valley Canal in order to capture the coal trade from Cannock Mines. After the top two locks the canal passes a golf course; beyond Sutton Road Bridge the banks are lined with canalside gardens, and the towpath is overhung with willow, flowering currant and berberis. There is a children's play-park at Gillity Bridge. Another golf course accompanies the route through the next flurry of locks on this long, drawn-out flight, and still the surroundings are wholly amenable. This is truly a fine length of urban canal, which would stand comparison with many others in the country.

Jerome K Jerome Birthplace Museum Belsize House, Bradford Street, Walsall (01922 653116 for information). Just south east of the Town Arm. A very small museum celebrating the life of the author of *Three Men in a Boat. Usually open Tue, Thur and Fri 09.00–16.00, Wed 09.00–12.30, Sat 12.00–14.00. Closed Sun and Mon. Free.*
Walsall Museum Lichfield Street, Walsall (01922 653116). East of the Town Arm, above the Central Library. *Open Tue–Sat 10.00–17.00. Free.*
The New Art Gallery Walsall Gallery Square (01922 654400). At the end of the Walsall Town Arm. Features the Garman Ryan Collection of works by artists such as Picasso, Van Gogh, Constable and Sir Jacob Epstein, plus feature exhibitions. *Open Tue–Sat 10.00–17.00, Sun and B Hols 12.00–17.00 (open daily during school summer holidays). Free.*
Walsall Leather Museum 54–57 Wisemore, Walsall (01922 721153). A short walk north east of the Town Arm. For two centuries Walsall has been the centre of British saddlery and leathergoods, and indeed a hundred or so companies still trade, producing wallets, purses, belts, bridles and saddles. Here you can see craftsmen at work, and perhaps even have a try yourself. There are also plenty of leathergoods for sale. *Open B Hols and Apr–Oct, Tue–Sat 10.00–17.00, Sun 12.00–17.00; Nov–Mar, closes 16.00. Free. Café.*
Birchills Canal Museum Walsall Top Lock, Walsall (01922 645778). Situated in the old Boatman's Rest, dated 1900, is a recreated boatman's cabin, canal ephemera and a fine collection of old photographs. You can also see the upstairs chapel with its iron range. The display is constantly expanding, with educational facilities. *Open Tue and Wed 09.30–12.30, Thur–Sun 13.00–16.00. Free.*
Rough Wood Walsall Countryside Services (0121 360 9464). In the 12th C Rough Wood was part of Bentley Hay, a district of Cannock Forest. Deer were hunted here, in what was a Royal Forest, until the 1500s when the king ordered all the trees to be felled. Coal was found here in the 1700s, and this was transported by canal to the furnaces of the Black Country. It used to be loaded onto boats by Bentley Wharf Bridge.

Today Rough Wood contains fine stands of oak, which in turn support vast numbers of insects, upon which a great variety of birds feed.
Park Lime Pits Walsall Countryside Services (0121 360 9464). Some 200 years ago this area was a thriving lime quarry, the lime being used as flux in the production of iron. Blocks of limestone were taken to the canal in trucks, to be transported to the furnaces of the Black Country. It is also possible that the Romans may have used stone from here in the building of Watling Street. When quarrying ended some 150 years ago the old workings were landscaped, beech trees were planted and the quarries filled with water. These pools now support coot, moorhen and other waterfowl. Daubenton's bats fly over the water at dusk. Limestone spoil heaps support plants such as burnet-saxifrage and potentilla.
Lime Pits Farm Walsall Countryside Services (0121 360 9464). This farm adjoins the reserve, and is a pioneering project which is endeavouring to combine nature conservation with productive farming. Follow the trail to see wheat and barley growing, with Jersey cows producing milk. The cattle drink from ponds which also support a variety of birds and insects. There is a wildflower hay meadow, small fields and rich hedgerows, protected from pesticides and fertilisers. Trees have been planted in field corners to provide both shelter and wildlife habitats. *If you visit, please do not leave the marked trail. This is a working farm.*
Hay Head Wood Walsall Countryside Services (0121 360 9464). Another limestone area, with evidence of mine shafts dating from the late 18th C still visible. The lime from here was found to be suitable for cement production, and much was used in the construction of canal buildings. The pond was once an arm of the canal, built to transport limestone from the mines, and the remains of old wharf buildings can still be made out. Follow the trail *Apr–Jun* and you will see (and smell) wild garlic, as well as dog's mercury, a plant which loves the lime. Old oak woods support varied birds and insects, and occasionally kingfishers and herons are seen in the remains of the old canal basin.

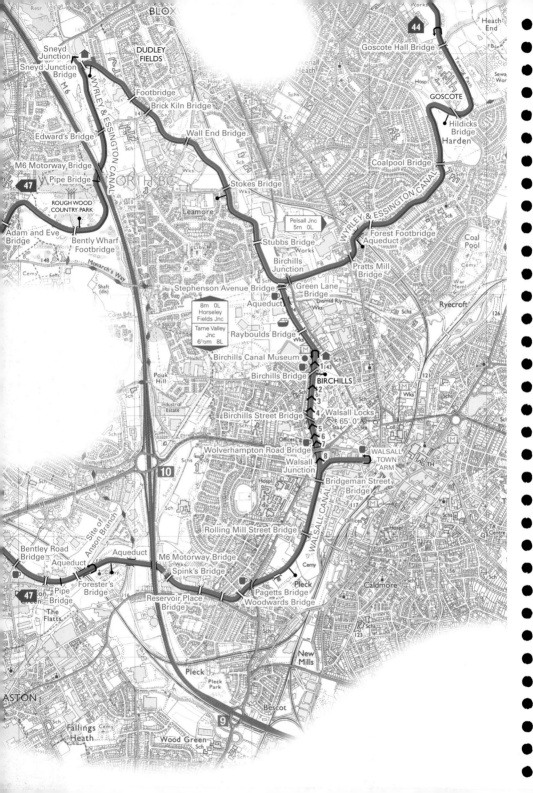

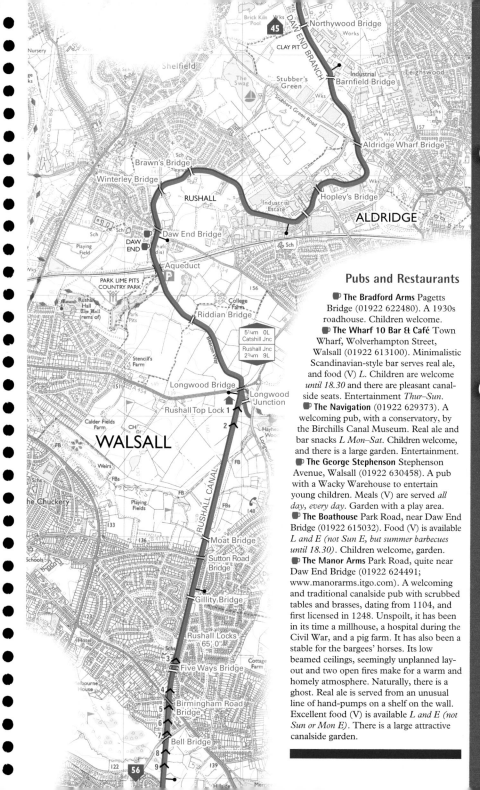

5¼m 0L
Catshill Jnc
Rushall Jnc 2¾m 9L

Pubs and Restaurants

The Bradford Arms Pagetts Bridge (01922 622480). A 1930s roadhouse. Children welcome.

The Wharf 10 Bar & Café Town Wharf, Wolverhampton Street, Walsall (01922 613100). Minimalistic Scandinavian-style bar serves real ale, and food (V) *L*. Children are welcome *until 18.30* and there are pleasant canalside seats. Entertainment *Thur–Sun*.

The Navigation (01922 629373). A welcoming pub, with a conservatory, by the Birchills Canal Museum. Real ale and bar snacks *L Mon–Sat*. Children welcome, and there is a large garden. Entertainment.

The George Stephenson Stephenson Avenue, Walsall (01922 630458). A pub with a Wacky Warehouse to entertain young children. Meals (V) are served *all day, every day*. Garden with a play area.

The Boathouse Park Road, near Daw End Bridge (01922 615032). Food (V) is available *L and E (not Sun E, but summer barbecues until 18.30)*. Children welcome, garden.

The Manor Arms Park Road, quite near Daw End Bridge (01922 624491; www.manorarms.itgo.com). A welcoming and traditional canalside pub with scrubbed tables and brasses, dating from 1104, and first licensed in 1248. Unspoilt, it has been in its time a millhouse, a hospital during the Civil War, and a pig farm. It has also been a stable for the bargees' horses. Its low beamed ceilings, seemingly unplanned layout and two open fires make for a warm and homely atmosphere. Naturally, there is a ghost. Real ale is served from an unusual line of hand-pumps on a shelf on the wall. Excellent food (V) is available *L and E (not Sun or Mon E)*. There is a large attractive canalside garden.

Great Bridge

The Walsall Canal runs from Ryder's Green Junction to Birchills Junction, connecting with the Tame Valley and Wyrley & Essington Canals. Its construction to Walsall was completed in 1799, with the link with the Wyrley & Essington being made via eight locks in 1841. The Wednesbury Old Canal was opened prior to this, in 1769, and still provides the vital link with the Walsall Canal. These two canals are still industrialised, and as such they give some impression of what the BCN was like in its heyday. The Wednesbury Old Canal leaves the main line at Pudding Green Junction under a flurry of bridges and hemmed in by factories. Immediately after Ryder's Green Junction, where the shortened Ridgeacre Branch heads half-a-mile to the north, eight locks descend to Doebank Junction. Access to shops is easily made by walking west from Great Bridge Bridge. Hempole Lane Bridge is one of the few BCN bridges dated in Roman numerals – MDCCCXXV – 1825, and just beyond here is the Ocker Hill Tunnel Branch. This once fed water to the Wednesbury Oak Loop via six pumping engines, a tunnel and shafts. Beside it is the British Waterways office. The branch has been tidied up, and is used for long-term moorings (so don't take your boat in!). Black and white cast iron bridges mark the junction with the Tame Valley Canal, and just beyond here the canal reaches what is left of the Gospel Oak Branch (no navigation). This whole area is now quite smart, with Holyhead and Darlaston Bridges looking particularly attractive.

Hall Green

Opened in 1844 to overcome the long delays which were occurring at Farmer's Bridge Locks, the canal is typified by its direct course, deep cuttings and high embankments. The $3^1/2$ mile section between Doebank Junction and Rushall Junction has the distinction of being the dreariest on the whole BCN. For those who would choose to stop along here, there is an art gallery, and shops south of Hateley Heath Aqueduct and north of Crankhall Lane Bridge.

The Wednesbury Oak Loop

This was the original course of the Old Main Line which followed a contour route around Coseley Hill, and was bypassed in 1837 with the building of Coseley Tunnel. Leaving the main line at Deepfields Junction, the canal passes through what was once a mining area, now landscaped and with wide views to south and north. Beyond Pothouse Bridge, land which at one time reverberated to the sound of iron making is now grassy fields, accompanying the waterway on its last $1/4$ mile to the terminus at British Waterways Midlands Regional Workshop. It is to this maintenance yard, where lock gates and boats are made and repaired, that the remaining section of the loop owes its survival. There is now little trace of the length which once connected to the Walsall and Tame Valley canals via the Bradley Locks Branch. Please DO NOT take your boat right to the end outside working hours.

CARING FOR BODY AND SOUL

The Walsall Iron Company's works once stood close to the canal at Birchalls, not far from the Boatman's Rest, which now houses the Birchills Canal Museum. A furnace in the works, loaded with more molten metal than was prudent, exploded on 15 October 1875, showering 17 men with molten metal and burning them badly. Three of the unfortunate victims jumped into the canal in an effort to find relief. Although lovingly nursed by Sister Dora (Dorothy Pattison), only two survived the incident, making it one of Walsall's worst industrial accidents.

Sister Dora, who died three years later, became famous in the area for her nursing skills, and did much to reduce the death rate from industrial accidents, giving Walsall a better track record in this respect than many of the London teaching hospitals. She came from Yorkshire in 1865, taking charge of Walsall's first hospital and soon gaining a reputation as a civilian Florence Nightingale.

The Boatman's Rest was one of three such institutions operated by the Incorporated Seamen and Boatman's Friend Society – the other two, at Gas Street Basin and Hednesford, have now been demolished. Caring for the physical and spiritual needs of the boatmen, the halls offered religious services, a clubroom (with no alcohol), overnight accommodation, letter writing and a semblance of education for the boat children. Stables were also provided for the horses.

Wednesbury Oak Loop

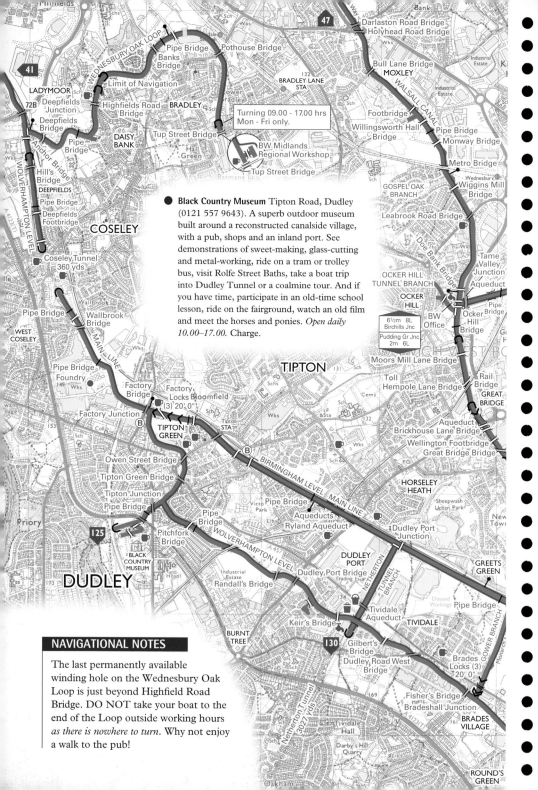

Black Country Museum Tipton Road, Dudley (0121 557 9643). A superb outdoor museum built around a reconstructed canalside village, with a pub, shops and an inland port. See demonstrations of sweet-making, glass-cutting and metal-working, ride on a tram or trolley bus, visit Rolfe Street Baths, take a boat trip into Dudley Tunnel or a coalmine tour. And if you have time, participate in an old-time school lesson, ride on the fairground, watch an old film and meet the horses and ponies. *Open daily 10.00–17.00.* Charge.

Turning 09.00 - 17.00 hrs Mon - Fri only.

NAVIGATIONAL NOTES

The last permanently available winding hole on the Wednesbury Oak Loop is just beyond Highfield Road Bridge. DO NOT take your boat to the end of the Loop outside working hours *as there is nowhere to turn.* Why not enjoy a walk to the pub!

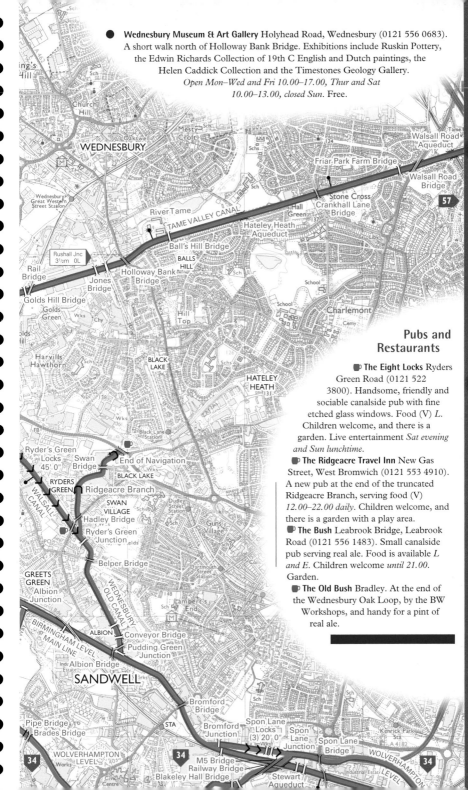

● **Wednesbury Museum & Art Gallery** Holyhead Road, Wednesbury (0121 556 0683). A short walk north of Holloway Bank Bridge. Exhibitions include Ruskin Pottery, the Edwin Richards Collection of 19th C English and Dutch paintings, the Helen Caddick Collection and the Timestones Geology Gallery. *Open Mon–Wed and Fri 10.00–17.00, Thur and Sat 10.00–13.00, closed Sun.* Free.

Pubs and Restaurants

⚑ **The Eight Locks** Ryders Green Road (0121 522 3800). Handsome, friendly and sociable canalside pub with fine etched glass windows. Food (V) *L.* Children welcome, and there is a garden. Live entertainment *Sat evening and Sun lunchtime.*

⚑ **The Ridgeacre Travel Inn** New Gas Street, West Bromwich (0121 553 4910). A new pub at the end of the truncated Ridgeacre Branch, serving food (V) *12.00–22.00 daily.* Children welcome, and there is a garden with a play area.

⚑ **The Bush** Leabrook Bridge, Leabrook Road (0121 556 1483). Small canalside pub serving real ale. Food is available *L and E.* Children welcome *until 21.00.* Garden.

⚑ **The Old Bush** Bradley. At the end of the Wednesbury Oak Loop, by the BW Workshops, and handy for a pint of real ale.

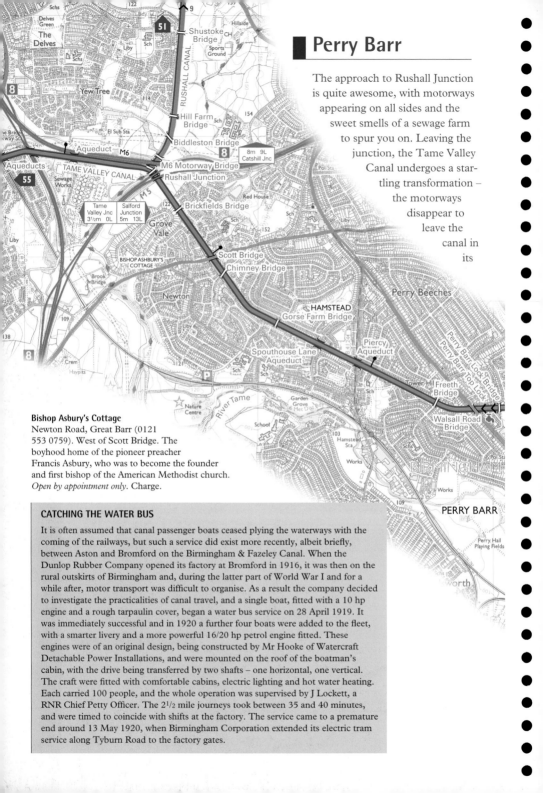

Perry Barr

The approach to Rushall Junction is quite awesome, with motorways appearing on all sides and the sweet smells of a sewage farm to spur you on. Leaving the junction, the Tame Valley Canal undergoes a startling transformation – the motorways disappear to leave the canal in its

Bishop Asbury's Cottage
Newton Road, Great Barr (0121 553 0759). West of Scott Bridge. The boyhood home of the pioneer preacher Francis Asbury, who was to become the founder and first bishop of the American Methodist church. *Open by appointment only.* Charge.

CATCHING THE WATER BUS

It is often assumed that canal passenger boats ceased plying the waterways with the coming of the railways, but such a service did exist more recently, albeit briefly, between Aston and Bromford on the Birmingham & Fazeley Canal. When the Dunlop Rubber Company opened its factory at Bromford in 1916, it was then on the rural outskirts of Birmingham and, during the latter part of World War I and for a while after, motor transport was difficult to organise. As a result the company decided to investigate the practicalities of canal travel, and a single boat, fitted with a 10 hp engine and a rough tarpaulin cover, began a water bus service on 28 April 1919. It was immediately successful and in 1920 a further four boats were added to the fleet, with a smarter livery and a more powerful 16/20 hp petrol engine fitted. These engines were of an original design, being constructed by Mr Hooke of Watercraft Detachable Power Installations, and were mounted on the roof of the boatman's cabin, with the drive being transferred by two shafts – one horizontal, one vertical. The craft were fitted with comfortable cabins, electric lighting and hot water heating. Each carried 100 people, and the whole operation was supervised by J Lockett, a RNR Chief Petty Officer. The 2½ mile journeys took between 35 and 40 minutes, and were timed to coincide with shifts at the factory. The service came to a premature end around 13 May 1920, when Birmingham Corporation extended its electric tram service along Tyburn Road to the factory gates.

own secluded world – tree lined and with small fields either side. Colourful suburban gardens are glimpsed here and there before the waterway enters a steep wooded cutting crossed by the high modern Scott Bridge, and the more agreeable Chimney Bridge, a footbridge supported on substantial brick pillars. Emerging from the cutting, the traveller then finds himself on a high embankment, with wide views all around; two aqueducts are crossed. By the second, Piercy, there are shops and an off-licence. Again the canal enters a deep cutting, this time through sandstone some 200 million years old. After passing the handsome brick arch of Freeth Bridge, Perry Barr Top Lock is reached, set between a fine red-brick BCN house (no. 86), old stables and the Gauging Weir House. The lock flight straggles along the canal, and passes through an area of private back gardens, public open spaces and sports fields. Little industry intrudes, although the M6 motorway crosses twice. There are petrol stations by College Road Bridge and a telephone kiosk and post box by Brookvale Road Bridge, where factories and other industrial premises close in. The Tame Valley Canal joins the Birmingham & Fazeley and Grand Union canals under Spaghetti Junction motorway interchange, where cast iron towpath bridges are dwarfed by flyovers, making a strangely mesmeric scene in complete and utter contrast to the tranquillity of the canals hidden below.

A unique experience.

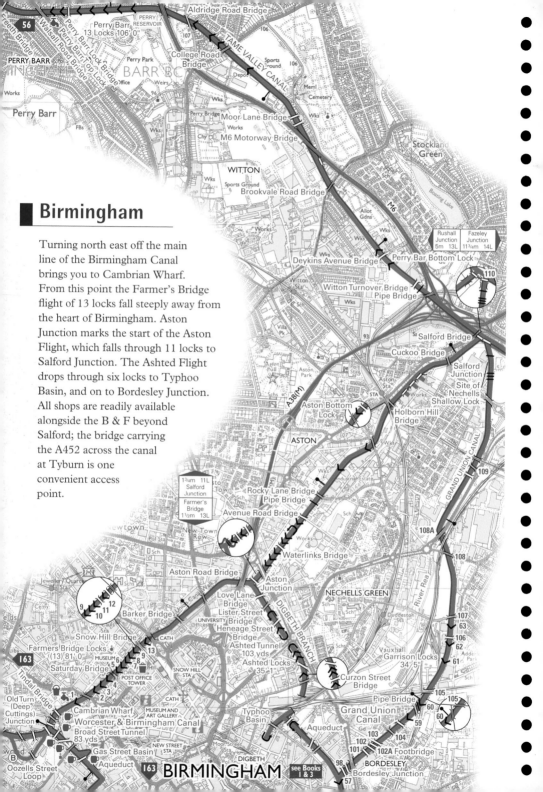

Birmingham

Turning north east off the main line of the Birmingham Canal brings you to Cambrian Wharf. From this point the Farmer's Bridge flight of 13 locks fall steeply away from the heart of Birmingham. Aston Junction marks the start of the Aston Flight, which falls through 11 locks to Salford Junction. The Ashted Flight drops through six locks to Typhoo Basin, and on to Bordesley Junction. All shops are readily available alongside the B & F beyond Salford; the bridge carrying the A452 across the canal at Tyburn is one convenient access point.

The Digbeth Branch This leaves the Birmingham & Fazeley main line at Aston Junction, and descends through six locks to Typhoo Basin, where it meets the former Warwick & Birmingham Canal, which became part of the Grand Union Canal when the GUC Company was formed in 1929. There was a stop lock – called Warwick Bar – at the junction by Bordesley Basin. One of the lesser-known tunnels on the canal system is on the Digbeth Branch – the Ashted.

National Sea Life Centre Waters Edge, Brindley Place, Birmingham (0121 633 4700; www.sealife.co.uk). Over 3000 British marine and freshwater creatures to see. Walk through a transparent underwater tube with sharks swimming around you, and visit the 'wreck' of the Titanic. *Open 10.00–17.00 daily.* Charge. Restaurant, shop.

Thinktank Curzon Street, Birmingham (0121 464 1977). Walk west from Curzon Street Bridge on the Digbeth Branch. A new science centre with ten galleries spread

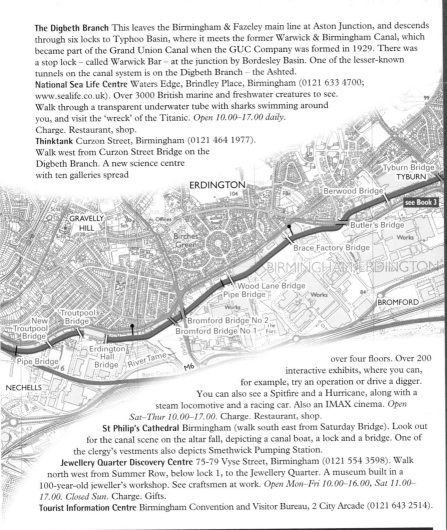

over four floors. Over 200 interactive exhibits, where you can, for example, try an operation or drive a digger. You can also see a Spitfire and a Hurricane, along with a steam locomotive and a racing car. Also an IMAX cinema. *Open Sat–Thur 10.00–17.00.* Charge. Restaurant, shop.

St Philip's Cathedral Birmingham (walk south east from Saturday Bridge). Look out for the canal scene on the altar fall, depicting a canal boat, a lock and a bridge. One of the clergy's vestments also depicts Smethwick Pumping Station.

Jewellery Quarter Discovery Centre 75-79 Vyse Street, Birmingham (0121 554 3598). Walk north west from Summer Row, below lock 1, to the Jewellery Quarter. A museum built in a 100-year-old jeweller's workshop. See craftsmen at work. *Open Mon–Fri 10.00–16.00, Sat 11.00–17.00. Closed Sun.* Charge. Gifts.

Tourist Information Centre Birmingham Convention and Visitor Bureau, 2 City Arcade (0121 643 2514).

NAVIGATIONAL NOTES

The lock keeper at Farmer's Bridge is on duty *07.30–17.00 Mon–Thur (until 16.30 Fri)*. Telephone 0121 236 1607.

Pubs and Restaurants

The Flapper & Firkin Cambrian Wharf, Kingston Row (0121 236 2421). Real ale in a student type pub, together with food (V) available *all day, every day.* Children welcome *until 19.00.* Outside terrace seating by the basin. *Open all day.* Light music most evenings.

The Malt House 75 King Edwards Road, Brindley Place (0121 633 4171). Overlooking Deep Cuttings Junction, this pub serves real ale and food *12.00–21.30 daily (not after 20.00 Fri and Sat).* Children welcome *until 19.00.* DJ and

disco *Fri and Sat.* Handy for the Sea Life Centre.

The James Brindley Gas Street Basin, Bridge Street (0121 644 5971). Modern pub overlooking Gas Street Basin. Bar meals (V) are served *L and E (not Sat E).* There is outside seating, and a jazz band entertains *Sat and Sun lunchtimes.*

Reservoir Cuckoo Bridge, Lichfield Road (0121 327 3336). Friendly pub undergoing refurbishment. Food. Children welcome. Disco *Fri and Sat.*

BCN – Birmingham & Fazeley Canal **Birmingham**

DROITWICH CANALS

MAXIMUM DIMENSIONS

Droitwich Barge Canal
Length: 71' 6"
Beam: 15'
Headroom: 8'

Droitwich Junction Canal
Length: 71' 6"
Beam: 7' 1"
Headroom: 8'

MILEAGE

RIVER SEVERN to:
Ladywood Lock: 2³/₄ miles
Barge Lock, Droitwich: 5³/₄ miles

HANBURY WHARF (Junction with Worcester & Birmingham Canal): 7¹/₄ miles

Locks: 15 (many awaiting restoration)

MANAGER

The Droitwich Canals Trust
Old Park
Plough Road
Tibberton
Droitwich
WR9 7NN
01905 345307;
mrowley@worcs.com

The Droitwich canals are unique in this country in that they owe their existence to salt. Authorised in 1768, engineered by James Brindley and opened on 12 March 1771, the Droitwich Barge Canal was one of the earliest canals built. As with many canals that were branches of existing river navigations, it was built to a wide gauge which allowed river craft to use it, transporting salt directly to the port of Bristol. The Droitwich Junction Canal, which connected Droitwich to the Worcester & Birmingham Canal and the new salt works at Stoke was completed in 1852, well after the end of the period of canal mania, and at the start of the railway age.

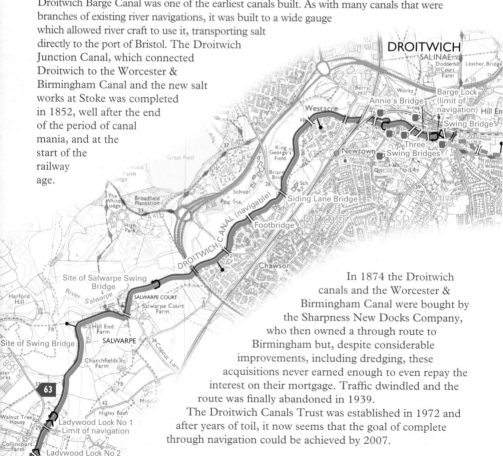

In 1874 the Droitwich canals and the Worcester & Birmingham Canal were bought by the Sharpness New Docks Company, who then owned a through route to Birmingham but, despite considerable improvements, including dredging, these acquisitions never earned enough to even repay the interest on their mortgage. Traffic dwindled and the route was finally abandoned in 1939.

The Droitwich Canals Trust was established in 1972 and after years of toil, it now seems that the goal of complete through navigation could be achieved by 2007.

Droitwich

The currently navigable stretch of the Droitwich Canals extends from the Barge Lock, through Vines Park and Salwarpe to Ladywood Lock No. 1. It is a fine example of the way in which an artificial waterway, mellowed with time and heavy use, adds a unique character to the surrounding urban environment. People come to the park to picnic by the canal, walk, jog or simply go about their daily business, connected to an industrious past and a better, cleaner future. Heading west the canal is soon out of the town and passing through countryside that is surprisingly peaceful, bearing in mind the close proximity of Worcester. Ladywood Lock No. 1 is soon reached, and illustrates how attractive this all will be when restoration is complete: there is a tidy black and white painted lock with a pretty lock cottage beside it, all enlivened with plantings of colourful flowers. For practical purposes this is the limit of navigation, although the next two locks are in a good state of repair.

To the east of Droitwich it is little more than a mile to Hanbury Wharf (on the Worcester & Birmingham), but much restoration work still needs to be done to secure this connection.

WALKING & CYCLING
The towpath makes an excellent walk west from Droitwich to Hawford Mill. Cyclists can ride west as far as Ladywood locks.

NAVIGATIONAL NOTES

Winding on the Droitwich Canal is currently restricted to about 45ft.

● **Droitwich Spa** *Worcs. All services.* St Andrew's Church stands at the top of the High Street, its tower removed (some now think unnecessarily) in 1928 due to subsidence caused by salt extraction from underground brine streams, which are close to the surface here. It was the Romans, in the 2nd C, who first began industrial salt extraction and a large, plank-lined tank built at the time has been uncovered during excavations. Following the Roman abandonment of Britain around AD410, the Angles and Saxons gradually spread west, and salt production increased, only to face disaster during the 7th or 8th C, when flooding spread vast quantities of silt and clay across the salt wells. But their economic importance was demonstrated with the clearance of the wells and reinforcement of the flood defences.

By the 8th C, under the control of the Mercian kings, the town was known as 'saltwic', and the salt wells were considered one of the wonders of Britain. A complete network of routes, or 'salt-ways', radiated from the town.

Salt was extracted from brine ($2^{1}/_{2}$ pounds of salt in each gallon of water, a concentration ten times that of sea water) by boiling in pans, and as a consequence vast quantities of timber was felled for fuel, even though coal was available from the 14th C. The result of all this burning and boiling was terrible pollution, but still salt production continued to increase and, inspite of a set-back during the Civil War, it rose to 3000 tons per annum in the late 1600s, and increased further when the town's monopoly on production ended and many private wells opened. When steam engines were intro-duced to drive pumps in the 18th C, production soared to 15,000 tons each year. Factories built in the 19th C exploited production, which peaked at an astonishing 120,000 tons per annum. Around this time the major salt producer was John Corbett, a philanthropist who decided to move his salt production to Stoke Prior, on the Worcester & Birmingham Canal, and transformed

Droitwich into a spa town following the realisation of the therapeutic qualities of salt water in the 1830s. He opened the Royal Brine Baths in Queen Street in 1836, and this was soon followed by further baths and some fine hotels. Salt production finally ended in Droitwich in 1922, although pumping at Stoke Prior continued, causing serious subsidence in the town until that in turn ceased. The last of the original brine baths, St Andrew's, closed on Christmas eve in 1975, but new baths were opened in 1984. A replica brine pit, and other remains of the salt industry, can be seen in Vines Park, by the canal. Droitwich was also known nationally, and internationally, for its powerful long-wave transmitter, which was built here in 1933. Marked on the dial of wireless sets (as they were then known) as 'Droitwich 1500 metres', transmissions began on 6 September 1934. During World War II the transmitter was initially used to broadcast to occupied Europe, and later used to jam signals to enemy aircraft. Today it broadcasts Radio 4 long wave, the World Service and Radio 5.
Radiating the friendly atmosphere typical of a small West Midland town, most of historic Droitwich lies to the south of the canal, in an area enclosed by Saltway, and is easily explored.
Tourist Information & Heritage Centre St Richard's House, Victoria Square, Droitwich (01905 774312). The Heritage Centre opened in 1980 and is housed on the former Brine Baths site, first established in the 1880s. There is a fascinating small museum devoted to the salt industry, and other exhibits illustrate the history of the BBC transmitting station. Extremely friendly and helpful. *Open Oct-Mar, Mon-Fri 09.00-16.30; Apr-Sep, Mon-Fri 09.00-17.00, Sat 09.30-16.00. Closed Sun.*
St Andrew's Church High Street, Droitwich. The structure of the church was greatly affected by subsidence due to salt extraction, with the result that the tower was dismantled in 1928, and the bells removed to the north aisle. Built around 1310 on the site of an earlier church destroyed by a fire in 1290, which also laid waste to most of the rest of the town, only the base of the tower and the plinth of the chancel survived. If you are lucky you might be offered a short guided tour of the church.

Boatyards

Droitwich Canal Co Ladywood Lock, Ladywood (01905 458352). A 24ft narrowboat available for day hire.

Pubs and Restaurants

🍺 ✕ **The Eagle & Sun** Hanbury Wharf (01905 770130). Canalside, at bridge 35. Smart, friendly and comfortable pub, with several cosy rooms, where real ale is served. Excellent food (V), including fish specials and a carvery *(not Sat L or Mon)* is served *L and E*. Booking is recommended. Children welcome, and there is a pleasant garden with plenty of seats.
🍺 **The Gardeners Arms** Vines Lane, Droitwich (01905 772936). Real ale is served, along with food (V) *L and E (not Wed)*. Children welcome if you are eating, and the garden has a play area.
🍺 ✕ **The Old Cock Inn** Friar Street, Droitwich (01905 774233/774728). First licensed in 1712, the ecclesiastical window was taken from nearby St Nicholas Church after it was destroyed in the 18th C. The carved head is thought to represent Judge Jeffreys, with a frog emerging from his mouth. Extensive menu (V) and bar meals *L and E (not Sun E)*. Real ale. Children welcome and there is a garden.
✕ ♆ **Rossini's** 6 Worcester Road, Droitwich (01905 794799). Italian and Mediterranean cuisine *L and E*.
🍺 **The Barley Mow** Hanbury Street, Droitwich (01905 773248). Food (V) is served *L and E*. Real ale. Children welcome, patio.
🍺 **The Talbot Hotel** High Street, Droitwich (01905 773331). Late 17th-C building, where a third storey was subsequently added. Real ale. Patio.

🍺 **The Railway Inn** Kidderminster Road, Droitwich (01905 770056). There is lots of railway memorabilia in this pub, which serves real ale and food (V) *L (not Sun)*. Children welcome *until 19.00*. First floor terrace, garden.
🍺 **The Star & Garter** High Street, Droitwich (01905 770234). Friendly local serving real ale, and food (V) *L Mon-Sat* (orders taken for *E*, and takeaways). Children welcome.
🍺 ✕ **The Raven Hotel** Droitwich (01905 772224). A large black and white hotel built on the site of the birthplace of St Richard de Wyche. Destroyed in the fire of 1290, it was later rebuilt as St Andrew's House and was bought by John Corbett, who opened it as a hotel in 1887. Charles I is said to have stayed here in May 1645, while on the way to storm Leicester. Meals in Platts restaurant (V) *L and E (not Sat L or Sun E)*. Children welcome, garden.
🍺 ✕ **The Hadley Bowling Green Inn** Hadley Heath (01905 620294; www.english-inns/hadleybowlinggreen). Walk north from lock 1, or take the path from Hill End Farm. There is a bowling green at this 16th-C pub, and they posses the actual bowls used by Sir Francis Drake. Meals (V) are served *L and E*, and there is real ale. Children welcome, garden. They also offer clay-pigeon shooting.

Hawford Mill

Beyond Porter's Mill Lock you will reach Linacre Bridge. This is worthy of close examination, since it is a rare surviving example of one of Brindley's original structures. The canal then continues on its extravagant way, passing Mildenham Lock before reaching a (presently) substantial obstacle at Hawford Mill: the main A449 road. There is a caravan and camping site here, with a nearby boatyard accessed from the River Severn via one of its tributaries, the Salwarpe. Following the canal on foot to the west of the main road is not entirely straightforward, but soon the River Severn is reached at the presently ungated Hawford Locks, which were considered at the time to be one of the canal engineer James Brindley's finest works. When the restoration of the Droitwich Canals is completed, this will certainly become a busy junction, with craft diverting off the natural course of the Severn to explore the meandering, river-like course of the canal to Droitwich, or completing (if they are no more than 7ft beam) a 22-mile cruising ring encompassing the Worcester & Birmingham Canal and the Severn.

WALKING & CYCLING
The towpath is virtually untraceable west of Hawford Mill to the River Severn. The Severn Way long distance path, which stretches from Plynlimon, Powys, to Severn Beach, near Bristol, a distance of 210 miles, can be joined near the junction.

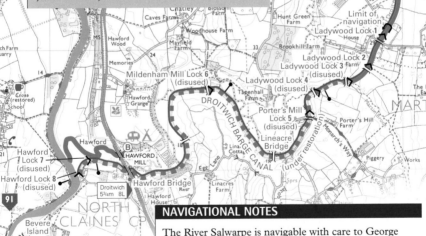

NAVIGATIONAL NOTES

The River Salwarpe is navigable with care to George Judge's boatyard for craft of around 30ft and drawing less than 2ft 6ins of water (and who have a valid reason to visit). Craft over 35ft long will be unable to turn.

Boatyards

Hawford Mill Caravan & Camping Site Mill House, Hawford (01905 451283; millhousecaravansite@ yahoo.co.uk). A pleasant site right by the canal and at the limit of navigation on the River Salwarpe. Gas, shop and restaurant.

ⒷGeorge Judge Mill House, Hawford (01905 458705). Just east of the A449 bridge on the River Salwarpe. Gas, winter storage, crane, boat sales and repairs, boat fitting out, DIY facilities, chandlery. There are no visitor moorings and craft over 35ft cannot turn.

GLOUCESTER & SHARPNESS CANAL AND RIVER SEVERN

GLOUCESTER & SHARPNESS CANAL

MAXIMUM DIMENSIONS
Length: 240' 0"
Beam: 30' 0"
Draught: 10' 0"
Headroom: 105' 0"

SPEED LIMIT
Gloucester & Sharpness Canal: 6 mph

MILEAGE
SHARPNESS Lock to:
Purton: 1¹/₂ miles
Saul Junction: 8 miles
GLOUCESTER Lock: 16¹/₂ miles

Locks: 2

RIVER SEVERN

MAXIMUM DIMENSIONS
Gloucester to Worcester
Length: 135' 0"
Beam: 21' 0"
Draught: 8' 0"
Headroom (at low summer level): 24' 6"

Worcester to Stourport
Length: 90' 0"
Beam: 19' 0"
Draught: 6' 0" (in low rainfall and with silting, this can be reduced to less than 5' 0" in places during the summer)
Headroom (at low summer level): 20' 0"

SPEED LIMIT
River Severn Navigation: 6 mph heading upstream – 8 mph heading downstream

MILEAGE
GLOUCESTER Lock to:
Ashleworth: 5 miles
Haw Bridge: 8¹/₄ miles
TEWKESBURY Junction with River Avon: 13 miles
Upton upon Severn: 19 miles
DIGLIS Junction with Worcester & Birmingham Canal: 29 miles
Holt Fleet: 36 miles
STOURPORT Junction with Staff & Worcs Canal: 43 miles

Locks: 5

MANAGER
01452 318000;
enquiries.gloucester@britishwaterways.co.uk

The River Severn has always been one of the principal navigations in England. Its great length has made it an important trade artery since the medieval period. With its tributary, the Avon, it cuts deep into the heart of England, linking the iron and coal fields with the Bristol Channel and the British coastal trade. By using the Severn, boats of a considerable size could sail into the Midlands, and into Wales as far as Welshpool. However, the navigation, especially above Worcester, was always difficult, owing to currents, shoals and the demands of water supply for milling, etc.

As boats increased in size, and the cargoes became heavier, the navigational problems increased. The larger boats in common use in the 18th C could rarely sail higher than Bewdley, and so by the end of the century this inland port was beginning to lose its significance. At the same time the sandbanks and shifting shoals in the Gloucester area were seriously affecting the trade on the river as a whole. In order for the river to survive as a viable trade route, it became necessary for drastic improvements to be made. Various Acts were passed to ensure the maintenance of the towing path, although the Severn maintained its tradition of using gangs of men to bow-haul boats until well into the 19th C. In 1803 over 150 men were still employed in what Telford called 'this barbarous and expensive slave-like office' on the section between Bewdley and Coalbrookdale.

The demands of increasing navigation, and the spread of canals in the West Midlands (the Staffordshire & Worcestershire Canal linked the Severn with Birmingham and the rest of the network was opened in 1772) led to the passing of an Act in 1793 that authorised a canal to be built from Berkeley Pill to Gloucester. Work began on Gloucester Docks in 1794, and over the next few years 5$^{1}/2$ miles of canal were cut. Shortage of money then caused work to be stopped, and so the canal remained useless and incomplete. In 1817 Telford was commissioned by the government to report on the feasibility of the canal, with particular reference to the maintenance of navigation on the Severn. He reported in favour of continuing and completing the canal, but recommended that it should run to Sharpness instead of to Berkeley. The government put up the money for the canal, mainly to relieve acute problems of unemployment, and after considerable delays the Gloucester & Sharpness Canal was opened throughout in 1827.

Some of the structural problems were caused by the decision to build the canal to ship standard. At the time of opening, this was the broadest, deepest canal in the world. But, although it greatly increased the cost, this far-sighted decision has ensured that the canal remains in use, and even today Sharpness Dock is still a commercial port.

Once the canal was completed, considerable dredging works and improvements became necessary to maintain the navigation of the upper Severn to Worcester and Stourport. This work, carried out extensively since the formation of the Severn Commission in 1842, included the building of locks and weirs, and the canalisation of parts of the river. The links with the Midlands canal network helped the Severn to flourish, and railway competition increased rather than decreased the traffic both in the docks and on the ship canal. In 1874 Sharpness docks were enlarged and modernised, to handle ships of up to 1000 tons. The same year the Gloucester & Berkeley Canal Company leased the Worcester & Birmingham Canal, to maintain their hold on the trade routes to the Midlands. By 1888 the Severn had a minimum depth of over 6ft, and in most places the depth was 8–9ft. Trade continued to thrive, and the recession in the 1920s was soon overcome by the rapidly growing oil traffic which became the mainstay of the river. The BW Waterway Office publish an excellent guide, giving detailed information on both the canal and river, obtainable from the manager above.

Sharpness

The Gloucester & Sharpness Ship Canal, which was built to bypass the dangerous winding stretch of the tidal River Severn between these two places, has its southern terminus at Sharpness, where there are docks and a large lock up from the Severn. The Gloucester & Sharpness Canal is nowadays the only navigable route between the Severn estuary and the Severn Navigation above Gloucester, so all boats heading upstream must pass through Sharpness Lock and Docks. It should be noted that the entrance to the lock dries out completely at low water, so boats heading in from the estuary should time their arrival for 1 hour before high water, notifying Sharpness in advance. The best time to arrive at the lock is about 2 hours before high water when locking down, and 1 hour before high water when locking up. (**It cannot be stressed too strongly** that craft should **not** attempt to arrive at Sharpness too early – i.e. *more than one hour before high water*). It is unlikely that any boat arriving after high water will be locked in, leaving a choice between an extremely unpleasant 12 hours in the estuary, or a return voyage to Portishead. (The lock is normally operated *2¹/₂ hours before, up until high water*). BW maintain free visitor moorings on the canal outside the docks, which are available for 48 hours. It is important to give prior notice of one's intentions to Sharpness pier head staff (VHF channel 13 or 01453 511968) who can be contacted within a core operating period of *5 hours before high water to 1 hour after high water. Boaters not equipped with VHF marine band radio should carry a mobile phone.*
Craft wishing to use the lock must also book the dock bridges with Sharpness pier head staff *24 hours in advance.* The Low Level Bridge must be swung for all craft; the High Level Bridge has an air draught of approx 16' 6" – it is important to state whether this bridge is required to be operated. Boaters wishing to proceed down the Severn estuary from Sharpness are advised not to do so without a pilot

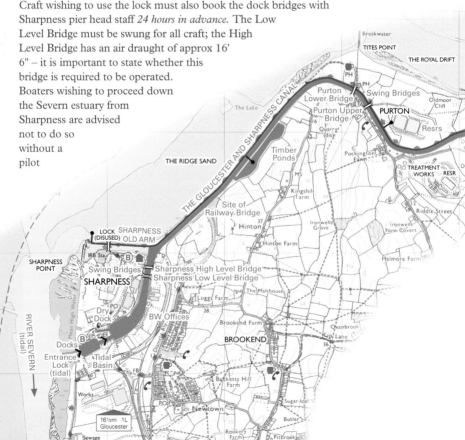

(*see* navigational note 1 on page 68). It is important to keep to the marked channel, and the tide runs extremely fast. Immediately above the lock are Sharpness Docks, which handle ships from Europe, North Africa, Scandinavia and the Mediterranean, making them a busy area. Pleasure boats are encouraged to move on quickly through the two swing bridges out of the docks and onto the ship canal itself. Just north of the swing bridges is an arm off to the west: this leads to a tidal basin which is now, unfortunately, disused. However the length of the arm leading to it is used for permanent and temporary pleasure craft moorings, and there is a small boatyard at the end of it. It is a fascinating place to walk round and see the tidal Severn flowing strongly at the foot of the stone walls. Across the river is the tree-lined west bank of the river, only $^1/_2$ a mile across at this point. A railway line runs along the bottom of the hills. However, the old 22-arched railway bridge that used to cross the river just north of here has been completely demolished, and only the merest traces of some of the stone piers can be seen at low water. The bridge was badly damaged one foggy night in November 1959, when a vessel collided with it; the bridge then stood with a hole in the middle until it was demolished and the iron girders sold to – of all places – Chile, where they now form a road-carrying viaduct. Along the main line of the canal, the circular stone

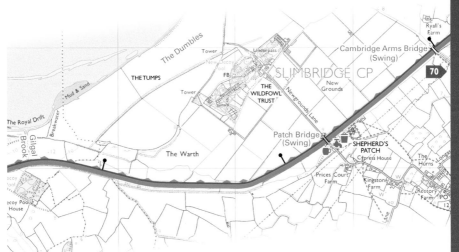

structure is all that remains of the railway's swing bridge over the canal. One mile from Sharpness Docks, the canal is lined with trees on each side – an uncharacteristically river-like stretch that is belied by the occasional glimpse of the Severn flowing alongside. Old timber ponds open off the canal to the right. Timber was stored afloat here in the round. A curve leads to the village of Purton and its two swing bridges: the Upper Bridge is remotely operated. The Lower Bridge keeper can be contacted on 01453 811384 (there are also disabled moorings here). The navigation snakes through the village, passing the large waterworks before settling down to a steady course of wide, straight reaches. It traverses a quiet, green and predictably flat landscape that is well studded with trees and always bounded to the north by saltings and the mud-flats of the Severn estuary – which is here much wider than at Sharpness. At Patch Bridge (01453 890324) there are two pubs; this is the best access point to the Slimbridge Wildfowl Trust (*see* page 69).

NAVIGATIONAL NOTES

1 The Severn Estuary is rightly regarded as no place for the inexperienced inland boater. However, safe passage is perfectly feasible for craft properly prepared and equipped for a short sea voyage and with a crew familiar with these waters, or with a qualified Severn Pilot. Pilotage can be arranged by telephoning Amalgamated Gloucester Pilots on 07774 226143. Safety Guidance Notes for Small Boat Passage of the Severn Estuary are available by sending a large SAE to: The Harbourmaster, Sharpness Port Authority, Sharpness Dock, Berkeley, Glos. GL13 9UD.

2 Once through the docks and onto the canal, remember that this is a commercial waterway; moor only at recognised sites: Old Arm, Sharpness; Purton Lower Bridge; Patch Bridge; Fretherne Bridge; Sandfield Bridge; Saul Junction Bridge; Sellars Bridge; Romans Quay; Bakers Quay; Gloucester Docks.

3 The mechanical swing bridges are manned *08.00–18.30 (until 16.15 winter), lunch break 13.00–13.30.* Last boat admitted *10 minutes before closing time.* Some bridges can be navigated, closed, by low air draught craft. All bridges are guarded by traffic lights and **under no circumstances** should you proceed without a green light.

4 Gloucester Lock and some bridge keepers operate a listening watch on marine band VHF channel 74. It is not necessary to contact each bridge or lock unless you are delayed, or have an emergency.

5 The canal is closed to navigation *on some days over Xmas and New Year.*

Sharpness

Glos. PO, tel. Stores and garage distant. Sharpness exists only for its docks with their tall cranes, old and new warehouses and ever-changing display of foreign ships. It has a strange atmosphere and an interesting situation beside the River Severn. The Severn is wide here, and wild: the tidal range at Sharpness is believed to be the second biggest in the world (only the Bay of Fundy, sandwiched between Nova Scotia and New Brunswick, has a greater range) and the current is swift, especially when accompanied by the high winds that often race up the estuary from the sea. Across the water is the hilly Forest of Dean, with a main railway line running almost along the shore. It is only half a mile away, but it could as well be another country, so remote does it seem. In terms of population, Sharpness is very strung out; here and there is a row of terraced cottages, inhabited mainly by dock workers. Along the lockside – the focus of the docks – are the buildings housing the offices of various shipping firms and the British Waterways Harbourmaster *open Mon–Thu 08.30–17.00 and Fri 08.30–16.30* (01453 811862; keithbadsey@britishwaterways.co.uk). The annual tonnage currently handled here is approximately 600,000 tons, with cargoes consisting mainly of animal feedstuffs, grain, fertilisers, coal, cement and scrap metal, coming from Europe, the Mediterranean, North Africa and Scandinavia. Ships handled average 3000 tons dead weight, with 5000 tons being the maximum: the limiting dimensions of the entrance lock are 55ft beam by 21ft 6in draught. An interesting development at Sharpness is the privatisation of the dock's operation, which should result in a significantly increased traffic flow through the port. However, BW remain as the port authority. Traffic along the canal is now limited to approximately half a dozen shipping movements a year – a coaster collecting bulky distillation plant and water separation units from a manufacturer on the outskirts of Gloucester.

Purton

Glos. Tel. A tiny village of lean, modest houses. It derives an unusual charm from being bisected by the Ship Canal. The canal is not particularly wide here, and to have a large coaster quietly throbbing past these diminutive dwellings seems an incredible distortion of scale. There used to be a ford for cattle across the river nearby – the herdsman had to judge the time to cross the treacherous river to within a few minutes. Just outside Purton, a huge waterworks has been built for the city of Bristol, where up to 24 million gallons of water can be drawn daily from the Ship Canal, purified and pumped through a new 4ft pipeline down to Bristol for drinking purposes. Small reservoirs have been constructed on the other side of the canal: these will provide a temporary feed if and when a monitoring device beside the canal nearer Gloucester indicates that the water is too heavily polluted to draw on.

● **Shepherd's Patch**

Glos. This little settlement existed long before the canal: it used to be where the shepherds watched over their flocks grazing the Severn estuary. There are two pubs here, a gift shop, café and youth hostel.

Slimbridge Wildfowl and Wetland Trust (WWT) Shepherd's Patch, Slimbridge (01453 890333; www.wwt.org.uk). Conveniently situated just half a mile north west of the canal at Patch Bridge, WWT Slimbridge is well worth visiting. Close to the River Severn, apart from containing the largest collection of captive wildfowl in the world (182 species), the grounds and adjacent reserve attract many thousands of migrant birds – Bewick's Swans, White-fronted Geese and all kinds of ducks and waders. Visitors are able to walk around the grounds and study and feed the inhabitants, which are fascinating for their variety, quantity and behaviour. WWT also incorporates an important research establishment that studies all aspects of wildfowl, with special reference to ecological trends. It also plays an important role in the defence of the various species from extinction and can already be credited with the rescue of several important species. Restaurant, gift, book and children's shops; exhibitions and binocular hire; children's activities. No dogs. *Open daily 09.30–17.00 (09.30–16.00 Nov–Mar) except Xmas day.* Charge. Full disabled access including wheelchair loan.

Boatyards

Ⓑ **Sharpness Shipyard** Sharpness Docks (01453 811261/811422). Overnight mooring, long-term mooring, winter and long-term storage, crane (18 tons), engine sales, DIY facilities, general marine engineering facilities.

Ⓑ **Sharpness Marine** Floating Yacht Services Store, The Old Dock, Sharpness (01453 811476). ♣ Gas, overnight and long-term mooring, winter storage, chandlery, boat building and fitting out, charts, toilets. Solid fuel available nearby.

WALKING & CYCLING

The towpath is passable for walkers and cyclists along the Gloucester & Sharpness Canal from Sharpness Old Arm to Hempstead Bridge. North of Gloucester there is an established footpath from Maisemore to Tewkesbury on the west bank, and from Gloucester to Tewkesbury (the Severn Way) on the east bank. A new length of the 128-mile Gloucester, Bristol and Newbury section of the National Cycle Network Route 41 uses the towpath between Slimbridge and Frampton.

Pubs and Restaurants

🍺 **The Pier View Hotel** Sharpness (01453 811255). East of dock area, in centre of village. Bar snacks (V) are available *L and E (not Sun)*. Garden and children's play area. Pool, darts, dominoes. Occasional live music *Sat.* B & B.

🍺 **The Lammastide Inn** New Brookend, Berkeley (01453 811337). 1 mile east of Sharpness at New Brookend, near Berkeley. Comfortable, welcoming pub dispensing a variety of real ales. Also a wide range of good value for money food (V) *L and E, daily.* Excellent *Sunday* roasts. Children and dogs welcome. Large enclosed garden with swings and climbing frame. *Monthly Fri* musical entertainment.

🍺 **The Berkeley Arms** Purton, near Berkeley (01453 811262). 150yds from the lower bridge. Situated beside the river with an excellent view along it. Real ale.

🍺 ✗ **The Tudor Arms** Shepherd's Patch, a few yards from Patch Bridge towards the Wildfowl Trust (01453 890306). A large, country pub (once a smallholding, then a beer and cider house for the canal-constructing Irish navvies) serving real ale. À la carte restaurant and bar meals (V) *L and E, daily.* Non-smoking family room with children's toys. Garden. Camping. B & B. Popular with Slimbridge's (human) visiting celebrities. *Open all day in summer.*

✗ **The Slimbridge Boat Station** Patch Bridge, Shepherd's Patch, Slimbridge (01453 899190/899191). Small canalside café serving teas, coffees and light meals (V) including breakfast. *Open weekends all year and Mon–Fri, Jun–Aug 08.00–16.45.*

Saul Junction

The Ship Canal continues towards Gloucester, with the spacious Severn estuary over to the west. Swing bridges punctuate the canal and at almost every bridge is a bridge keeper's cottage (Cambridge Arms Bridge – 01453 890272, Junction Bridge – 01452 740444). These cottages are peculiar to the Gloucester & Sharpness Canal and have great charm – they are only small single-storey buildings, but each one has a substantial classical façade with fluted Doric columns and a pediment. At Cambridge Arms Bridge there is an unnavigable arm which feeds the canal with water from the Cotswolds. At Frampton on Severn the church is passed on the east side, then after a long straight the navigation bends to the north east. Between Fretherne Bridge and Sandfield Bridge, on the offside, there is solid fuel and red diesel for sale. Trees encroach here on one side, and several bridges lead past scattered houses to Saul Junction. Over to the east the great Cotswold scarp marches parallel to the canal.

UPPER DUMBALL

RIVER SEVERN (tidal)

CROWN POINT

Lea Court Farm

FRAMILODE

Stroudwater Canal (dis)

Baldwins

UPPER FRAMILODE

Saul Bridge

PO

Glebe Farm

Passage Road

Saul Junction Bridge (Swing)

SAUL

Sch

Lock (dis)

B

Square Covert

Saul Farm

Church

Whitminster House

NE WITH SAUL CP

Sandfield Bridge (Swing)

Grain Store

WALK BRIDGE

Malthouse Farm

Oatfield

WHITMINSTER BRIDGE

Dunstalls Wood

MS

4071

Hock Ditch

Dunstalls

Sewage Works

Fretherne Bridge (Swing)

Factory

Sch

12

Saul Lodge

Pol Ho

Saul Warth

PO

FRAMPTON ON SEVERN

Manor Farm

The Green

FRAMPTON COURT

12

Works

Mean High Water

Pit (dis)

Townfield Farm

Pp Ho

Cont & CP Bdy

Splatt Bridge (Swing)

Frampton Pill

CHURCH END

Park Corner Cottage

Nastfield Farm

FRAMPTON BREAKWATER

THE SPLATT

10m 1L Gloucester

Sharpness 6½m 0L

FRAMPTON ON S

Parkfield Covert

BLACK ROCK BREAKWATER

THE GLOUCESTER AND SHARPNESS CANAL

Oegrove Covert

Mincepie Covert

Severn Way

Old Withy Bed

MIDDLE POINT BREAKWATER

NEW GROUNDS

Marsh Lane Track

Blackthorn Covert

9

Nebrow Hill

The Marshes

Park Fm

New Decoy Pool

FB

Ryall's Farm

Cambridge Arms Bridge (Swing)

67

Cambridge Arm (unnavigable feeder)

SLIMBRIDGE CP

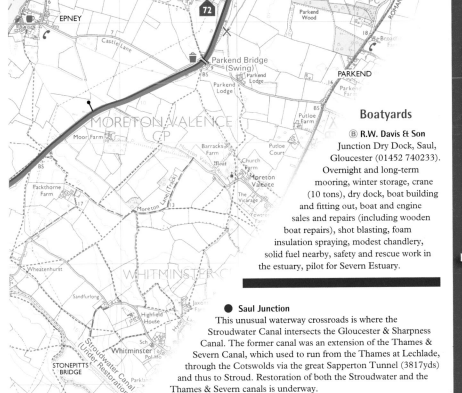

Boatyards

Ⓑ **R.W. Davis & Son**
Junction Dry Dock, Saul,
Gloucester (01452 740233).
Overnight and long-term
mooring, winter storage, crane
(10 tons), dry dock, boat building
and fitting out, boat and engine
sales and repairs (including wooden
boat repairs), shot blasting, foam
insulation spraying, modest chandlery,
solid fuel nearby, safety and rescue work in
the estuary, pilot for Severn Estuary.

● **Saul Junction**
This unusual waterway crossroads is where the
Stroudwater Canal intersects the Gloucester & Sharpness
Canal. The former canal was an extension of the Thames &
Severn Canal, which used to run from the Thames at Lechlade,
through the Cotswolds via the great Sapperton Tunnel (3817yds)
and thus to Stroud. Restoration of both the Stroudwater and the
Thames & Severn canals is underway.

● **Frampton on Severn**
Glos. PO, tel, stores, garage. A beautiful linear village notable mainly for its
green, which is about 100yds wide and fully half a mile long. The Church of
St Mary at the south end of the village, near the canal, is mainly of the 14th C.
Frampton Court Facing the village green is this Georgian mansion (1731–3)
whose gardens contain a Gothic Orangery (1745) and an octagonal dovecote.
Visits only by written application to the owners in residence.

Pubs and Restaurants

🍺 ✕ **The Three Horseshoes**
Frampton on Severn (01452 740463).
Half-way along the green towards Splatt
Bridge. Real village pub serving home-
cooked food (V) *L and E (not Sun E)*, six
real ales, cider and table wines. Children and
dogs welcome. Patio seating. Very occasional
live music.

🍺 **The Bell Inn** The Green, Frampton on
Severn (01452 740346). ¹/4 mile south east
of Fretherne Bridge. Delightful village inn
offering warmth and hospitality beside the
longest village green in England, together with
an excellent selection of real ales and regional
ciders. Home-cooked English country food
(V) using local produce served *L and E (until
21.30 unless pre-arranged)*. Children and dogs
welcome in prescribed areas. Large gardens
overlooking cricket green and with children's

play equipment. Log fires *in winter*; cream
teas *in summer*. Camping. B & B.

🍺 **The Ship Inn** Framilode, Saul (01452
740260). Where the disused arm of the
Stroudwater Canal meets the B4071 – walk-
able, with care, from Saul Junction! An
excellent hostelry serving real ale together
with an interesting selection of food (V) *L
and E (last orders 21.30)*. Children welcome in
family room and dining room. Large garden
with children's play area. Pub games, camping, and real fires *in winter*. Non-smoking
area. Regular *Sun* jazz evenings.

🍺 **The Anchor** Epney (01452 740433).
Country pub beside the River Severn dispensing real ales and good food (V) *L and E, daily*
– home-made pies a speciality. Children
welcome inside; dogs outside on a chain. Large
gardens. Quiz *Sun*. Very busy *during the summer*.

Hardwicke

Heading more or less north from Parkend, the canal continues through undramatic country, which is slightly wooded. There are no villages on this section, but several farms are situated near the canal. Towards Sellars Bridge (01452 720251), the navigation enters a cutting for the first time since Sharpness. There is a pub by this bridge, and just to the north is a disused oil wharf for small ships. This was the furthest (northernmost) point which the oil traffic reached on the navigation once carrying had ceased on the river – originally as far as Stourport in barges – but this is all finished now. North of Quedgeley Wharf the canal approaches the River Severn (hidden behind a flood bank and far narrower up here than downstream); turning sharply eastward, the canal reaches Rea Bridge.

NAVIGATIONAL NOTES

1 The three bridges, Sellars, Rea and Sims have a greater head-room (over 7ft) than the others on the Gloucester & Sharpness Canal. Boats normally used on the narrow canals will find no difficulty in getting under these bridges without them being opened, although they do so at their own risk. Boats *should not* pass under these bridges without receiving a green light from the keeper.

2 It is anticipated that by summer 2003 there will be a new facilities block at Saul Junction that will include showers, toilets, laundry, telephone and possibly an information centre. Contact BW to confirm on (01452) 318000 or email enquiries. gloucester@britishwaterways.co.uk.

Boatyards

Ⓑ **A & D Marine Services** Hempstead Dry Dock, 338 Bristol Road, Gloucester (01452 307674; www.admarineservices.co.uk). Boat sales and repairs, engine sales and repairs (inboard and outboard), dry dock, boat fitting out, DIY facilities, books and maps.

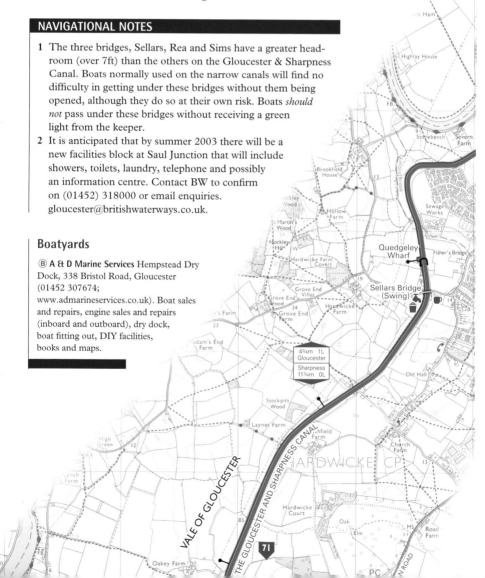

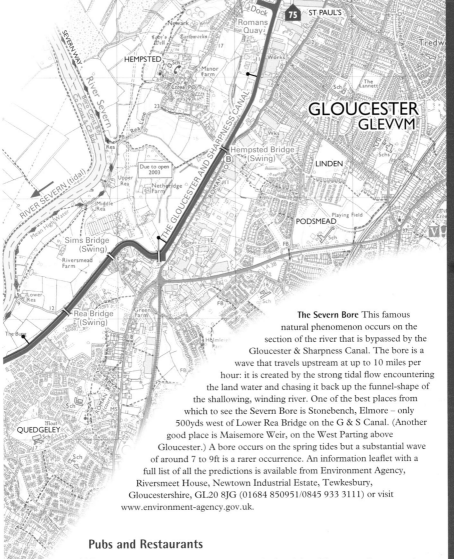

The Severn Bore This famous natural phenomenon occurs on the section of the river that is bypassed by the Gloucester & Sharpness Canal. The bore is a wave that travels upstream at up to 10 miles per hour: it is created by the strong tidal flow encountering the land water and chasing it back up the funnel-shape of the shallowing, winding river. One of the best places from which to see the Severn Bore is Stonebench, Elmore – only 500yds west of Lower Rea Bridge on the G & S Canal. (Another good place is Maisemore Weir, on the West Parting above Gloucester.) A bore occurs on the spring tides but a substantial wave of around 7 to 9ft is a rarer occurrence. An information leaflet with a full list of all the predictions is available from Environment Agency, Riversmeet House, Newtown Industrial Estate, Tewkesbury, Gloucestershire, GL20 8JG (01684 850951/0845 933 3111) or visit www.environment-agency.gov.uk.

Pubs and Restaurants

✕ ♀ **The Castle Restaurant** (01452 720328). Canalside, 300yds north of Parkend Bridge. Originally built in 1930 as a boathouse for the development of experimental electric yachts, this establishment now offers *morning coffees, L and afternoon teas.* All food is fresh from local markets and everything is prepared on the premises without recourse to microwaves or fryers. A battery of six electric ovens hold sway and in consequence meals are traditional British roasts. All dietary needs are catered for. Children welcome, and large canalside gardens. *L must be booked a day in advance* in order to accommodate the marketing régime. The owners have recently celebrated 34 years' residence here: something of a record in the catering trade! Mooring.

🍺 **The Pilot Inn** (01452 720252). Canalside, at Sellars Bridge, Hardwicke. Privately owned, traditional pub serving quality cuisine (V) at affordable prices *L and E (not Sat).* All food freshly cooked to order. Real ales. Nooks, crannies and open fires. Children welcome; dogs in garden only. Garden with excellent view overlooking the ship canal. No regular entertainment but themed events on selected dates.

Gloucester

At Rea Bridge the canal enters a cutting and describes a sharp double bend, from which one emerges into a completely different landscape: the quiet countryside has disappeared, its place taken by outlying industrial works on either side of the main road that runs noisily parallel to the navigation. The Ship Canal, strangely enough, has never played a large part in the generation of wealth that this industry represents, but north of Hempstead Bridge (01452 521880) there was a large timber wharf for discharging ships bringing imported wood. Further north there was an oil dock, a grain silo and a general cargo quay. Ahead is Gloucester, and the extensive docks that are laid out virtually in the town centre. These are superb docks, for all around are great warehouses ranged along the quays. Boatmen wishing to moor here – the best place for visiting Gloucester – should go to the office by the lock and seek advice from the BW official. Gloucester Lock (VHF channel 74 or 01452 318007) marks the northern end of the Gloucester & Sharpness Canal, and lowers boats back into the River Severn, reminding one that the ship canal is well above the river level. It has to be kept filled with water by pumping up from the river. No boats should follow the river to the south west at the tail of Gloucester Lock, for Llanthony Lock is closed and only a weir awaits them. North of Gloucester Lock, the river is bounded on the town side by a high quay, with moorings more suitable for larger vessels than for motor cruisers. Gloucester gaol is nearby. Proceeding upstream, boatmen will find themselves on a dull length of river, narrow and hemmed in by high banks. A sharp bend requires a careful lookout; beyond it are road and rail bridges. The river winds along in its own isolated way, flanked mainly by trees. At one point it approaches a minor road; the former pub here is now a private house. Further upstream is the junction with the big western channel of the Severn, whose separate course between here and Gloucester explains the narrowness of the navigation channel. There is in fact a lock (Maisemore Lock, now closed) just 300yds along the western channel of the Severn. This is a relic of the days before the Ship Canal was built; it used to give access from the upper Severn to the Herefordshire & Gloucestershire Canal (now undergoing restoration, *see* page 96), which joined the Severn near Gloucester.

NAVIGATIONAL NOTES

1 Gloucester Lock Bridge and Llanthony Bridge (01452 312143) will not be opened for pleasure craft during peak road traffic flows *Mon–Fri 08.20–09.00 and 16.30–17.30*.
2 As with all river navigations, the Severn must be treated with respect, especially after periods of prolonged rain, when the current increases. If you are in any doubt regarding your safety on the river, moor up out of the main stream and seek expert advice.
3 All locks on the River Severn are manned. They are open: *Nov–Feb 08.00–16.00; Mar, Sep and Oct 08.00–17.30; Apr–early Jul 08.00–18.30 and early Jul–early Sep 08.00–20.00. Last boat admitted 15 mins before lock closes. These dates are approximate and can vary from year to year.* Contact Gloucester Lock (VHF channel 74 or 01452 318007) for further details. Do not enter a lock unless the green light is showing.
4 Gloucester Docks is *48hr* visitor mooring only. Safety ladders must not be obstructed by moored craft at any time.
5 There is a self-operated pump out on Llanthony Pontoons.

Boatyards

(B) **T. Nielsen & Co** The Shipyard, Gloucester Docks, Gloucester (01452 301117). ⚓ Winter storage, crane (9 ton), boat repairs (specialising in wooden boats), boat building and fitting out, dry dock (170ft).

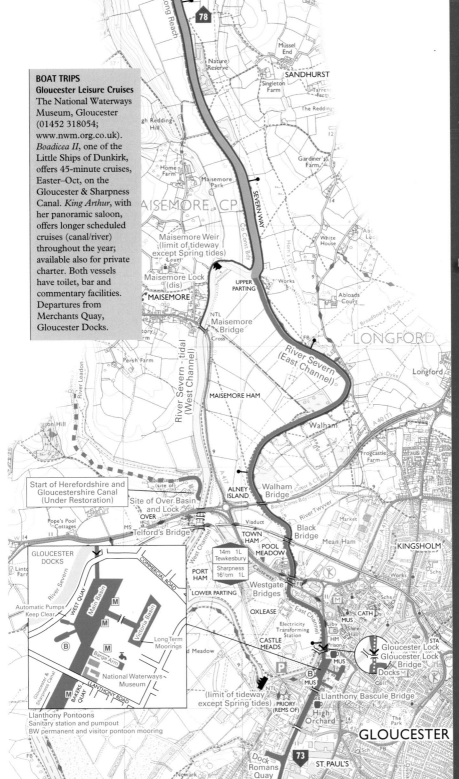

BOAT TRIPS

Gloucester Leisure Cruises

The National Waterways Museum, Gloucester (01452 318054; www.nwm.org.co.uk). *Boadicea II*, one of the Little Ships of Dunkirk, offers 45-minute cruises, Easter–Oct, on the Gloucester & Sharpness Canal. *King Arthur*, with her panoramic saloon, offers longer scheduled cruises (canal/river) throughout the year; available also for private charter. Both vessels have toilet, bar and commentary facilities. Departures from Merchants Quay, Gloucester Docks.

Gloucester & Sharpness Canal — Gloucester

Gloucester

Glos. All services. Now a busy manufacturing town and commercial centre, Gloucester was once the Roman colony of Glevum. The town was laid out in a cross plan, with north, south, east and west gates. This geography still survives, if only in name. Traces of Roman habitation are much more difficult to find than in other Roman towns in Britain, but when the Bell Hotel was being demolished in recent years, excavations revealed 1000 sq ft of paved courtyard, believed to be the site of the Roman forum. There are a few interesting old buildings in the town centre, notably the 12th-C Fleece Hotel and numbers 11–15 Southgate, but otherwise the town centre is of less interest than one might expect. However the glorious cathedral provides an oasis of peace and beauty in the town. The other area of real interest is the docks; many of the splendid warehouses only just escaped demolition in a less enlightened time.

Bus Enquiries Bus Station, Market Parade, Gloucester (01452 527516). Also Traveline 0870 608 2 608.

Cathedral College Green, Gloucester (01452 528095; www.gloucestercathedral.com). Founded as an abbey in 1089 by Abbot Serlo, this splendid building is essentially Norman, but extensive remodelling of the choir and transepts between 1330 and 1370 shows fine examples of early Perpendicular architecture. But perhaps the most interesting part of the present building is the adjacent cloisters: they feature the earliest known fan-vaulting (mid-14th C). **Orchids Restaurant** (01452 308920). *Open Mon–Sat 10.00–17.00 for coffee, lunch and tea, Sun 11.30–16.30 for lunch and tea.*

City Museum & Art Gallery Brunswick Road (01452 524131; www.gloucester.gov.uk). Exhibits of furniture, glass, silver, costumes and coins; also local archaeology, geology and natural history. *Open Mon–Sat 10.00–17.00 (including B Hol Mon) and Sun (Jun–Sep only) 10.00–16.00. Closed public holidays.* Charge. Joint ticket with Folk Museum available.

Dean Forest Railway Forest Road, Lydney (01594 845840; www.deanforestrailway.co.uk). A living memory in steam of all those branch lines that used to serve small local communities. Currently open between Lydney Junction (direct access to Regional Railways services from Gloucester) and Norchard in the Forest of Dean, the line will eventually run to Parkend. Railway centre at Norchard with museum, souvenir shop (*open Easter–Xmas daily and winter weekends*) and cafeteria car. Riverside walk and woodland trail. For the energetic there is a 3-mile round walk to Lydney Harbour. The railway operates a mix of steam and diesel traction on *selected days Apr–Dec.* Telephone the talking timetable for further details

on (01594) 843423. Connecting trains from Gloucester station (telephone 08457 484950).

Eastgate Viewing Chamber Eastgate, Gloucester. Access to the medieval east gate of the city and original city walls. *Open May–Sep, 10.15–11.15 and 15.15–16.15.* Charge.

Folk Museum 99–103 Westgate Street (01452 526467; www.gloucester.gov.uk). Fine collection of local history and bygones: there is a whole section on the River Severn, its vessels and the salmon and eel fishing industries that it once supported. Also schoolroom, shoemaker's, carpenter's and wheelwright's workshops. Dairy, toys and games and model steam engines. *Opening as for City Museum & Art Gallery.* Charge. Joint pass with City Museum available.

Gloucester Antique Centre 1 Severn Road, Gloucester (01452 529716; www.antiquescentre.com). On the north west side of the docks. A complete grain warehouse packed with stalls selling antiques and collectables. Charge. *Open Mon–Sat 10.00–17.00 and Sun 13.00–17.00.* Free entry.

Gloucester Docks These extensive docks close to the centre of Gloucester are, to many people, really much more interesting than the town itself. They are at the north end of the Gloucester & Sharpness Ship Canal, where it locks down into the Severn, and were built around 1827. Imported timber and grain are two of the main cargoes that used to be brought up here – they arrived mostly in big barges from ports down the Bristol Channel. The seven-storey dock warehouses are magnificent. For further information on the contemporary commercial scene, together with details about organised, guided walks on *summer Suns,* telephone (01452) 311190 or email info@glosdocks.co.uk.

Guildhall Arts Centre 23 Eastgate Street, Gloucester (01452 505089; www.gloucester.gov.uk). Lively, friendly venue for an imaginative range of theatre, music, dance, films and visual arts. Licensed bar and snacks.

House of The Tailor of Gloucester 9 College Court, Gloucester (01452 422856; www.heroes-shop.com). Tiny shop and museum in the home that Beatrix Potter chose for her tailor in the famous story *The Tailor of Gloucester. Open Apr–Oct 10.00–17.00 and Nov–Mar 10.00–16.00.*

National Waterways Museum Llanthony Warehouse, The Docks, Gloucester (01452 318054; www.nwm.org.co.uk). Journey the waterways of Britain. Unravel the 200-year story of inland waterways through touch, working models and archive film. Board historic boats moored at the two quaysides. Specialist book/gift shop stocked with traditional Roses & Castles painted ware. *Open daily 10.00–17.00, closed Xmas day. Last admission 1 hour before closing.* Charge. Full disabled access. Joint ticket for museum and boat trip.

Nature in Art Wallsworth Hall, Main A38, Twigworth, Gloucester (01452 731422; www.nature-in-art.org.uk). Dedicated to all forms of art – from any period, in any medium – inspired by nature. A grand diversity of artists and a collection that is continually changing and developing. From *Feb–Nov* a variety of artists from around the world can be seen at working in a range of media and styles in a studio setting. Nature garden and pond as a focus for painting or relaxing. Outdoor play area for children, and animal brass rubbing. Gift shop and coffee shop serving home-made snacks, meals and drinks. *Open Tue–Sun and B Hol Mon 10.00–17.00. Closed 24–26 Dec.* Charge. Bus service to the entrance gate then ¹/₂ mile walk. Full disabled facilities.

Regiments of Gloucester Museum Custom House, The Docks, Gloucester (01452 522682; www.glosters.org.uk). The story of Gloucestershire's two regiments told with photographs, reconstructed scenes and displays of uniforms, medals, etc. An altogether more lively experience than many of its ilk. Gift shop. *Open Oct–May Tue–Sat 10.00-17.00; Jun-Sep also Mon and B Hols.* Charge. Disabled access.

Shopmobility Hampden Way, Gloucester (01452 302871/396898). Free hire of battery powered scooters and wheelchairs and chairs to push.

Gloucester Tourist Information Centre 28 Southgate Street Gloucester (01452 396572/504273; www.gloucester.gov.uk/ tourism). *Open Mon–Sat 10.00–17.00 and Sun 11.00–15.00.* Tourist Information available in National Waterways Museum (01452 330152) *open daily 10.00–17.00 (staffed from 11.00– 15.00 only).* Regular scenic guided coach tours of the local (and not so local) area *Jun–Sep* bookable at these offices (nearest departure point Cheltenham). Also guided walks.

Pubs and Restaurants

🍺 **The Linden Tree** 73–75 Bristol Road, Gloucester (01452 527869). South of the intersection between Llanthony Road and Bristol Road. Attractive Grade II listed building dispensing as many as eight different real ales. Good food (V) *L and E (not Sun E).* Children welcome, outside seating. No machines. Open fires, and excellent accommodation.

🍺 ✕ **Dr Foster's** Kimberley Warehouse, The Docks, Gloucester (01452 300990). At north east corner of the docks. Real ale served. Families welcomed in the airy conservatory area overlooking the docks. There is also an upstairs restaurant. Food (V) is available in all three areas *L and E, daily.* Disabled facilities. *Open all day.*

🍺 **The Black Swan Inn** 68–70 Southgate Street, Gloucester (01452 523642). North east of the docks. Comfortable city-centre inn offering an excellent selection of real ales, cider and perry. Good value, home-made food (V) is served *L and E, Mon–Sat.* Children and dogs (downstairs only) welcome. Patio seating area. Reasonably priced accommodation. Disabled access. *Tue evening* jazz and blues. *Open all day.*

✕ ♀ **Topoly's** 49 Southgate Street, Gloucester (01452 331062). North east of the docks. Good value Italian food (V) served in a friendly, family-run, welcoming restaurant close to the docks. All your favourite Italian dishes free from the chain-run, fast food format. *Open L and E, Mon–Sat* (booking advisable *E*).

🍺 **The Regal** Kings Square, Gloucester (01452 332344). A converted cinema in typical Wetherspoons style serving real ale. Food (V) available *all day, every day.* Children welcome. Outside seating and disabled access. Non-smoking area. *Open all day.*

🍺 **The Windmill** 83-85 Eastgate Street, Gloucester (01452 500370). Bottled beers and continental lagers vie with real ale and real cider in a smart, city centre pub. Food (V) available *Mon–Fri 12.00–19.00 and Sat–Sun 12.00–17.00.* No children. Limited outside seating. Non-smoking area and disabled access. DJ and live music *Fri and Sat. Open all day.*

🍺 **The Whitesmiths Arms** 81 Southgate Street, Gloucester (01452 414770). Opposite the eastern dock gates. Traditional English pub dispensing real ales and named after nautical metalworkers. Food (V) served *L and E.* Children welcome *until 21.00.* Outside seating, open fires and traditional pub games. Live music *Fri.* Disabled access. *Open all day except Sun.*

🍺 ✕ **The New Inn** 16 Northgate Street, Gloucester (01452 522177). Fine old Grade I listed building that has finally been restored as a superb example of a medieval, galleried inn. A restaurant, coffee shop and three bars surround the cobbled courtyard and as many as six real ales are available, together with real cider. Food (V) is served *L and E.* Children welcome, outside seating and pub games. B & B. *Open all day.*

Haw Bridge

Leaving the junction (known as the Upper Parting) of the east and west channels of the River Severn, from this point northwards the river is predictably wider. Its character changes very little in all its journey to Stourport – most of the way it is lined by trees and high banks. The surrounding countryside is quite pretty but because of the banks, the boater will see little except for the occasional hills. The walker along the banks is luckier in having good views of the river and the surrounding countryside. Away from the centre the river is often extremely shallow; there are anyway limited mooring places, so access to the villages on either side is restricted. After a series of long reaches, the spire of Ashleworth Church appears on the left side as the river bends to the east towards the hills that rise steeply from the river bank. There are visitor moorings on the west bank, just upstream of the pub. The main hill here is Wainlode Hill, which reaches a height of almost 300ft. The silted-up lock on the east bank is the entrance to the former Coombe Hill Canal, now partly restored, but land-locked. The modern bridge to the north is Haw Bridge. There are pubs and visitor moorings on the west bank, downstream of the bridge. Navigators should keep away from the east bank near this bridge – there is a submerged obstruction. The river winds through an S-bend, passing a riverside pub and a line of hills to the east; then it straightens out somewhat as it heads for Tewkesbury. Yet another riverside pub, the Yew Tree Inn, is passed – a half-sunk barge serves as a mooring. A sailing club is based here. Opposite is Odda's Chapel, but access is difficult because of the rocky banks.

NAVIGATIONAL NOTES

Because of Wainlode Hill's susceptibility to erosion by the river, old barges have been sunk in the river near the south east bank, in order to protect it. All boats should keep to the north side of the river to avoid the hulks. The area is marked by posts.

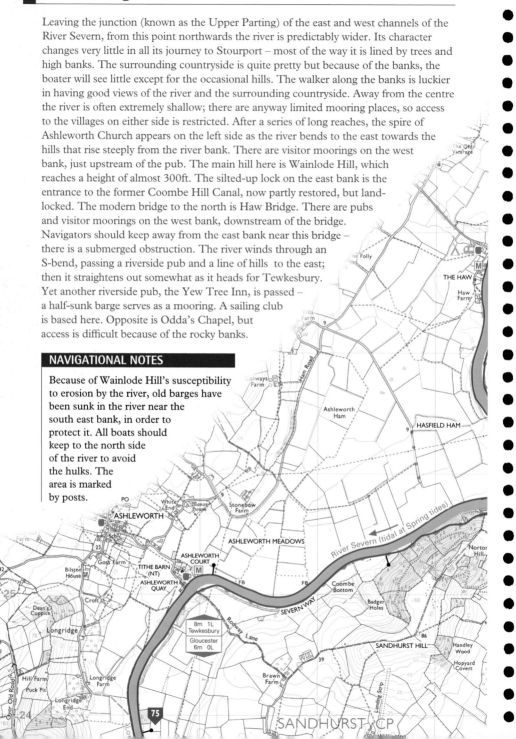

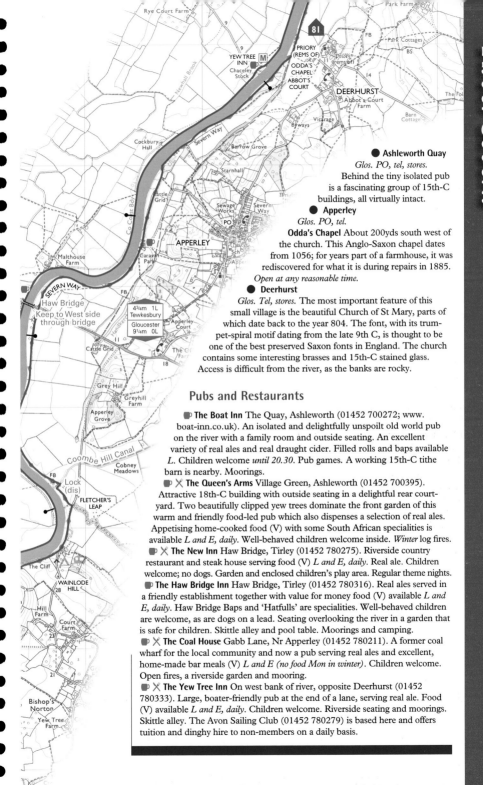

● **Ashleworth Quay**
Glos. PO, tel, stores.
Behind the tiny isolated pub
is a fascinating group of 15th-C
buildings, all virtually intact.
● **Apperley**
Glos. PO, tel.
Odda's Chapel About 200yds south west of
the church. This Anglo-Saxon chapel dates
from 1056; for years part of a farmhouse, it was
rediscovered for what it is during repairs in 1885.
Open at any reasonable time.
● **Deerhurst**
Glos. Tel, stores. The most important feature of this
small village is the beautiful Church of St Mary, parts of
which date back to the year 804. The font, with its trum-
pet-spiral motif dating from the late 9th C, is thought to be
one of the best preserved Saxon fonts in England. The church
contains some interesting brasses and 15th-C stained glass.
Access is difficult from the river, as the banks are rocky.

Pubs and Restaurants

🍺 **The Boat Inn** The Quay, Ashleworth (01452 700272; www.
boat-inn.co.uk). An isolated and delightfully unspoilt old world pub
on the river with a family room and outside seating. An excellent
variety of real ales and real draught cider. Filled rolls and baps available
L. Children welcome *until 20.30*. Pub games. A working 15th-C tithe
barn is nearby. Moorings.

🍺✗ **The Queen's Arms** Village Green, Ashleworth (01452 700395).
Attractive 18th-C building with outside seating in a delightful rear courtyard. Two beautifully clipped yew trees dominate the front garden of this
warm and friendly food-led pub which also dispenses a selection of real ales.
Appetising home-cooked food (V) with some South African specialities is
available *L and E, daily*. Well-behaved children welcome inside. *Winter* log fires.

🍺✗ **The New Inn** Haw Bridge, Tirley (01452 780275). Riverside country
restaurant and steak house serving food (V) *L and E, daily*. Real ale. Children
welcome; no dogs. Garden and enclosed children's play area. Regular theme nights.

🍺 **The Haw Bridge Inn** Haw Bridge, Tirley (01452 780316). Real ales served in
a friendly establishment together with value for money food (V) available *L and
E, daily*. Haw Bridge Baps and 'Hatfulls' are specialities. Well-behaved children
are welcome, as are dogs on a lead. Seating overlooking the river in a garden that
is safe for children. Skittle alley and pool table. Moorings and camping.

🍺✗ **The Coal House** Gabb Lane, Nr Apperley (01452 780211). A former coal
wharf for the local community and now a pub serving real ales and excellent,
home-made bar meals (V) *L and E (no food Mon in winter)*. Children welcome.
Open fires, a riverside garden and mooring.

🍺✗ **The Yew Tree Inn** On west bank of river, opposite Deerhurst (01452
780333). Large, boater-friendly pub at the end of a lane, serving real ale. Food
(V) available *L and E, daily*. Children welcome. Riverside seating and moorings.
Skittle alley. The Avon Sailing Club (01452 780279) is based here and offers
tuition and dinghy hire to non-members on a daily basis.

Mythe Bridge

The river now passes another pub with excellent BW visitor moorings. One of the two channels of the Warwickshire Avon enters here from Tewkesbury: the Battle of Tewkesbury was fought just to the east of here in 1471. Marked by the abbey, Tewkesbury can be seen to the north east, but the Severn sweeps round to the west of the town, leaving an enormous expanse of flat, empty meadow between them. Upper Lode Lock (01684 293138) is well concealed on a corner between the weir and a backwater. (The weir is, incidentally, the highest point to which normal spring tides flow.) Upstream of the lock is a junction with the main (navigable) course of the River Avon – boats heading for the Lower and Upper Avon navigations should turn east here, as should boats intending to visit Tewkesbury. Beware of the shallow spit projecting south west from the tip of the junction. Continuing up the Severn, one reaches the single 170ft-span of the cast iron Mythe Bridge over the river, built by Thomas Telford in 1828. Steep wooded hills rise on the east bank by this bridge, but the river bears off to the north west and soon leaves them behind. Its character remains virtually unchanged – it is lined by high banks and trees, untouched by villages or towns, and seemingly isolated from the countryside that its wide course divides so effectively.

THE RIVER AVON IN TEWKESBURY It is certainly worth turning off the Severn into the River Avon – this is the way to Tewkesbury, Evesham and Stratford-upon-Avon. Boaters not wishing to buy the short-term pass on to the Lower Avon Navigation may tie up just below the big Healing's Mill to visit Tewkesbury (charge), but those who decide to go through the pretty Avon Lock (operated by a lock keeper – 01684 292129) will find it a worthwhile diversion. *See* page 14 and the River Avon section for all details and boatyard services in the town.

SEVERAL SEVERN CROSSINGS

For thousands of years the river has been a barrier to communication. It has served both as a defence, keeping one marauding horde from the throats of another, and as a bar to pedestrian and road communication. Initially it was crossed via fords – or lodes as they were known locally – and by using tree trunks supported by stones on some of the upper, shallower reaches.

The first records of bridge building date from the 13th C when a flurry of fine structures, mainly of stone, were constructed in the pursuit of commerce. None have survived the vagaries of flood, war and the ravages of time. The most famous surviving bridge is at Coalbrookdale where Darby, a succesful local ironmaster, built Ironbridge – opened in 1781 – to a design by Thomas Pritchard. Thomas Telford was responsible for many of the existing major crossings including Holt Fleet, Mythe and Over – just to the west of Gloucester – and now disued. Further upstream he constructed the cast iron Haw Bridge, inadvertently demolished by an oil barge in December 1958 when the river was in spate. Two other cast iron bridges, at Arley and Coalbrookdale, were built by John Fowler in the mid-19th C. Spanning the non-tidal Severn, the more modern crossings are no more than utilitarian concrete affairs lacking the beauty and grace of their forebears. Downstream the two tidal Severn crossings are not without style and an element of daring, although it is the aviator rather than the boater, who is best placed to appreciate their aesthetic appeal.

Pubs and Restaurants

🍺 ✕ **The Lower Lode** Forthampton (01684 293224). 3/4 mile below Upper Lode Lock. 15th-C inn with excellent BW visitor moorings close by. This pub, in a delightful riverside setting, dispenses a selection of real ales and has an informal restaurant serving meals *L and E, daily.* Children welcome *until 21.00*; well-behaved dogs at all times. Food is available *all day during the summer* as are morning coffee and afternoon cream teas. Riverside gardens and slipway. *Weekend* barbecues and camping. B & B with en suite facilities. Picnic park opposite. The pub operates a ferry for walkers and cyclists *Easter–Sep.*

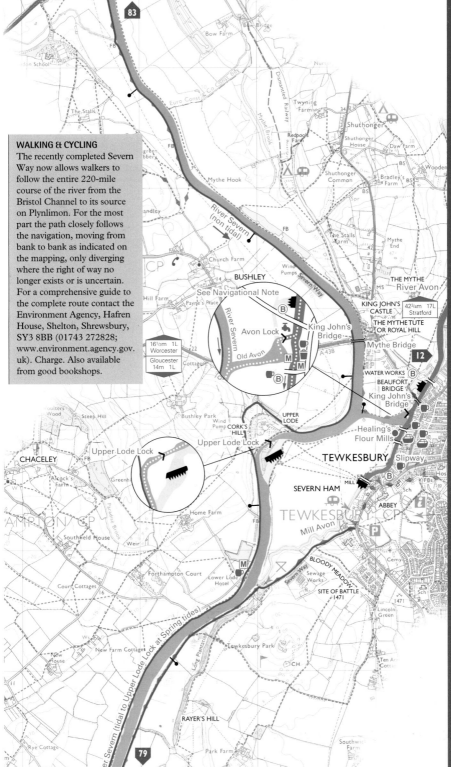

WALKING & CYCLING
The recently completed Severn Way now allows walkers to follow the entire 220-mile course of the river from the Bristol Channel to its source on Plynlimon. For the most part the path closely follows the navigation, moving from bank to bank as indicated on the mapping, only diverging where the right of way no longer exists or is uncertain. For a comprehensive guide to the complete route contact the Environment Agency, Hafren House, Shelton, Shrewsbury, SY3 8BB (01743 272828; www.environment.agency.gov.uk). Charge. Also available from good bookshops.

Upton upon Severn

The River Severn continues on its predictable, undramatic course northwards, flanked by wooded banks that prevent any views of the countryside. There are few signs of habitation or human activity apart from boats and anglers. The big steel viaduct carrying the M50 motorway provides a rare feature of interest. The significant-looking pipes sticking out of the ground on the east bank at this point betray the existence of an old underground oil depot, but it is now disused. A mile further on, the view improves as the old church tower at Upton upon Severn appears, followed by the graceful modern bridge and interesting waterfront of this attractive small town. Plenty of boats are moored here – there are visitor moorings on the west bank, just upstream of the bridge. Leaving Upton, the river resumes its high-banked course through the countryside. On the west bank, but hardly visible from a boat, is the village of Hanley Castle.

Boatyards

(B) **Upton Marina** Upton upon Severn (01684 593111/594287; www.waltonmarine.co.uk). 🛢 🚽 🛒 D E Pump out, gas, overnight and long-term mooring, winter storage, slipway, crane, chandlery, books and maps, boat building, boat and engine sales and repairs, café, groceries, toilets, showers, telephone. Licensed club.

(B) **Starline Narrowboats** Upton Marina, Upton upon Severn (01684 574774; www.starline.demon.co.uk). 🛢 🚽 🛒 D Pump out, gas, narrow-boat hire (including boats for disabled groups),

slipway, crane, narrowboat sales, engine sales, boat repairs, boat building and fitting out, wet dock, DIY facilities, chandlery, books and maps, toilets, showers, disabled facilities. *24hr emergency call out Mar–Oct.*

(B) **Gullivers** Upton Marina, Upton upon Severn (07771 860030). Broad beam boat for hire.

(B) **Handy Boat Hire** Upton Marina, Upton upon Severn (01684 594087). Fibreglass cruisers for day and long-term hire.

Pubs and Restaurants

🍺 **The Railway** Ripple (01684 592225). Follow the footpath into the village. Friendly village local dispensing real ale together with bar meals (V) *L and E, daily*. Children welcome. Outside seating. Skittle alley, darts and pool.

The only riverside pubs on this section are in Upton upon Severn.

🍺 **The Plough Inn** Waterside, near the bridge (01684 593182). A nicely situated, welcoming pub, where real ale is available. Bar meals (V) available *L and E, daily*. Children welcome inside, dogs outside. Paved outside seating area overlooking the river.

🍺 **Ye Olde Anchor Inn** High Street (01684 592146). This pub is dated 1601 and was once the haunt of body snatchers. It now serves a range of guest real ales and bar meals (V) *L, daily*. Patio seating.

✗ 🍷 **Pundits** 9 Old Street (01684 591022/591119; www.pundits-upton.co.uk). Bangladeshi restaurant serving appetising food (V) *E* (and *L* by prior arrangement). Children welcome. Garden seating *in summer*. Takeaway service.

🍺 ✗ **The Swan Hotel & Hoopers Restaurant** Waterside (01684 592299). Real ales together with an interesting range of bar snacks and restaurant meals (V) available *L and E, daily*. Fine riverside views. Mooring available. Children and dogs (not in restaurant) welcome. Outside seating. B & B.

✗ 🍷 **The Bell House** 9 New Street (01684 593828; vince.hogan@talk21.com). Pretty 17th-C black and white tea shop and restaurant open for *breakfast* and home-cooked meals (V) *all day*. Also *Sunday* lunches. Children welcome; dogs welcome in attractive, walled courtyard. B & B.

🍺 **The Three Kings** Church End, Hanley Castle (01684 592686). In the village centre. An attractive 15th-C country pub, unspoilt by progress, run by the same family for 90 years, serving a wide range of real ales and real draught cider. Bar meals *L and E (not Sun E)*. Toasted mushroom and bacon sandwiches a speciality. Well-behaved children and dogs welcome. Guitar and piano music *Sun and some Sat evenings*. Open fires, no machines, and pub games. The pub also has a family room, garden, camping and B & B.

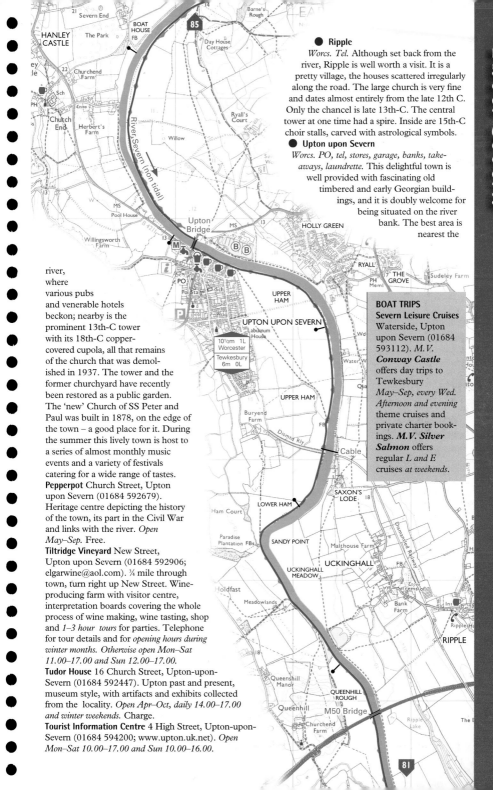

Ripple

Worcs. Tel. Although set back from the river, Ripple is well worth a visit. It is a pretty village, the houses scattered irregularly along the road. The large church is very fine and dates almost entirely from the late 12th C. Only the chancel is late 13th-C. The central tower at one time had a spire. Inside are 15th-C choir stalls, carved with astrological symbols.

Upton upon Severn

Worcs. PO, tel, stores, garage, banks, take-aways, laundrette. This delightful town is well provided with fascinating old timbered and early Georgian build-ings, and it is doubly welcome for being situated on the river bank. The best area is nearest the river, where various pubs and venerable hotels beckon; nearby is the prominent 13th-C tower with its 18th-C copper-covered cupola, all that remains of the church that was demol-ished in 1937. The tower and the former churchyard have recently been restored as a public garden. The 'new' Church of SS Peter and Paul was built in 1878, on the edge of the town – a good place for it. During the summer this lively town is host to a series of almost monthly music events and a variety of festivals catering for a wide range of tastes.

Pepperpot Church Street, Upton upon Severn (01684 592679). Heritage centre depicting the history of the town, its part in the Civil War and links with the river. *Open May–Sep.* Free.

Tiltridge Vineyard New Street, Upton upon Severn (01684 592906; elgarwine@aol.com). ¾ mile through town, turn right up New Street. Wine-producing farm with visitor centre, interpretation boards covering the whole process of wine making, wine tasting, shop and *1–3 hour tours* for parties. Telephone for tour details and for *opening hours during winter months. Otherwise open Mon–Sat 11.00–17.00 and Sun 12.00–17.00.*

Tudor House 16 Church Street, Upton-upon-Severn (01684 592447). Upton past and present, museum style, with artifacts and exhibits collected from the locality. *Open Apr–Oct, daily 14.00–17.00 and winter weekends.* Charge.

Tourist Information Centre 4 High Street, Upton-upon-Severn (01684 594200; www.upton.uk.net). *Open Mon–Sat 10.00–17.00 and Sun 10.00–16.00.*

BOAT TRIPS
Severn Leisure Cruises Waterside, Upton upon Severn (01684 593112). *M.V.* ***Conway Castle*** offers day trips to Tewkesbury *May–Sep, every Wed. Afternoon and evening* theme cruises and private charter book-ings. *M.V.* ***Silver Salmon*** offers regular *L and E* cruises *at weekends.*

Severn Stoke

Beyond Hanley Castle, on the east bank, is a wooded ridge with a curious turreted house projecting from the trees. The village of Severn Stoke is to the east; it is reached by a lane from a jetty on the river. North from here is an enjoyably romantic stretch of river, where tall, steep red cliffs rise sharply from the water to over 100ft. Trees and shrubs struggle to grow from this treacherous slope, and somewhere hidden at the top is Rhydd Court. The steep hill recedes, allowing a large caravan site to nestle by the river. A scattering of bungalows appears; then the river leaves houses and hills and wanders off north east. Distantly, to the west, can be seen the grey lumps of the Malvern Hills. The river winds past the hamlet of Pixham, then the bold tower of Kempsey church appears on the east bank, and a line of moored boats betrays the presence of a boatyard. There are temporary moorings along here for visitors to the village. Upstream, the river straightens out as it makes for Worcester.

Boatyards

Ⓑ ▣ ✕ **Seaborn Yacht Company** Court Meadow, Kempsey, Worcester (01905 820295). 🔧 Winter storage, slipway, hoist, engine repairs, toilets, showers, licensed club house.

Pubs and Restaurants

▣ **The Rose & Crown** Off the main road near the church, Severn Stoke (01905 371249). Dating back to 1490 this pub serves real ale together with bar meals and an à la carte menu (V) *L and E, daily. Sunday* lunches. Children welcome. Large garden with children's play area. No-smoking room. Floods occasionally!

▣ ✕ **Elgar Hotel** The Old School House, Severn Stoke (01905 371368). Converted 17th-C farmhouse-cum-Victorian school offering a varied menu (V) *L and E (not Sun E or Mon L and E)*. Children welcome. Large garden with views over the Malvern Hills. Jazz evenings *1st Tue in month*. Log fires. B & B.

▣ **The Farmers Arms** Kempsey Common (01905 820252; paulbrooker@farmersarms.com). Real ales together with bar meals and an à la carte menu (V) *served all day, every day*. Children welcome. Garden with play area and a skittle alley.

▣ **The Walter de Cantelupe Inn** Main Road, Kempsey (01905 820572; www.walterdecantelupeinn.com). A small, intimate village inn with warm décor, offering reliable food, real ale and accommodation, 15 minutes' walk from the river. All food is made on the premises and this establishment is renowned for its hefty ploughman's lunch with local cheese and home-made pickle. Food (V) is available *L and E (until 21.00 Tue–Thur and 22.00 Fri–Sat)* but no food *Sun E*. Well-behaved children welcome – under 14's *until 20.15*. Dogs welcome, but restricted to one per person and must be neither Pekinese nor Rottweiler. Walled garden. *Closed Mon all day except B Hols*.

▣ **The Anchor** Main Road, Kempsey (01905 820411). Popular main road hostelry dispensing real ale and real cider. Food (V) *L and E, daily*. Children welcome. Garden. B & B.

● **Severn Stoke**
Worcs. Tel. The village is scattered along the main road, and has no real centre. The best part is near the pretty half-timbered pub with its rose garden. Nearby is the church with its curious 14th-C side tower.

● **Kempsey**
Worcs. PO, tel, stores. A dull village in which acres of new housing have swamped the original settlement. One or two beautiful thatched cottages have survived to defy the invasion of modernity. However, it is the church that should be visited, for the enormous scale of this building is matched by its interior grandeur. It was constructed to cater for the Bishop of Worcester and his huge retinue – the Bishop's Palace used to stand just a few yards west of the church. Hence the generous proportions of, especially, the chancel and sanctuary. Note the medieval glass in the chancel.

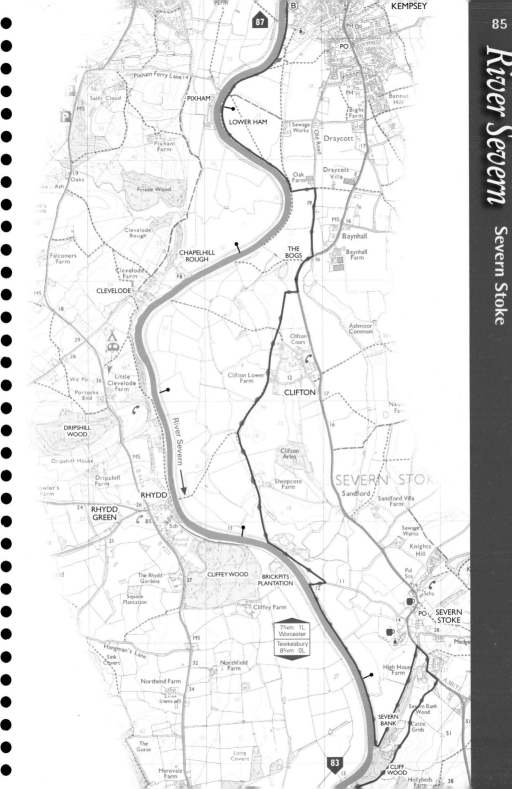

Worcester

Soon the Severn narrows somewhat as a wooded ridge encroaches from the east. The Severn Motor Yacht Club is based here – it is well-named, for the cruisers moored along here are lavish and grand. There is a pub up among the trees near the club. The Battle of Worcester was fought in 1651 near where the little River Teme joins the Severn. Above here is the pair of Diglis Locks (01905 354280), on the outskirts of Worcester. There is a BW maintenance yard and a large freight depot above the locks, so dredgers and tugs are often seen. Just above Diglis Locks is the terminal basin where the oil tankers used to come to unload before the traffic finished some years ago. A few hundred yards on are the disused wharves and the two locks that lead into Diglis Basin (01905 358768) and the Worcester & Birmingham Canal (*see* page 148). Worcester Cathedral is well in view now; the big square tower commands the town and the riverside. Two other church towers contribute to the scene and the unspoilt nature of the west bank makes Worcester's riverside a pretty one. Anglers fish from a path along the east bank, seemingly just below the great west window of the cathedral, while fours and eights appear from rowing clubs. There are three bridges over the river in Worcester – a 5-arched stone road bridge and, just north of it, a curious iron railway bridge and a new foot bridge. The best temporary moorings are above Diglis Lock and north of the railway bridge. The west bank is built up while the east bank is green and tree-lined, with the racecourse right by the river. At the river's northern end is a busy waterworks, contrasting with the bijou houses which adjoin it. North of here the river moves out into pleasantly wooded country; the only trace of civilisation is the glimpse of the occasional farm and a pretty, secluded riverside pub with good moorings.

BOAT TRIPS

M.V. Marianne operates daily trips *Mar–Oct on the hour, every hour, starting 11.00.* Departures from South Quay, near the cathedral. Bar and refreshments. Charter bookings. Telephone Bickerline on (01905) 422499 or 07702 523140.

Severn Leisure Cruises operate *M.V. Silver Salmon* restaurant boat for a variety of *dinner and daytime cruises.* Telephone (01684) 593112 for further details.

Pitchcroft Boating Station (01905 27949). Traditional rowing boats and motor boats for hire *Apr–Oct.*

Worcester Steamer Company Croft Road, Worcester (01905 354991). Riverboat available for charter *throughout the year,* departing from North Quay.

Boatyards

Ⓑ **M. W. Marine** Wharf Cottage, Diglis Basin (01905 763249/07940 071416/01905 453479 *after 17.00*). Marine engineer carrying out all types of boat fitting and engine work.

Ⓑ **Grist Mill Boatyard** Diglis Basin (01905 350814). Boat builders specialising in traditional craft, they also work on narrowboats, cruisers and commercial craft. Boat sales.

Ⓑ **Worcester Yacht Chandlers** Unit 7, 75 Waterworks Road, Barbourne, Worcester (01905 22522). ⛽ Gas, long-term mooring, winter storage, slipway, crane, boat sales and repairs, engine sales and repairs (including outboards), chandlery, books and maps, gifts, DIY facilities. *24hr emergency call out.*

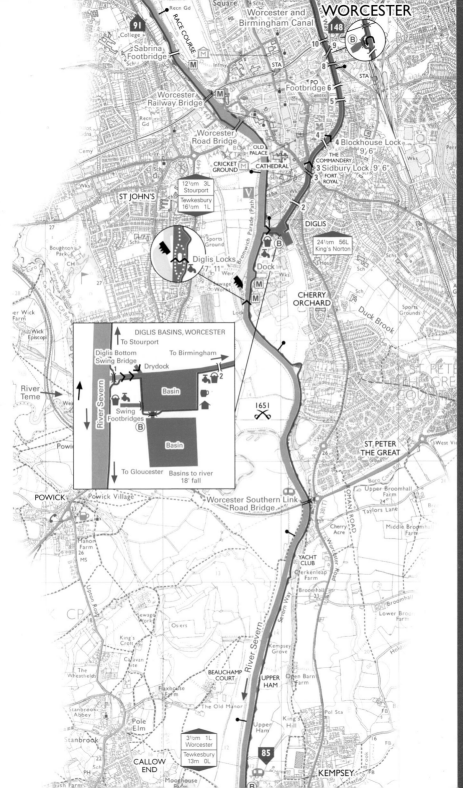

WORCESTER

Worcester and Birmingham Canal

CP 91

College

RACE COURSE

Sabrina Footbridge

148

10
9
8

B

STA

PO
Footbridge 6

Worcester Railway Bridge

STA

Worcester Road Building

OLD PALACE

CATHEDRAL

CRICKET GROUND

ST JOHN'S

12½m   3L
Stourport
Tewkesbury 1L
16½m   1L

4 4 Blockhouse Lock
            9' 6"

THE COMMANDERY

3 3 Sidbury Lock 9' 6"
3
FORT ROYAL

2

DIGLIS

24½m   56L
King's Norton

Diglis Locks
7' 11"
Weir

Dock

B

M
M

CHERRY ORCHARD

Duck Brook

Sports Grounds

DIGLIS BASINS, WORCESTER

To Stourport

Diglis Bottom
Swing Bridge

Drydock

To Birmingham

River Severn

Basin

Swing
Footbridges

B

Basin

To Gloucester   Basins to river
                         18' fall

1651

POWICK

Powick Village

Worcester Southern Link
Road Bridge

ST PETER
THE GREAT

Upper Broomhall
Farm

Taylors Lane

Middle Broomhall
Farm

Cherry
Acre

Manor
Farm

YACHT
CLUB

Clerkenleap
Farm

Broomhall

Lower Broomhall
Farm

Broomhall

River Severn

BEAUCHAMP
COURT

UPPER
HAM

Open Barn
Farm

Kempsey
Grove

King's
Hill

Stanbrook
Abbey

Pole
Elm

The Old Manor

Upper
Ham

3½m   1L
Worcester
Tewkesbury
13m   0L

85

CALLOW
END

KEMPSEY

Battle of Worcester, 3 September 1651 On 22 August 1651 Charles Stuart (later Charles II), having been proclaimed king by the rebels at Scone, reached Worcester with his Scottish army of 17,000 men. The Roundhead General Lambert was sent off in pursuit with his northern cavalry, and captured the Severn Bridge at Upton upon Severn, cutting off Charles' retreat. Meanwhile, another army of 28,000 under Cromwell advanced on Worcester from Nottingham. Charles, realising that he would have to fight at Worcester, organised his defences around the rivers Severn and Teme. After receiving further reinforcements from Banbury, the Roundhead armies advanced across the Severn, using a pontoon made of boats; meanwhile their cavalry crossed by a ford south of Powick Bridge, on the Teme. Heavy fighting broke out, and Charles' Scottish infantry, taken by surprise, were soon driven back. Charles tried to redeem the battle by leading a brave charge out of the east gate of Worcester; supported by cavalry this might have succeeded, but by this time the Scottish cavalry had fled. Cromwell held his ground and forced the Royalists back into the town, killing many in the narrow streets. This Roundhead victory ended the Royalist hopes; Charles fled with a few followers, and after the famous Boscobel Oak episode he made his way back to France.

● **Worcester**

Worcs. All services. A bishopric was founded in the Saxon town of Wigorna Ceaster around the year 680, and a castle was built here following the Norman conquest. During the Civil War the city was the first to declare for Charles I, and the last place where the Royalists rallied around Charles II. They were subsequently defeated in 1651 by Cromwell's army. These days Worcester has plenty to offer the visitor, although the enjoyment is lessened by the constant flow of heavy traffic through the city. A railway bridge at Foregate Street does not intrude, for the girders are suitably decorated and trains are infrequent. However the best area is around Friar Street, and of course the splendid cathedral.

Worcester Cathedral (01905 28854; info@worcestercathedral.org.uk). An imposing building which dates from 1074 (when Bishop Wulstan started to rebuild the Saxon church), but has work representative of the five subsequent centuries. There is a wealth of stained glass and monuments to see – including the tomb of King John, which lies in the chancel. Carved out of Purbeck marble in 1216, this is the oldest royal effigy in England. When he was dying at Newark, King John demanded to be buried at Worcester Cathedral between two saints: but the saints have gone now. The best way into the cathedral is from the Close with its immaculate lawns and houses, passing through the cloisters where one may inspect five of the cathedral's old bells, two of which were cast in 1374. The gardens at the west end of the building look out over the Severn and on to the Malvern Hills – a particularly fine sight at sunset. Gift shop and tearoom. *Open daily 07.30–18.00.* Donations. Disabled toilet. **The Three Choirs Festival** is held annually in rotation at the cathedrals of Worcester, Gloucester and Hereford, during the last week in *Aug.* This famous festival has inspired some fine music, one notable composer being Vaughan Williams. For further information about the festival, contact the Tourist Information Centre in any of the three cities.

City Museum and Art Gallery Foregate Street (01905 25371). Opened in 1896, it contains collections of folk life material and natural history illustrating man and his environment in the Severn valley. In the Art Gallery are a permanent collection and loan exhibitions. Children's activities. Also museum of the Worcestershire Regiment. Balcony Café. *Open Mon–Sat 09.30–17.30 (Sat 17.00). Closed Xmas Day, Box. Day, New Year's Day and G Fri.* Free. Teas. Disabled access.

The Greyfriars NT. Friar Street, Worcester (01905 23571; greyfriars@ntrust.org.uk). Dating from 1480, this was once part of a Franciscan priory and is one of the finest half-timbered houses in the country. Charles II escaped from this house after the Battle of Worcester on 3 September 1651. It has a delightful walled garden. *Open Apr–Oct, Wed, Thur and B Hol Mon 14.00–17.00 and during the Three Choirs Festival.* Charge.

Museum of Local Life Tudor House, Friar Street, Worcester (01905 722349). A museum of local antiquities, furniture and porcelain housed in traditional Elizabethan buildings (the wattle and daub that make up the walls can be clearly seen in places). Amongst other exhibits are a modern copy of a traditional coracle, a tiny fishing craft used for thousands of years on the River Severn, and a painting of the Waterman's Church in Worcester – a chapel on a floating barge, last used in the 1870s, when it was taken ashore and set up on dry land. *Open Mon–Wed, Fri and Sat 10.00–17.00.* Free. Shop. Limited disabled access.

Royal Worcester & The Museum of Worcester Porcelain The Royal Porcelain Works, Severn Street, Worcester (01905 23221; www.royal-worcester.co.uk). Here, where it should be, is the most comprehensive collection of Worcester porcelain in the world, from 1751 to the present day. Visitor Centre. *Open Mon–Sat 09.00–17.30, Sun 11.00–17.00.* Tours of the porcelain works. Seconds, whiteware and clearance shop. Family restaurant.

Swan Theatre The Moors, Worcester (01905 27322; swan_theatre@lineone.net). Year-round drama, music and dance from local and national companies.

The Guildhall High Street, Worcester (01905 723471). Built in 1721–3 by a local architect,

Thomas White, this building has a splendidly elaborate façade with statues of Charles I and Charles II on either side of the doorway and of Queen Anne on the pediment. It contains a fine assembly room and **The Assembly Rooms Restaurant** (01905 722033) which offers a tempting range of food (including appetising sweets made by their own patisseurs) and snacks *during Guildhall opening hours, Mon–Sat 09.00–16.30.* Free.

Tourist Information Centre Guildhall, High Street, Worcester (01905 726311; touristinfo @cityofworcester.gov.uk). Enquire here about local guided walks.

Diglis Basin This is a fascinating terminus at the junction of the River Severn and the Worcester & Birmingham Canal. It consists of basins, old warehouses and a dry dock. Commercial craft have been entirely replaced by a mixture of pleasure boats designed for narrow canals, rivers and the sea. The locks will take boats up to 72ft by 18ft 6in, although obviously only narrowboats can proceed along the canal. The locks are under the supervision of the basin attendant, who is available *from 08.00–19.30 (16.00 winter) with breaks for meals.* Craft are not permitted to use the locks

outside these times. The BW basin attendant can be contacted on (01905) 358758, or enquire through the Lapworth Office, (01564) 784634. Near the first lock is a small pump-house that raises water from the river to maintain the level in the basin.

The Commandery Civil War Centre Sidbury Lock (01905 361821; thecommandery@ cityofworcester.gov.uk). Founded as a small hospital just outside the city walls by Bishop Wulstan in 1085: from the 13th C the masters of the hospital were referred to as commanders, hence the building's name. The present timbered structure dates from the reign of Henry VII in the 15th C, and served as Charles II's headquarters before the Battle of Worcester in 1651. The glory of the building is the superb galleried hall with its ancient windows and Elizabethan staircase. The museum is devoted entirely to the story of the Civil War, with recreations using life-size figures, sound systems and a video presentation of the Battle of Worcester, including Oliver Cromwell writing his dispatch before the battle. *Open all year Mon–Sat 10.00–17.00, Sun 13.30–17.00.* Charge.

Pubs and Restaurants

✕♀ **The King Charles II Restaurant** New Street, Worcester (01905 22449). Famous for fine food (V) served in one of the city's oldest buildings *L and E, Mon–Sat.* Oak panelled restaurant with open fires. Beef Wellington and saddle of lamb are specialities. Children welcome. Booking essential.

✕ **Saffrons Bistro** 15 New Street, Worcester (01905 610505). An internationally inspired menu in relaxed, pine-clad surroundings. Food (V) is available *L and E, daily.* Children welcome.

🍺 **The Postal Order** 18 Foregate Street, Worcester (01905 22373). The old telephone exchange with the Wetherspoon treatment now connected to handpumps dispensing real ale, together with real cider. Popular with a wide-ranging clientele this pub serves reasonably priced food (V), available *all day, every day.* No children or dogs. Non-smoking area and disabled access. *Open all day.*

✕ **Natural Break** 4 The Hopmarket, Worcester (01905 26654). Excellent coffee, home-made snacks and meals (V). The chance to eat al fresco in a delightful courtyard. The thinking, non-smoking, non-music person's café. Children of similar ilk also welcome. Quick and friendly service. *Open Mon–Sat 09.00–17.00.*

🍺 **The Farriers Arms** 9 Fish Street (off High

Street), Worcester (01905 27569; 1134. farriersarms@greyarcher.co.uk). Grade II listed building dispensing real ales. Old paintings promoting the Wychwood Brewery and outside seating. Traditional, home-made food (V) available *L, daily.* Children welcome at all times; dogs when food is not being served. Beer garden and pub games. *Open all day.*

✕♀ **Ruby Tuesday's** 26–32 Friar Street, Worcester (01905 25451). A cocktail and wine bar upstairs and lively bistro downstairs, all housed in Tudor timber-framing. American and Mexican cuisine in intimate surroundings. *Open daily 11.00–23.30.*

🍺 **The Olde Talbot Hotel** Friar Street, Worcester (01905 23573). This cosy, original coaching inn, dating back to the 13th C, is situated in the centre of the city, close to the cathedral. Food (V) is served from *12.00–22.00, daily* together with a selection of real ales. Children welcome, outside seating. B & B. *Open all day.*

🍺 **The Plough** 23 Fishgate, Deansway, Worcester (01905 21381). Down to earth local serving real ales and tasty bar snacks (V) *L.* Set in an historic, listed building, this pub spurns all intrusive machines and offers a non-smoking area when food is served. No children. Outside seating area. *Closed Mon and Tue all day and Sun L.*

Grimley

Just upstream of the Camp House Inn is Bevere Lock
(01905 640275), which is certainly one of the prettiest on
the Severn. Half a mile north the little River Salwarpe and
the disused Droitwich Canal enter together from the east.
The Salwarpe is navigable for craft up to 35ft as far as Judge's
Boatyard at Hawford, but there are no visitors' moorings. Plans
are afoot for the complete restoration of the canal. The village
of Grimley is at the end of a lane leading up from the river,
but it is difficult to distinguish this track, and there are
currently no official moorings. The river continues
north west now, until Holt Castle is reached, a curious
composite building overlooking the river.
The Droitwich Barge Canal is an attractive rural
waterway, which leaves the Severn ½ mile north
east of Bevere Lock. Surveyed and built by James
Brindley, it used to go to Droitwich – 6¾ miles
and eight locks away. Linacre bridge is an
original accommodation bridge constructed to a
Brindley design. The navigation was then joined
by the Droitwich Junction Canal, whose seven
locks led it a further 1½ miles to terminate in a
junction with the Worcester & Birmingham
Canal at Hanbury Wharf (*see* page 153). Both
the Droitwich canals have been derelict for
most of this century, but they are now being
revived, and the summit pound of 3 miles
from Droitwich to Ladywood is now navigable.
Wychavon District Council and the Droitwich
Canals Trust are implementing a scheme to
open up the Droitwich Canal from the town to
the River Severn and it is hoped later to extend
the restoration to the Junction Canal. When this
happens, it will restore a 22-mile ring of cruising
waterways (*see* Droitwich Canal, page 60).

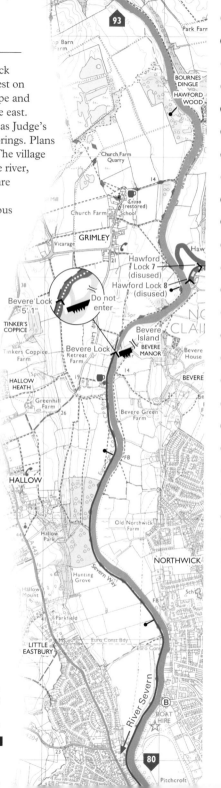

● **Grimley**
Worcs. Tel. A small farming village close to, but hidden
from, the river. The well-placed church has some Norman
work, but has been heavily restored; it has a curious outside
staircase by the door. Access from the river is not easy.

Boatyards

ⓑ **George Judge** Mill House, Hawford (01905 458705).
Just east of the A449 bridge on the River Salwarpe. Gas,
winter storage, crane, boat sales and repairs, boat fitting out,
DIY facilities, chandlery, provisions and café *weekends during
camping season*, toilets, showers, camping and caravan site.
There are no visitor moorings and craft over 35ft *cannot turn*.

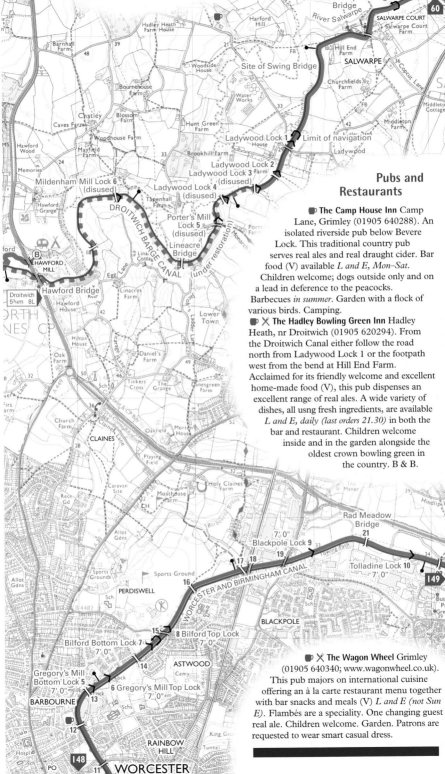

Pubs and Restaurants

🍺 **The Camp House Inn** Camp Lane, Grimley (01905 640288). An isolated riverside pub below Bevere Lock. This traditional country pub serves real ales and real draught cider. Bar food (V) available *L and E, Mon–Sat*. Children welcome; dogs outside only and on a lead in deference to the peacocks. Barbecues *in summer*. Garden with a flock of various birds. Camping.

🍺 ✕ **The Hadley Bowling Green Inn** Hadley Heath, nr Droitwich (01905 620294). From the Droitwich Canal either follow the road north from Ladywood Lock 1 or the footpath west from the bend at Hill End Farm. Acclaimed for its friendly welcome and excellent home-made food (V), this pub dispenses an excellent range of real ales. A wide variety of dishes, all usng fresh ingredients, are available *L and E, daily (last orders 21.30)* in both the bar and restaurant. Children welcome inside and in the garden alongside the oldest crown bowling green in the country. B & B.

🍺 ✕ **The Wagon Wheel** Grimley (01905 640340; www.wagonwheel.co.uk). This pub majors on international cuisine offering an à la carte restaurant menu together with bar snacks and meals (V) *L and E (not Sun E)*. Flambés are a speciality. One changing guest real ale. Children welcome. Garden. Patrons are requested to wear smart casual dress.

Holt Fleet

Beside Holt Castle is the discreet tower of a small church, while further on is the delicate iron span of Holt Fleet Bridge. Above Holt Lock (01905 620218) steep wooded hills continue, rising straight up from the river bank. It is a pleasant scene, and there is a riverside pub nearby. The next few miles form an attractive reach, with tree-lined hills rising from the river banks first on one side, then on the other. Another riverside hostelry lies close by. The reach from Lenchford to Stourport is one of the most pleasant on the Severn. Unlike much of its journey further downstream, the river runs here through a well-defined valley, with steep rising ground never far away from either bank. The hills on the west bank are the more impressive and the more thickly wooded, although the old church at Shrawley can sometimes be seen peering over the woods. Roads keep their distance, but at the site of Hampstall Ferry (Astley Burf) there is a small village and a riverside pub, with good moorings.

PLUMBING THE DEPTHS

It may come as something of a surprise to discover that the longest river in Britain is so little used by commercial traffic, considering its size and proximity to the industrial midlands. However its width belies its depth which throughout history has always been somewhat unreliable. Above Stourport shoals and a rocky, shelving bed have always restricted regular traffic, making it difficult for barges to penetrate above Shrewsbury, into Wales. Downstream, between Tewkesbury and Gloucester, spring tides carry silt up from the estuary which is then trapped by the weirs on the East and West Partings, unable to return with the ebb. Consequently the bottom rapidly starts to approach the top, causing considerable problems for any commercial craft still determined to exploit this navigation's potential.

This situation is further exacerbated by the exuberant performance of the Severn Bore: a spring tide *in extremis*. It shovels literally hundreds of tons of unwanted material over the weirs demanding continuous dredging to redress. Reputedly, one of its more bizarre victims was a Blue Peter camera crew, their boat swamped when overtaken by the 6ft wave, whilst filming a surfer. Boat and camera went to the bottom, as did plans for screening the event. However the BBC reckoned without the combined forces of chance and a somewhat bewildered fisherman who, some several weeks later, contacted them with news of a most unusual catch.

Pubs and Restaurants

🍺 **The Wharf Inn** Holt Heath (01905 620289). North bank by caravan site. Large family pub serving real ales and food (V) *L and E, daily.* Riverside seating and children's play area. Fishing and boating available. Free overnight moorings available to patrons. Gas and water. *Open all day Easter–Oct.*

🍺 ✕ **The Holt Fleet Hotel** Holt Heath (01905 620286). By the bridge. Rambling, Tudor brewery-style establishment tucked in between the river and the steep bank below Holt Heath. Bar meals (V) together with an à la carte and carvery restaurant serving food *L and E, daily.* Children welcome. Riverside seating in large garden. Moorings.

🍺 ✕ **The Lenchford Hotel** Shrawley (01905 620229). Riverside, upstream of Holt Lock. Real ales are served in this riverside hotel with B & B accommodation. Restaurant offering full à la carte menu (V) *L and E* and bar snacks available *all day, every day. Sunday* carvery. Children welcome at all times; dogs when food is not being served. Riverside garden and moorings (free to patrons only). Pool and cards.

🍺 **The Hamstall Inn** Astley Burf (01299 822600). Originally known as the Old Cider House, overlooking the river 1/2 mile below Lincomb Lock. Real ale together with six different real ciders are served in this friendly pub with good moorings and a riverside garden. Bar food (V) available *L and E, daily.* Garden, children's play area and patio seating. Darts, dominoes and pool *(in the winter).*

● Holt

Worcs. Tel. Holt is a scattering of assorted settlements, around the river. The elegant narrow bridge here was built by Telford in 1828. Holt Fleet exploits the river in a most unattractive fashion, being composed of a large sprawling caravan site, whose television aerials and wires swamp the riverside. There are two large pubs. Holt Castle is up on the hill, overlooking the river. The castle is a 14th-C tower, the rest of the building is a 19th-C battlemented mansion. Nearby, set among the fruit fields, is the church, a fine late Norman building with interesting carving around the doorways, and rich in interior ornamentation. There is a *PO and garage* at Holt Heath whilst gas is available by the bridge.

River Severn near Stourport-on-Severn (see page 94)

● Astley Burf

Worcs. Tel. An isolated riverside settlement, comprised mainly of new housing for retired persons. The word Burf is thought to mean an enclosure below a hill.

Stourport-on-Severn

North of Astley Burf steep hills encroach on the east bank of the river, almost hanging over it at Lincomb Lock (01299 822887). This pretty lock is now the northernmost on the river, for signs of Stourport soon come into view. First there are the abandoned oil wharves, now frequented by the occasional fisherman. On the opposite side of the river, at the foot of a cliff, is the Redstone Rock – an unexpected outcrop of crumbling red sandstone. There was once a hermitage in caves here. Before reaching the canal junction the Severn is joined first by the River Stour and then by the little River Salwarpe, flowing in from the east, just as to the north the Staffordshire & Worcestershire Canal drops down into the Severn from the unseen basins. There are two sets of locks – narrow canal boats should use the upstream set. Just above these locks is Stourport Bridge, a heavy iron structure built in 1870. There are visitor moorings either side of the Broad Lock entrance leading into the basin (01299 877667) and a floating sanitary station and water point *Easter–Oct*. The River Severn is not officially navigable for more than a couple of hundred yards above Stourport Bridge, at which point BW's jurisdiction as navigation authority ends. However, in suitable conditions small boats drawing not more than 1ft 9in can penetrate upstream to within a mile of Bewdley Bridge. A shoal across the river impedes further progress, and boatmen must tie up or wade ashore when they reach the shoal. Bradshaw's *Canals and Navigable Rivers Of England and Wales* (1904) stated that a few craft, in times of full water, proceeded as far as Arley Quarry, 5 miles above Bewdley, although the trade was small. There is a road into Bewdley on either side of the river (the B4194 on the west bank being the most direct). Alternatively, one can avoid all this by leaving the boat in Stourport and either walking along the riverside path (which continues to Bridgenorth) or by taking a bus to Bewdley; an excursion well worth the effort.

RIVER SEVERN ABOVE BEWDLEY

In the 19th C the Severn was fully navigable for a long way past Stourport: it was a vital trade artery right up into Wales, through Bridgnorth, Shrewsbury and Newtown. It used to connect with the Montgomery Canal north of Welshpool, and the Shropshire Canal at Shrewsbury. It is unfortunate that this upper section is unnavigable, for the river is much prettier than further south: it runs along a narrow valley, hemmed in by steep and wooded hills. However, there is a public right of way along one or both banks up to Bridgnorth and beyond, and this can form an interesting walk. Another attraction north of Bewdley is the Severn Valley Railway, a private railway which runs a service of steam trains between Bridgnorth, Bewdley and Kidderminster (*see* page 97).

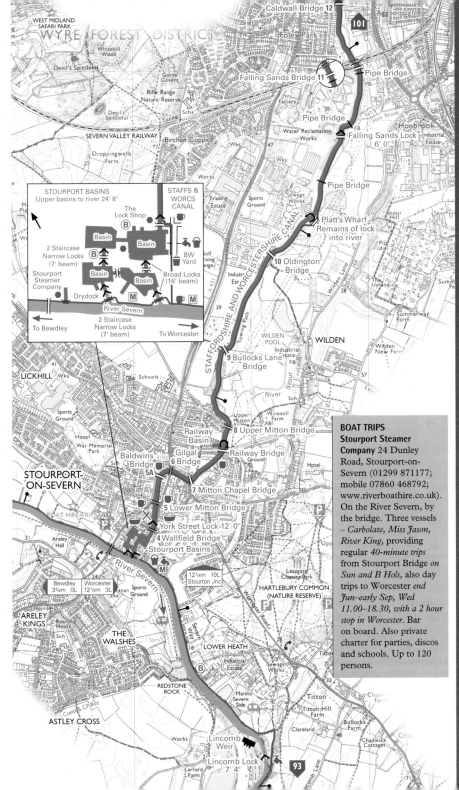

Caldwall Bridge 12

WEST MIDLAND
SAFARI PARK
WYRE FOREST DISTRICT

Whitehill
Wood

Devil's Spittleful

Gorse
Covert

Rifle Range
Nature Reserve

Devil's
Spittleful

Foley Park

Pipe Bridge

Falling Sands Bridge 11

Pipe Bridge

SEVERN VALLEY RAILWAY

Birchen Coppice

Factory

Water Reclamation
Works

Hoobrook

Pipe Bridge

Falling Sands Lock
6' 0"

Industrial
Estate

Droppingwells
Farm

Tunnel

Schs

Wks

Wks

Works

Pipe Bridge

Sewage
Works

Stour
Hill

STOURPORT BASINS
Upper basins to river 24' 8"

STAFFS &
WORCS
CANAL

Trading
Estate

Sports
Ground

Platt's Wharf
Remains of lock
into river

The
Lock Shop

B

Basin

Basin

BW
Yard

10 Oldington
Bridge

Wilden Lane

2 Staircase
Narrow Locks
(7' beam)

B

Basin

Basin

Broad Locks
(16' beam)

Stourport
Steamer
Company

Drydock

M

River Severn

M

2 Staircase
Narrow Locks
(7' beam)

To Bewdley

To Worcester

STAFFORDSHIRE AND WORCESTERSHIRE CANAL

Industrial Est

Towing Path

WILDEN
POOL

WILDEN

Widen
New Farm

Summerway
Farm

9 Bullocks Lane
Bridge

Wiremill
Farm

LICKHILL

Wks

Schools

River

Sch

Sports
Ground

Upper
Mitton

8 Upper Mitton Bridge

Railway
Basin

Hospl
War Memorial
Park

Railway Bridge

Baldwins
Bridge

Gilgal
6 Bridge

Hotel

STOURPORT-
ON-SEVERN

5A

7 Mitton Chapel Bridge

5 Lower Mitton Bridge

BOAT HIRE TRIPS

York Street Lock 12' 0"

4 Wallfield Bridge
Stourport Basins

Areley
Hall

M

Bewdley | Worcester
3¾m 0L | 12½m 3L

12¼m 10L
Stourton Jnc

Sports
Ground

Leapgate
Country Park

ARELEY
KINGS

River Severn

Round
House

Sch

HARTLEBURY COMMON
(NATURE RESERVE)

Severn Way

THE
WALSHES

Sprs

LOWER HEATH

Industrial
Estate

Sewage
Works

Titton

Titton
Farm

REDSTONE
ROCK

Marina
Severn
Side

Titton
Hill
Farm

Bullocks
Farm

Chadwick
Cottages

ASTLEY CROSS

Works

Clareland

Lincomb
Weir

Lincomb Lock
7' 4"

Larford
Farm

93

BOAT TRIPS
Stourport Steamer
Company 24 Dunley
Road, Stourport-on-
Severn (01299 871177;
mobile 07860 468792;
www.riverboathire.co.uk).
On the River Severn, by
the bridge. Three vessels
– *Carbolate, Miss Jason,*
River King, providing
regular *40-minute trips*
from Stourport Bridge *on*
Sun and B Hols, also day
trips to Worcester *end*
Jun–early Sep, Wed
11.00–18.30, with a 2 hour
stop in Worcester. Bar
on board. Also private
charter for parties, discos
and schools. Up to 120
persons.

Boatyards

Ⓑ **BW Stourport Yard** Stourport Basin, Stourport (01299 877661). 🛉 🛈 ⚓ Dry dock.

Ⓑ **Stroudwater Cruisers** Engine Lane, Stourport (01299 877222; www.stroudwater-cruisers.co.uk). (🛉 🛈 ⚓ nearby) **D** Pump out, gas, narrowboat hire, overnight and long-term mooring, boat building, boat sales and repairs, toilet, books and maps. *Emergency call out.*

Ⓑ **Severn Valley Cruisers** York Street Boatyard, Stourport (01299 871165; www.severnboat.co.uk).(🛉 🛈 ⚓ nearby) **D** Pump out, long-term mooring, winter storage, crane (25 tons), boat building, boat and engine sales and repairs, large chandlery, books and maps, DIY facilities.

WATERWAYS UP THE SEVERN

Inevitably an arterial waterway like the Severn encouraged the construction of branch navigations at various points along its course. Near Stourport a canal was proposed to run west to the coalfields at Mamble and thence on to Leominster and Kington on the Welsh border. Only the section between the mines at Mamble and Leominster was ever completed. Further south the River Salwarpe, in conjunction with a stretch of canal, was made navigable to Droitwich, whilst the Coombe Hill Canal – just upstream of the city of Gloucester – ran eastwards 2¾ miles to aid coal transport to Cheltenham. Nearby, the Herefordshire and Gloucestershire Canal – a truly rural canal started in 1792 and completed in 1845 – linked the two cities of its title. Its 34 wandering miles followed a route via Newent, Dymock and Ledbury, required 3 tunnels and 22 locks, and appeared on the canal scene just as railway mania was taking hold. Closed in 1881 to allow part of its bed to be used as a railway (in turn axed by Dr Beeching in the 1960s), it is now firmly fixed in the sights of a very professional and dedicated canal trust, committed to its complete restoration. Equally important, the Trust now has the full policy backing of all five councils along the route who are determined to preserve the line against any future, compromising developments. Now that the comparatively easy canal restorations are complete, or at least well in hand, it is the turn of the difficult ones, considered impossible 10–15 years ago. Some 10 per cent of the canal is restored or under restoration. Work is now completed on the first phase at Over, where the canal entered the River Severn and a delight-ful, landscaped basin complements the new housing development. The lock down into the Severn will be the focus for the next phase of activity. The sheer dogged determination and tenacity shown in the face of not inconsiderable adversity, whilst meeting a demanding schedule, will surely stand as an inspiration to all those engaged in future waterway restoration. A detailed account, setting out the ups and downs of the waterway, is entitled *The Hereford and Gloucester Canal*, by David E. Bick, and is available from the Herefordshire and Gloucestershire Canal Trust, 6 Castle Street, Hereford, HR1 2NL. The trust also publish *The Wharfinger*, keeping its healthy membership abreast of progress.

● **Stourport-on-Severn**

Worcs. PO, tel, stores, garage, bank. When the engineer James Brindley surveyed the line for the Staffordshire & Worcestershire Canal in the early 1760s, he chose to meet the River Severn at the hamlet of Lower Mitton, 4 miles downstream from Bewdley, where the River Stour flowed into the Severn. Basins and locks were built for the boats, warehouses for the cargoes and cottages for the workmen. In 1788 the canal company even built the great Tontine Hotel beside the locks. The hamlet soon earned the name of Stourport, becoming a busy and wealthy town. The two basins were expanded to five (one has since been filled in) and the locks were duplicated.

Much still remains of Stourport's former glory, for the basins are always full of moored boats, with plenty of other craft passing to and from the river. The delightful clock tower still functions and a canal maintenance yard carries on in the old workshops by the locks. Mart Lane, on the north east side of the basins, is well worth a look – the original 18th-C terrace of workmen's cottages still stands, with numbers 2, 3 and 4 listed as ancient monuments. In contrast with the basin area, the town of Stourport is not particularly interesting and, although it was built on account of the canal, the town has no relationship at all with the basins now.

● **Bewdley**

Worcs. PO, tel, stores, garage, bank, takeaway. Bewdley is a magnificent small 18th-C riverside town, still remarkably intact. It is blessed with a fine river frontage and elegant bridge that make the most of the wide Severn, and a handsome main street that leads away from the river to terminate at the church. The scale of the whole town is very pleasing, a comfortable mixture of old timber-framed buildings and plainer, more elegant 17th- and 18th-C structures. Most of the town is on the west bank, and so Telford's three-arch stone bridge, built in 1798 to replace an earlier medieval structure, forms a fitting entrance to Bewdley. The Queen Elizabeth Jubilee gardens are well worth a visit and the Civic Society runs guided walks around the town.

Bewdley Museum Load Street, Bewdley (01299 403573; museum_wfdc@online.rednet.co.uk). A fascinating insight into the area and the lives of its people in a town where river trade played an important part. Interactive displays, changing exhibitions, workshops and special events. Gift shop.

Open Apr–Sep, daily (including B Hols) 11.00–17.00; Oct daily 11.00–16.00. Closed Nov–Mar. Last admission 30 mins before closing. Charge.

Safari Park Mid-way between Bewdley and Kidderminster (01299 404604; www.wmsp.co.uk). Whilst the park area is not accessible to the car-less boater, there are a wide range of thrilling rides and more static animals to be seen. *Open daily Apr–Oct 10.00–dusk.* Charge.

Severn Valley Railway The Station, Bewdley (01299 403816; www.svr.co.uk). Arguably the premier restored steam line, running trains along 16 miles of one of the most beautiful sections of the Severn Valley. Trains operate *May–Sep daily, and at weekends for the remainder of the year.* Most trains have licensed buffet cars and several stations have gift shops. Charge. Disabled facilities available by *prior booking. 24hr* talking timetable (01299) 401001.

Tourist Information Centre Bewdley Museum, Load Street, Bewdley (01299 404740; bewdleytic@btconnect.com). *Open daily Easter–Sep 10.00–17.00 and Oct–Easter 12.00–16.00.* Information about guided town and country walks can be obtained from here.

Pubs and Restaurants

🍺 **The Angel** (01299 822661). In a fine riverside situation, this compact bar serves real ale and real cider. Food (V) is served *L, and Thur–Sat E in summer.* Children welcome, and there is a riverside garden, where barbecues are held.

✗ 🍷 **Spice Valley** Lion Hill, (01299 877448/822988). Smart Indian restaurant, in a building listed as an ancient monument, serving Tandoori and Balti meals and Indian lager. Children welcome. *Open Sun–Thur 17.30–11.30, Fri and Sat 17.30–midnight.*

✗ **The Lock Shop & Tearooms** 18 York Street, Stourport (01299 829442). Right beside York Street Lock. An extremely handy shop for hot pies, bread, milk, sandwiches, ice cream and drinks. Also takeaway casseroles and crafts.

🍺 ✗ **The Swan** 56 High Street, Stourport (01299 871661). Just west of Lower Mitton Bridge. Friendly town pub serving a choice of real ales and bar and restaurant meals (V) *L and E (not Sun E).* Children welcome if eating. Karaoke on *Thur.*

🍺 **The Black Star** (01299 822404). Canalside, by Lower Mitton Bridge, next to the Remembrance Gardens. A long, narrow, friendly pub with a low and beamy tap-room. Real ale is served and bar meals (V) are available *L.* Children welcome and there are seats outside by the canal. On *Tue evenings* there is live jazz, on *Thur evenings* other live music, and on *Wed evenings* a quiz.

🍺 **The Rising Sun** 50 Lombard Street, Stourport (01299 822530). Canalside, between Baldwins (5A) and Gilgal (6) bridges. Small friendly pub serving real ale. Food (V) is available *L and E (not Sun E).* Children welcome away from the bar, and there is a garden. Singer on *Sat,* quiz on *Tue.*

🍺 **The Bird in Hand** 5 Holly Road (01299 822385). Real ale is served in this black and white canalside pub, which has a pleasant garden and a bowling green. Food (V), including baltis and fresh fish, is served *L and E.* Children welcome. Have a look at the canal company cottages next door. Irish folk music *once a month.* B & B.

STAFFORDSHIRE & WORCESTERSHIRE CANAL

MAXIMUM DIMENSIONS	MILEAGE
Length: 70'	*STOURPORT to:*
Beam: 7'	Kidderminster Lock: 4^1/$_2$ miles
Headroom: 6' 6"	Wolverley Lock: 6 miles
	STOURTON JUNCTION: 12^1/$_4$ miles
MANAGER	Swindon: 16^3/$_4$ miles
01785 284253	Bratch Locks: 19 miles
enquiries.norbury@britishwaterways.co.uk	*ALDERSLEY JUNCTION:* 25 miles
	AUTHERLEY JUNCTION: 25^1/$_2$ miles
	GREAT HAYWOOD JUNCTION: 46 miles
	Locks: 43

Construction of this navigation was begun immediately after that of the Trent & Mersey, to effect the joining of the rivers Trent, Mersey and Severn. After this, only the line down to the Thames was necessary to complete the skeleton outline of England's narrow canal network.

Engineered by James Brindley, the Staffordshire & Worcestershire was opened throughout in 1772, at a cost of rather over £100,000. It stretched 46 miles from Great Haywood on the Trent & Mersey to the River Severn, which it joined at what became the bustling canal town of Stourport. The canal was an immediate success. It was well placed to bring goods from the Potteries down to Gloucester, Bristol and the West Country; while the Birmingham Canal, which joined it halfway along at Aldersley Junction, fed manufactured goods northwards from the Black Country to the Potteries via Great Haywood. Stourport has always been the focal point of the waterway, for the town owed its birth and rapid growth during the late 18th C to the advent of the canal. It was here that the cargoes were transferred from narrowboats into Severn Trows for shipment down the estuary to Bristol and the south west.

The Staffordshire & Worcestershire Canal soon found itself facing strong competition. In 1815 the Worcester & Birmingham Canal opened, offering a more direct but heavily locked canal link between Birmingham and the Severn. The Staffordshire & Worcestershire answered this threat by gradually extending the opening times of the locks, until by 1830 they were open 24 hours a day. When the Birmingham & Liverpool Junction Canal was opened from Autherley to Nantwich in 1835, traffic bound for Merseyside from Birmingham naturally began to use this more direct, modern canal, and the Staffordshire & Worcestershire lost a great deal of traffic over its length from Autherley to Great Haywood. Most of the traffic now passed along only the 1/2-mile stretch of the Staffordshire & Worcestershire Canal between Autherley and Aldersley Junctions. This was, however, enough for the company, who levied absurdly high tolls for this tiny length. In 1836 the B & LJ Company, therefore, cooperated with the Birmingham Canal Company to promote a parliamentary Bill for the Tettenhall & Autherley Canal and Aqueduct. This remarkable project was to be a canal flyover, going from the Birmingham Canal right over the profiteering Staffordshire &

Worcestershire and locking down into the Birmingham & Liverpool Junction Canal. In the face of this serious threat to bypass its canal altogether, the Staffordshire & Worcestershire company gave way and reduced its tolls to a level acceptable to the other two companies. In later years the device was used twice more to force concessions out of the Staffordshire & Worcestershire.

In spite of this set-back, the Staffordshire & Worcestershire maintained a good profit, and high dividends were paid throughout the rest of the 19th C. When the new railway companies appeared in the West Midlands, the canal company would have nothing to do with them; but from the 1860s onwards railway competition began to bite, and the company's profits began to slip. Several modernisation schemes came to nothing, and the canal's trade declined. Like the other narrow canals, the Staffordshire & Worcestershire had faded into obscurity as a significant transport route by the middle of this century, although the old canal company proudly retained total independence until it was nationalised in 1947. Now the canal is used by numerous pleasure craft – it is certainly most delightful for cruising, walking and cycling.

Entering wide lock at Stourport (see page 101)

Stourport

The Staffordshire & Worcestershire Canal is, without doubt, one of the prettiest and most interesting waterways in England. The locks and basins at Stourport make for a fascinating start, having an intriguing combination of all kinds of engineering features and fine buildings, with the famous clock tower looking out over all. There are two sets of locks here, narrow and broad – *and they are open 24 hours.* The narrow locks are those most commonly in use, and form a staircase – the lock keeper is usually around to help if you have difficulties. To reach the Staffordshire & Worcestershire Canal itself, boats should proceed to the eastern corner of the upper basins, pass under the bridge and climb the deep lock at York Street. There is a useful tearoom and craft shop by the lock, and above the lock there are good temporary moorings. The canal soon acquires a secluded, unspoilt character, flanked by discreet houses and walls. Keep a look out for the lovely old red-brick canalside building, with a terrace, by Gilgal Bridge. The navigation continues to creep through the town, soon emerging into the country. It follows the west side of a valley, the steep slopes rising sharply from the water. The River Stour approaches, and at Pratt's Wharf the towpath rises over the remains of a lock that once joined the canal to the Stour. This river used to be navigable from here for 1^1/$_4$ miles down to the Wilden Ironworks. Soon the canal's surroundings change, for the hillside on the west bank becomes a dramatic cliff of crumbling red rock rising sheer from the canal. This is the southern end of a geological feature that stretches almost to Wombourn, 15 miles away. Falling Sands and Caldwall locks both enjoy delightful situations at the foot of the sandstone, and both have split iron bridges of a type usually associated with the Stratford-on-Avon Canal. Beyond Falling Sands Bridge look out for the steam trains of the Severn Valley Railway on the viaduct. Kidderminster now engulfs the canal: its course through the centre of the town is truly private, passing through a corridor of high walls, factories and warehouses which clearly date from the arrival of the canal. There are shops by bridge 5A.

A LATE 18TH-CENTURY VIEW OF STOURPORT

'About 1766, where the river Stour empties itself into the Severn below Mitton stood a little ale house called Stourmouth. Near this Brindley has caused a town to be erected, made a port and dockyards, built a new and elegant bridge, established markets and made it a wonder not only of this county but of the nation at large.'

Nash, a Worcestershire historian.

Boatyards

Ⓑ **BW Stourport Yard** Stourport Basin, Stourport (01299 877661). 🛁 🚾 ⚓ Dry dock.

Ⓑ **Stroudwater Cruisers** Engine Lane, Stourport (01299 877222; www.stroudwater-cruisers.co.uk). (🛁 🚾 ⚓ nearby) D Pump out, gas, narrowboat hire, overnight and long-term mooring, boat building, boat sales and repairs, toilet, books and maps. *Emergency call out.*

Ⓑ **Severn Valley Cruisers** York Street Boatyard, Stourport (01299 871165; www.severnboat. co.uk).(🛁 🚾 ⚓ nearby) D Pump out, long-term mooring, winter storage, crane (25 tons), boat building, boat and engine sales and repairs, large chandlery, books and maps, DIY facilities.

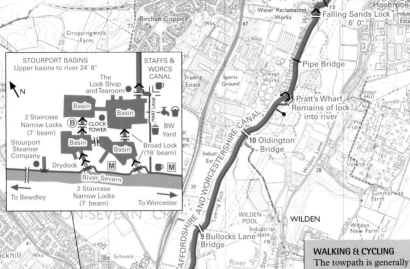

BOAT TRIPS
Stourport Steamer Company 24
Dunley Road, Stourport-on-Severn
(01299 871177; mobile 07860
468792; www.riverboathire.co.uk).
On the River Severn, by the bridge.
Three vessels – *Carbolate, Miss
Jason* and *River King* – provide
regular *40 minute* trips from
Stourport Bridge *on Sun and B
Hols*, and also day trips to
Worcester *end Jun–early Sep, Wed
11.00–18.30*, with a 2 hour stop in
Worcester. Bar on board. Also
private charter for parties, discos
and schools. Up to 120 persons.

KIDDERMINSTER

15 Caldwall Hall Bridge
Pipe Bridge
14 Caldwall Mill Bridge
13 Round Hill Bridge
Caldwall Lock 5' 6"
Caldwall Bridge 12
Pipe Bridge
Falling Sands Bridge 11
Pipe Bridge
Falling Sands Lock 6' 0"
Pipe Bridge
Pratt's Wharf
Remains of lock into river
10 Oldington Bridge

STOURPORT BASINS
Upper basins to river 24' 8"

STAFFS & WORCS CANAL

The Lock Shop and Tearoom
Basin
Basin
2 Staircase Narrow Locks (7' beam)
CLOCK TOWER
Basin
Basin
BW Yard
Stourport Steamer Company
Broad Lock (16' beam)
Drydock
River Severn
2 Staircase Narrow Locks (7' beam)
To Bewdley
To Worcester

9 Bullocks Lane Bridge

WILDEN POOL
WILDEN

8 Upper Mitton Bridge

Railway Basin
Gilgal
Baldwins Bridge 5A
6 Bridge
Railway Bridge

7 Mitton Chapel Bridge

STOURPORT-ON-SEVERN

5 Lower Mitton Bridge
York Street Lock 12' 0"
4 Wallfield Bridge

94

River Severn

12¼m 10L
Stourton Jnc

HARTLEBURY COMMON

95

WALKING & CYCLING
The towpath is generally
in good condition
throughout the length of
the canal. There is an
excellent 6-mile walk
from Stourport Basin to
visit Hartlebury
Common. Walk along the
canal to bridge 10, then
turn sharp right to reach
Wilden, and continue
south east to reach
Wilden Top. Now walk
south along the road and
continue across
Hartlebury Common, a
haven for wildlife and a
rare expanse of inland
sand dunes. Continue
south through Titton to
join the River Severn,
where you turn right to
return to Stourport.

Stourport-on-Severn

Worcs. PO, tel, stores, garage, bank. When the engineer James Brindley surveyed the line for the Staffordshire & Worcestershire Canal in the early 1760s, he chose to meet the River Severn at the hamlet of Lower Mitton, 4 miles downstream from Bewdley, where the little River Stour flowed into the Severn. Basins and locks were built for the boats, warehouses for the cargoes and cottages for the workmen. In 1788 the canal company even built the great Tontine Hotel, which is now, alas, closed, beside the locks. The hamlet soon earned the name of Stourport, becoming a busy and wealthy town. The two basins were expanded to five (one has since been filled in) and the locks were duplicated. Much still remains of Stourport's former glory, for the basins are always full of moored boats, with plenty of other craft passing to and from the river. The delightful clock tower still functions and a canal maintenance yard carries on in the old workshops by the locks. Mart Lane, on the north east side of the basins, is well worth a look – the original 18th-C terrace of workmen's cottages still stands, with numbers 2, 3 and 4 listed as ancient monuments. In contrast with the basin area, the town of Stourport is not particularly interesting, and, although it was built on account of the canal, it has no relationship at all with the basins now.

Hartlebury Common To the east of Stourport. This is regarded by naturalists as one of the most important surviving areas of heathland in the West Midlands, recognised by the Nature Conservancy Council in 1955 and designated a SSSI. Originally owned by the Church Commissioners, it was purchased by the County Council in 1968. It covers an area of 216 acres rising to a height of 184ft, and consists mainly of dry lowland or scrub heath on river terraces of sand, over a bedrock of Triassic sandstone. The sand has, in places, formed into dunes, which can shift with the wind – a feature rare so far inland. There is a pond and marshy areas which support aquatic plants, dragonflies and frogs. Birds to look out for include long-tailed tits, tree pipits and stonechats. Plants to be seen include ling and bell heather, bogbean, marsh cinquefoil, heath milkwort and shepherds purse. The particularly sharp-eyed may notice dung beetles, green tiger beetles, large skipper butterflies and common lizards. The views from the top are splendid.

Pubs and Restaurants

The Angel (01299 822661). In a fine riverside situation, this compact bar serves real ale and real cider. Food (V) is served *L, and Thur–Sat E in summer*. Children welcome, and there is a riverside garden, where barbecues are held.

Spice Valley Lion Hill, (01299 877448/ 822988). Smart Indian restaurant, in a building listed as an ancient monument, serving Tandoori and Balti meals and Indian lager. Children welcome. *Open Sun–Thur 17.30–11.30, Fri and Sat 17.30–24.00.*

The Lock Shop & Tearooms 18 York Street, Stourport (01299 829442). Right beside York Street Lock. An extremely handy shop for hot pies, bread, milk, sandwiches, ice cream and drinks. Also takeaway casseroles and crafts.

The Swan 56 High Street, Stourport (01299 871661). Just west of Lower Mitton Bridge. Friendly town pub serving a choice of real ales and bar and restaurant meals (V) *L and E (not Sun E)*. Children welcome if eating. Karaoke on *Thur*.

The Black Star (01299 822404). Canalside, by Lower Mitton Bridge, next to the Remembrance Gardens. A long, narrow, friendly pub with a low and beamy tap-room. Real ale is served and bar meals (V) are available *L*. Children welcome and there are seats outside by the canal. On *Tue* there is live jazz, on *Thur* other live music, and on *Wed* a quiz.

The Rising Sun 50 Lombard Street, Stourport (01299 822530). Canalside, between Baldwins (5A) and Gilgal (6) bridges. Small friendly pub serving real ale. Food (V) is available *L and E (not Sun E)*. Children welcome away from the bar, and there is a garden. Singer on *Sat*, quiz on *Tue*.

The Bird in Hand 5 Holly Road (01299 822385). Real ale is served in this black and white canalside pub, which has a pleasant garden and a bowling green. Food (V), including baltis and fresh fish, is served *L and E*. Children welcome. Have a look at the canal company cottages next door. Irish folk music *once a month*. B & B.

The Watermill Kidderminster (01562 66713). By Round Hill Bridge (13). A fine pub with gardens onto the canal, and offering real ale. Food (V) is served *12.00–20.00 daily*. Children are welcome *until 20.30*. Karaoke on *Tue*, quiz on *Wed*, DJs *Thur–Sun*.

Kidderminster (see *page 104*)

Kidderminster

As the buildings of Kidderminster appear, the navigation narrows until it escapes by diving into a short tunnel-like bridge, at the end of which is a deep lock and a split bridge. Emerging from the lock the scene is very different: open townscape, with traffic all around, shopping streets close by and a church just ahead, on a rise. There are good moorings here, by the gardens and the old wharf crane, with easy access to the town. Nearby is a statue of Richard Baxter, the 17th-C thinker who advocated unity and comprehension in religion. Just above Kidderminster Lock the River Stour appears, and the canal crosses it on an aqueduct. There is a supermarket by bridge 17. Leaving the town behind, the navigation moves into an area of quiet water meadows created by the River Stour, which is now on the west side. Past an isolated lock, the village of Wolverley on the other side of the valley is marked by its unusual Italianate church standing on a large outcrop of rock. The approach to the deep Wolverley Lock is lined by trees. There is a pub beside the lock, and good moorings above and below it. Beyond here the course of the canal becomes really tortuous and narrow as it proceeds up the enclosed and thickly wooded valley, forced into endless diversions by the steep cliffs of friable red sandstone. Vegetation of all kinds clings to these cliffs, giving the impression of jungle foliage. At one point the navigation opens out, becoming momentarily like a normal canal; but soon the rocks and trees encroach again, returning the waterway to its previous constricted width. An impressive promontory of rock compels the canal to double back on itself in a great horseshoe sweep that takes it round to the pretty Debdale Lock. A doorway reveals a cavern cut into the solid rock here; this was used as an overnight stable for towing horses. Beyond Cookley Tunnel the steep rocks along the right bank used to culminate in a remarkable geological feature where Austcliff Rock overhung the canal. It was removed when it became unstable. Thick woods keep the nearby A449 road at bay. Across the River Stour, 1/4 mile west of bridge 26, is the small settlement of Caunsall. There are farms here, and two pubs, but little else. Between bridges 26 and 27 the canal passes from Worcestershire into Staffordshire, but the surroundings of this remarkable waterway do not change: it continues through secluded woodlands, the rocky hillside on the east bank steepening as the valley narrows again. The nearby main road remains unnoticed while the canal reaches Whittington Lock, which has a pretty lock cottage beside it and a seat made from an old balance beam and dedicated to Jim Robbins, Chairman of the Staffs & Worcs Canal Society 1964–7. The bridge at the lock tail is typical of this navigation, its parapet curving fluently round and down to the lower water level.

Kidderminster

Worcs. All services. Kidderminster once existed above all for carpet weaving. The industry was first introduced in 1735, when the town was already a prosperous cloth manufacturing centre, and today there are still factories in Kidderminster involved in the production of carpets. Rowland Hill, founder of the Penny Post, was born here in 1793. His statue, in front of the head post office, commemorates his 'creative mind and patient energy'. The best place for access to the town is from Kidderminster Lock, where there are moorings just below the church. The inner ring road unfortunately passes the door of the impressive, dark church of St Mary and All Saints, cutting it off completely from Church Street, in which Kidderminster's few Georgian houses are situated.

Severn Valley Railway The Station, Kidderminster (01299 403816/talking timetable, telephone 0800 600900 and ask). A fine preserved steam railway on which you can travel the 16 miles to Bewdley, Arley, Highley, Hampton Loade and Bridgnorth. Most trains have buffet and bar facilities, and you may book in advance for special dining car services on

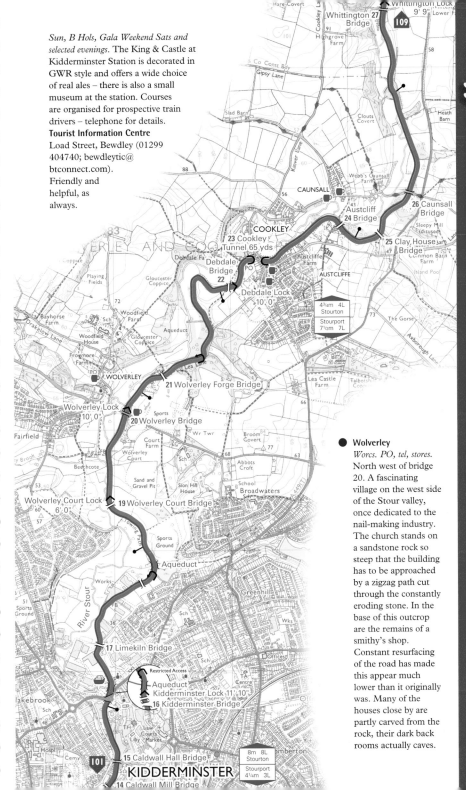

Sun, B Hols, Gala Weekend Sats and selected evenings. The King & Castle at Kidderminster Station is decorated in GWR style and offers a wide choice of real ales – there is also a small museum at the station. Courses are organised for prospective train drivers – telephone for details.

Tourist Information Centre
Load Street, Bewdley (01299 404740; bewdleytic@ btconnect.com). Friendly and helpful, as always.

● **Wolverley**
Worcs. PO, tel, stores.
North west of bridge 20. A fascinating village on the west side of the Stour valley, once dedicated to the nail-making industry. The church stands on a sandstone rock so steep that the building has to be approached by a zigzag path cut through the constantly eroding stone. In the base of this outcrop are the remains of a smithy's shop. Constant resurfacing of the road has made this appear much lower than it originally was. Many of the houses close by are partly carved from the rock, their dark back rooms actually caves.

Most of the village is clustered just to the north of the church, near the little-used but dignified stone buildings of the Old Court House, which has also seen service as both a grammar school and council offices. The school was endowed in 1629, but most of the buildings date from 1820. Around it is the bulk of this small village, where gardens make the most of the brook that flows through. There is an attractive pub in the centre of the village, and another, with spacious gardens, up the hill. Wolverley is certainly a village worth visiting – easily accessible from Wolverley Lock.

St John the Baptist Wolverley. A predominant dark red structure built in 1772 in a precise Italianate style, succeeding earlier churches which have stood on this site since Anglo-Saxon times. In legend the Lord of the Manor, a crusader called Attwood, was found in chains in the meadow, having been miraculously transported from a prison after seeing a vision of the Virgin Mary. Indeed the field by the lock is still called the Knight's Meadow. Fragments of the knight's effigy can be seen in the church.

● **Cookley**
Worcs. PO, tel, stores, garage, fish & chips. The village is set well above the canal, which passes underneath it in a tunnel. Although it has an attractive situation, Cookley is not a particularly pretty village, and there is little to visit. Down in the valley, near the River Stour, there are older, more attractive cottages, and clearly visible are the entrances to caves in the cliff face. Mooring, to gain access to the village, is not easy, as the towpath is often overgrown.

Cookley Tunnel This is 65yds long and is rough hewn from the living rock. It is unusual, in having a towpath running through it, but this probably reflects the ease with which sandstone can be worked.

Pubs and Restaurants

◖ **The King & Castle** The Railway Station, Kidderminster (01562 747505). A fine bar, decorated in GWR style and offering real ales and home-cooked meals *L daily and E Fri–Sun.* Children welcome, and there are seats outside on the platform.

◖ **The Lock** Wolverley Road (01562 850581). Canalside at Wolverley Lock. A fine canalside pub, which was previously 16th-C cottages. It was converted in stages to a pub and once had a brewhouse. There are stories of one landlord, Harry Davies, who held the licence for 55 years, taking his payment for ale in cargoes from passing boats. This resulted in drunken boatmen with their wallets still full but their boats half-empty. But the pub predates the canal, and originally drew its trade from the drove road which passed between the Black Country and Wales. The basic and beamy public bar has wooden settles and a real fire; there is an intimate Edwardian saloon with a more formal, but friendly, layout. Real ale, and excellent bar meals (V) are served *L and E*, with a children's menu. Children welcome *until 21.00*, and there is outside seating in the canalside garden, with a patio service and children's amusements. Pleasant camp site nearby. Look out for the ghost of a 1900s school mistress who plays tricks. Can get busy.

◖ **The Queens Head** Wolverley Village (01562 850433). Near the old school. Real ale in a quiet and traditional two-room village local, with a fine public bar and a smarter lounge. This pub apparently has the longest-serving pub regular in Britain. Bar meals (V) are served *L and E (not Sun E)*. Children welcome in the lounge. There is a garden, with the remains of rock houses in the car park.

◖ **The Live & Let Live** Blakes Hall Lane, Wolverley (01562 850139). Up the hill from the village, this is a friendly pub with a spacious bar, a fine conservatory and a pretty garden. Five regularly changing real ales are offered, and food (V) is available *L and E daily.* Children welcome.

◖ **The Bulls Head** Bridge Road, Cookley (01562 850242). Popular village local up the hill from the tunnel, near the shops, serving real ale. Bar meals *L and E (no food Mon)*. There is a family room and a garden with a play area. A decked area overlooks the canal. Live music *Sun*. Mooring.

✕ **Cookley Fisheries** 1 Bridge Road, Cookley (01562 850554). Excellent fish & chips, kebabs, burgers and chicken. *Closed Mon L and Sun.*

◖ ✕ **The Eagle & Spur** 176 Castle Road, Cookley (01562 850184). Bar and restaurant meals (V), are served *L and E (not Sun E)*. Children very welcome, there are two gardens. Jazz on *Wed*, folk on *Fri*.

◖ **The Anchor** Cookley Road, Caunsall (01562 850254). A short walk west of bridge 26. Real ale in an old-fashioned pub, which has been in the same family for over 70 years. Food (V) is served *L and E.* Children welcome, garden.

◖ **The Rock Tavern** Cookley Road, Caunsall (01562 850416). Old, pleasantly refurbished and haunted country pub serving real ale. Home-cooked food (V) is available *L and E (not Sun E) – please telephone and book.* Children welcome, and there is a patio.

Kinver

This stretch of the canal begins with yet another delightful scene – on both sides of the canal are cottages, pretty gardens, moored boats and a low bridge. Tall, steep, hills rising to over 250ft appear on the east bank. The canal leaves this damp, mossy area and bends round to Kinver Lock. There is a pub here, and a road leading round to the village, behind the bold modern waterworks, built in 1939. The waterworks pump water from the vast underground lake that lies deep below the great sandstone ridge stretching from Kidderminster to Wombourne. Beyond the particularly pretty Hyde Lock, the canal wanders along the edge of woods on the east side of the valley, where in one place the sandstone, eroded away, is supported on brick pillars – it then passes through the charmingly diminutive (25yds long) Dunsley Tunnel, a rough-hewn bore carved out of the rock, with overhanging foliage at each end. The next lock is at Stewponey, accompanied by a toll house. The Stourbridge Canal leaves at Stourton Junction, north of the wharf: the first of the many locks that carry this canal up towards Dudley and the Birmingham Canal Navigations is just a few yards away (*see page 124*). Beyond Stourton Junction, a 90-degree bend to the left takes the canal to an aqueduct over the River Stour: this river now disappears to the north east and is not seen again. Its place near the canal is taken by the Smestow Brook as far as Swindon. At the far end of the aqueduct is a curious narrowboat-house, known as the Devil's Den, cut into the rock. Prestwood Park is concealed in the woods above the east bank. The hall is now a hospital: it used to be the home of the Foleys, a family of Black Country ironmasters. Beyond Prestwood Bridge (34), now rebuilt in red brick to the original design, the canal makes a remote journey through Gothersley and Rocky locks: at Gothersley a memorial marks the site of the Roundhouse, built in 1805 as part of the ironworks, and lived in until the 1930s. After Rocky Lock, where rooms have been carved into the sandstone, the canal comes to a fork: the narrow entrance on the right leads into the long Ashwood Basin, where there is a marina. Now the outcrops of sandstone appear less frequently, and the countryside becomes flatter and more regular. The locks, however, do not disappear, for the canal continues the steady rise up the small valley of the Smestow Brook, through southern Staffordshire towards Wolverhampton. At Greensforge Lock there is an attractive pub, and another of the circular weirs that are found, often hidden behind a wall or a hedge, at many of the locks along this delightful canal.

● **Kinver**
Staffs. PO, tel, stores, garage, bank, laundrette.
Kinver deservedly has a reputation as a very pretty village. It is surrounded by tall hills and consists of a long main street of reasonably attractive houses, but its chief glory is its situation – it nestles among tall wooded hills, a position that must strike the visitor as remark-able for a village so close to the industries of the West Midlands. Kinver Edge (National Trust), west of the village, is a tremendous ridge covered in gorse and heather, and for anyone prepared to toil up to the top from the valley it provides a splendid view of the Cotswold and Malvern Hills. The church of St Peter is near the Edge, and is reached by a steep zigzag road. It overlooks the village and contains several items of interest, including plaques recording the Charter granted by Charles I in 1629 and the Charter granted by Ethelbad in 736, giving '10 cessapis of land to my general Cyniberte for a religious house'. If you walk up Stone Lane, close to the White Harte Hotel, until trees appear on your left, then follow the path into the trees, you will come to some superb examples of rock houses at Holy Austin Rock. Here you will see rooms, windows, cupboards, doorways and chimneys carved out of the cliffs. One of these houses, which from the inside appeared just like normal dwellings (apart from a lack of windows) was in continuous occupation for 150 years until

1935. Rock dwellings were first recorded here in 1777, and it is likely that the name, Holy Austin, originated from an Augustinian Friar who lived here prior to that time. The film *Bladys of the Stewponey* was made here in 1919 by the folklorist and novelist Sabine Baring-Gould. Take care when exploring, as the rock can be slippery underfoot.

● **Stewponey Wharf**
An interesting wharf at the head of Stewponey Lock, with a restored octagonal toll office, where you can buy souvenirs and canalware, or partake in some clairvoyance or healing (01384 877110). From near the wharf the long-abandoned Kinver Valley Light Railway used to run from Stourbridge to Kinver. From Stewponey to Kinver it followed a route close to the canal. Note also the fine circular weir by the lock. Just across the river from the wharf is the impressive bulk of Stourton Castle, while in the opposite direction – but shielded by trees – is a fast main road and a built-up area. There is an excellent tearoom just across the road, and a petrol station not far away.

Stourton Castle Just a few yards west of Stewponey Wharf, this building is a curious mixture of building styles and materials. The castle is notable as the birthplace of Cardinal Pole in 1500. A friend of Mary Tudor, Pole became Archbishop of Canterbury in her reign after Cranmer had been burned at the stake. The castle is privately owned.

● **Ashwood Basin**
This used to be a railway-connected basin owned by the National Coal Board. After the line was closed the basin was disused for some years, but now it provides a pleasant mooring site for a large number of pleasure boats. There is a marina and a boatclub here. A road is carried over the basin by a small viaduct.

WALKING & CYCLING
Stone Lane, Kinver makes a fine start for a walk which visits the rock houses by Holy Austin Rock, and then climbs south to Kinver Edge, Nanny's Rock and Kingsford Country Park. You can then return across Blakeshill Common to Cookley, where you join the canal and turn left.

Boatyards

ⓑ **Ashwood Marina** Kingswinford (01384 295535). Just past bridge 36 at Ashwood Basin. 🔧 D Gas, (overnight mooring – telephone in advance), long-term mooring, books and maps, solid fuel. *Emergency call out.*

Many of these services are provided by Orion Narrowboats:
ⓑ **Orion Narrowboats** At Ashwood Marina, Kingswinford (01384 401464). Crane, boat and engine sales and repairs, boat building, chandlery.

Pubs and Restaurants

🍺 ✕ **The Whittington Inn** (01384 872110). 300yds east of bridge 28, along a footpath, and well worth the walk. Dating from 1310, this building has an impressive history. It was the home of Dick Whittington's grandfather, and much later of Lady Jane Grey, whose ghost is sometimes encountered. There are also priest holes and a tunnel to the nearby Whittington Hall. Restaurant and bar meals (V) *all day, everyday*, with real ale to enjoy. Children welcome if you are eating. Garden.

🍺 **The Vine** 1 Dunsley Road, Kinver (01384 877291). Pretty lockside pub with a lovely canalside garden. Choice of real ales, and food (V) is available *L and E*. Children welcome *until 21.30*, and there is a garden with a children's play area and a bouncy castle in summer. Quiz *Mon*,

music *Wed*. Outside servery during *summer*, and a barbecue wagon.

✕ ♀ **Berkleys Brasserie** 47 High Street, Kinver (01384 873679; www.berkleys.co.uk). Mediterranean food (V) and a good choice of wine *L and E*. Children welcome.

🍺 **Ye Old White Hart Hotel** High Street, Kinver (01384 872305). A large pub serving real ale, and food *all day, every day*. Children welcome and there is outside seating with a children's play area.

🍺 **The Navigation Inn** Canalside at Greensforge Lock, near Kingswinford (01384 273721). Refurbished pub, with log fires, built in 1767. Real ale and home-made food (V) *L and E*. Children welcome *until 21.00*, and there is canalside seating in the pretty garden.

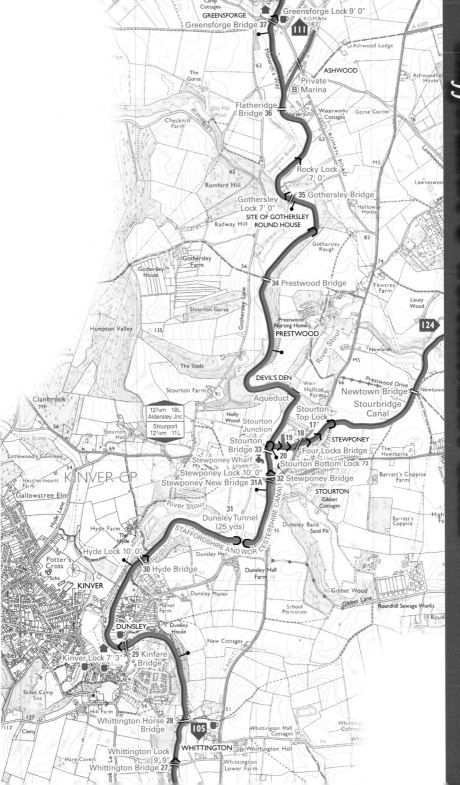

Greensforge Lock 9' 0"
GREENSFORGE
Greensforge Bridge 37

ASHWOOD
Private
Marina

Flatheridge
Bridge 36

Rocky Lock
7' 0"

Gothersley Bridge 35
Gothersley
Lock 7' 0"
SITE OF GOTHERSLEY
ROUND HOUSE

34 Prestwood Bridge

PRESTWOOD

DEVIL'S DEN
Aqueduct

Newtown Bridge
Stourton
Top Lock
17
Stourton
Junction
19 18
Stewponey
Stourton
Bridge 33
20
Four Locks Bridge
Stewponey Wharf
Stourton Bottom Lock 72
32 Stewponey Bridge
Stewponey Lock 10' 0"
Stewponey New Bridge 31A
STOURTON

12¾m 18L
Aldersley Jnc
Stourport
12¼m 11L

31
Dunsley Tunnel
(25 yds)

Hyde Lock 10' 0"

30 Hyde Bridge

KINVER

DUNSLEY

Kinver Lock 7' 3"
29 Kinfare
Bridge

Whittington Horse 28
Bridge

Whittington Lock
9' 9"   WHITTINGTON
Whittington Bridge 27

The Bratch

Another wooded, rocky section soon gives way to more open country. Passing through the isolated Hinksford Lock, the navigation bends round to Swindon where the canal is flanked by the tidy gardens of new houses. There are four locks hereabouts – Botterham Lock is a two-step staircase with a bridge crossing in the middle. Now the canal begins to lose its rural character as it encounters the modern outskirts of Wombourn, passing under a new bridge that, happily, retains the original cast iron name plates. There is a pub by this bridge (43) and a few shops not far to the north east of the next one. Yet another pub is at the next bridge (45); and beyond it is Bumblehole Lock. The three Bratch Locks are next, raising the canal level by over 30ft. From the top there is a good view back down the valley, with the spire of Wombourn Church backed by the great ridge of the Orton Hills to the east. Leaving The Bratch, the canal wanders through open farmland parallel to a long-closed railway, now the course of the Kingswinford Railway Walk, arriving at the pleasantly situated Awbridge Lock, accompanied by a fine circular weir.

● **Swindon**
Staffs. PO, tel, store, fish & chips. A small village, once a mixture of farming and industry. The 19th-C ironworks has been demolished, replaced with a housing estate.

● **Wombourne**
Staffs. PO, tel, stores. A village much expanded by housing development.

● **Bratch Locks**
With their octagonal toll office, attractive situation and unusual layout, these three locks are well known among students of canal engineering and architecture. At first sight they appear curiously illogical, with an impossibly short pound between the bottom of one lock and the top gate of the next; but the secret of their operation is the side ponds hidden behind the towpath hedge, and the culverts that connect these to the intermediate pounds. In fact, to work through these locks, boaters should simply treat each one as a separate lock, like any other. *Carefully study the operating instructions before use, and consult the lock keeper if you are in any doubt. It is especially important when locking through to close the gates and paddles of each lock before operating the paddles of the next.*

Boatyards

Ⓑ **Wombourne Canal Services** Giggety Wharf (01902 892242). Pump out, gas, chandlery, shop, coal.

Pubs and Restaurants

🍺 **The Old Bush Inn** Swindon Road, Hinksford (01384 294572). Two minutes' walk north east of bridge 38. A friendly pub.

🍺 **The Old Bush Inn** High Street, Swindon village (01384 279235). East of bridge 40. Real ale in a homely pub. Food (V) is served *L and E, Mon–Sat.* Children welcome, and there is a garden. *PO and stores opposite.*

🍺 **The Green Man** High Street, Swindon (01384 400532; www.westmidlandspubs.co.uk). West of bridge 40. A friendly, family-oriented traditional local, with open fires, a separate games room and a quiet snug with old books, serving real ale and real cider. Bar meals *L and E.* Children welcome, and there is outside seating in a small attractive garden. Quoits and pub games.

🍺 **The Greyhound** High Street, Swindon (01384 287243). Large beamy pub with open fires, offering real ale and serving food *L and E (not Sun or Tue E).* Children welcome if eating, and there is a patio.

🍺 **The Waggon & Horses** Bridgnorth Road, Wombourne (01902 892828). Near the canal at bridge 43. Sociable and recently refurbished real ale pub, serving food (V) *all day, every day.* Children welcome and there is a pretty garden.

🍺 **The Round Oak** 100 Ounsdale Road, Wombourne (01902 892083). Canalside, at bridge 45. A real ale pub, dating from the 1800s, serving food (V) *L and E.* There is a family room, and a garden with amusements. Note the old post box set into the wall. Quiz on *Tue.*

Sand Pit

Church Lane

The Grotto

Osiers

Manor House

CP

Trysull

Hunters Green

Fiershill Farm

Courtenay

Smestow Gate

Smestow

Church Cottage

Church Farm

Monks Path

Monkspath Farm

Clee View

Nursery

Woodford Grange

Woodford Lane

Bratch Common Road

Bell Road

Trysull Road

Awbridge Lock 10' 0"
49 Awbridge Bridge

Aw 112 Farm

Towpath

Monarch's Way

Little Covert

Fox Hill

Orton Hill

Bearnett House

WOMBOUR

Ladywell Wood

Bearnett Lane

Toll House

Upper Bratch Bridge 48

Bratch Locks 30' 2"
47 Bratch Bridge

Bullmeadow Coppice

Rushford Bridge

THE BRATCH

Bumblehole Lock 10' 0"
46 Bumblehole Bridge
45 Houndel Bridge

WOMBOURNE

Ounsdale

Pipe Bridge

44 Giggetty Bridge

GIGGETTY

Blakeley

Greenhill Farm

STAFFORDSHIRE AND WORCESTERSHIRE CANAL

43 Wombourne Bridge

Bridgnorth Road

Botterham Lane

Himley Plantation

WALKING & CYCLING
Walk north along the canal from The Bratch to Awbridge Bridge, and turn left. Turn left again at the church in Trysull and then veer across country to pass Woodford Grange and back to the canal at Wombourne Bridge. Turn left to return to the start, passing Bumblehole. East of Bratch Locks you can pick up the Kingswinford Railway Walk.

Botterham Bridge 42
Footbridge

Botterham Staircase Locks 20' 3"
Pipe Bridge

8½m 14L
Aldersley Jnc
Stourton Jnc
4½m 4L

Marsh Lock 9' 9"
Marsh Bridge 41

SWINDON

Swindon Lock 9' 0"
Swindon Bridge 40

Swindon Rough

Hinksford Lock 39 Bridge

Hinksford Farm

Hinksford Lock 7' 9" 60' only

Chasepool Farm

Hollow Mill

Hinksford Bridge 38

Aqueduct

HINKSFORD

Caravan Park

Greensforge Rough

ROMAN ROAD (course of)

Mile Flat Rd

Dismd Rly

Camp Cottages

Bank Farm

Greensforge Farm

109

GREENSFORGE

ROMAN FORT

Wightwick

North of Greensforge, the countryside becomes less interesting and, although it is still quiet and remote from roads and railways, the canal is accompanied by overhead power lines for a mile as it rises through Awbridge, Ebstree and Dimmingsdale locks. At bridge 53 an arm provides moorings for a fine array of traditionally painted working boats, amidst overhanging trees. Beyond the bridge a pretty lake to the west closes in – this is a canal-feeder reservoir of considerable interest to fishermen. Ahead, the hills of Wightwick overlook the navigation as it approaches a shallow valley and a busy main road. This valley – in places an artificial cutting – contains the canal right through to the flatter land at Aldersley. Houses, mostly modern, are never far away, although the canal manages to preserve its rural character all the way through what are in effect the western outskirts of Wolverhampton. Compton Lock marks the end of the 31-lock climb from the River Severn at Stourport, a rise of 294ft. There is a supermarket nearby. From here northwards, a 10-mile level pound takes the Staffordshire & Worcestershire on to Gailey, where the first of 12 locks begin the fall towards the Trent & Mersey Canal.

Boatyards

ⓑ **Lime Kiln Narrowboats** 4 Bridgnorth Road, Compton (01902 751147). By Compton Bridge. ♣ D Pump out, gas, boat building, boat sales and repairs, chandlery, toilets, books and maps, solid fuel.

ⓑ **Wolverhampton Passenger Boat Services** The Wharf, Oxley Moor Road (01902 789522). 🛉 🛉 (♣ charge) D Pump out, gas, overnight and long-term mooring, winter storage, slipway, crane, boat sales, boat and engine repairs, telephone, toilets.

BOAT TRIPS
Nb Stafford (01902 789522). A 42-seater available for private charter from Wolverhampton Passenger Boat Services. They also run a *3-hour walk-on trip at 15.00 on the first Sun of every month.*

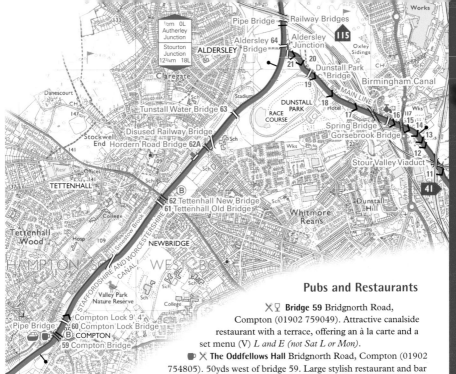

Pubs and Restaurants

✕ ♀ **Bridge 59** Bridgnorth Road, Compton (01902 759049). Attractive canalside restaurant with a terrace, offering an à la carte and a set menu (V) *L and E (not Sat L or Mon)*.

◗ ✕ **The Oddfellows Hall** Bridgnorth Road, Compton (01902 754805). 50yds west of bridge 59. Large stylish restaurant and bar serving real ale and food (V) *L and E*. Children welcome *until 21.00*. Large-screen TV.

◗ ✕ **The Mermaid** Bridgnorth Road, Wightwick (01902 760021). 100yds west of bridge 56. A large, warm and friendly pub serving real ale, and meals (V) *all day, every day*. Children welcome, and there is a patio.

● **Wightwick**
Staffs. (pronounced Wittick). Once a village but now a suburb. There is a hill and plenty of trees, and in spite of the busy road it is a pleasant scene around the canal bridge and the pub. It is worth the short walk to Wightwick Manor.
Wightwick Manor (NT) Wightwick Bank, Wolverhampton (01902 761108; wightwickmanor@ntrust.org.uk). About 300yds north west of bridge 56, across the busy road and up the hill. Built between 1887 and 1893 for Theodore Mander, a paint and varnish maker, and designed by Edward Ould. The manor has an exterior that embodies many of the idiosyncrasies of the time. Inside, it is furnished with original wallpapers and fabrics by William Morris and various contributions by the Pre-Raphaelites. This certainly makes a pleasing change from the usual venerable stone or timbered buildings that are open to the public. The drawing room is perhaps the most richly decorated, with a Jacobean-style ceiling, a 16th-C alabaster carved fireplace and William Morris Dove and Rose silk wall

hangings. The Great Parlour is the main room of the house, and gives the impression of a Tudor hall, richly timbered and glowing with stained glass, tiles and porcelain. It contains what is considered to be the finest of Burne-Jones' later works *Love among the Ruins*. Other superb rooms include the kitchen and nursery. The beautiful 17-acre Edwardian gardens were laid out from plans by Alfred Parsons and Thomas Mawson drawn in 1904 and 1910. *Open Mar–Dec, Thur, Sat and B Hols 13.30–16.30*. Also family openings *Aug, Wed 13.30–17.00*. The Old Manor (01902 761108) is *open Wed and Thur 11.00–17.30, Sat and B Hols 13.30–17.30*. The garden is *open Wed, Thur, Sat and B Hols 11.00–18.00*. Charge. Tea room.

● **Compton**
Staffs. PO, tel, stores, laundrette. A busy but uninteresting village with a modern shopping centre, a pub, and a restaurant by the bridge. The canal lock here was the first that James Brindley built on the Staffordshire & Worcestershire Canal in the late 1760s, but unfortunately the cottage that accompanied it has been demolished.

Autherley Junction

Autherley Junction is marked by a big white bridge on the towpath side. The stop lock just beyond marks the entrance to the Shropshire Union: there is a useful boatyard just to the north of it. Leaving Autherley, the Staffordshire & Worcestershire runs through a very narrow cutting in rock, once known as 'Pendeford Rockin', after a local farm: there is only room for boats to pass in the designated places, so a good look out should be kept for oncoming craft. After passing the motorway and a rather conspicuous sewage works at Coven Heath, the navigation leaves behind the suburbs of Wolverhampton and enters pleasant farmland. The bridges need care: although the bridgeholes are reasonably wide, the actual arches are rather low.

● **Autherley Junction**
A busy canal junction with a full range of boating facilities close by.
● **Coven**
Staffs. PO, tel, stores, garage, fish & chips. The only true village on this section, Coven lies beyond a dual carriageway north west of Cross Green Bridge. There is a large number of shops, including a laundrette.

Near Gailey (see page 116)

Boatyards

ⓑ **Water Travel** Autherley Junction, Oxley Moor Road, Wolverhampton (01902 782371). 🛢 🔧 D Pump out, gas, narrowboat hire, slipway, boat and engine repairs, chandlery, toilets.
ⓑ **Oxley Marine** The Wharf, Oxley Moor Road, Wolverhampton (01902 789522). 🛢 D Pump out, gas, overnight and long-term mooring, slipway, crane, boat and engine sales and repairs. Licensed bar *each evening*, snacks.

WALKING & CYCLING
The towpath is generally in good condition for both walkers and cyclists.

BOAT TRIPS
Nb Stafford Carrying up to 42 passengers, with a bar and food. Public trips on the *first Sun each month*, plus private charter. For details telephone (01902) 789522.

Pubs and Restaurants

🍺 ✕ **Fox & Anchor Inn** Brewood Road, Cross Green (01902 790786). Canalside by Cross Green Bridge. Large and friendly pub with roof-top terrace. Real ale, and meals (V) available *all day*. Menu is traditional English, along with steaks and *Sunday* roast. Children's menu, garden and good moorings.

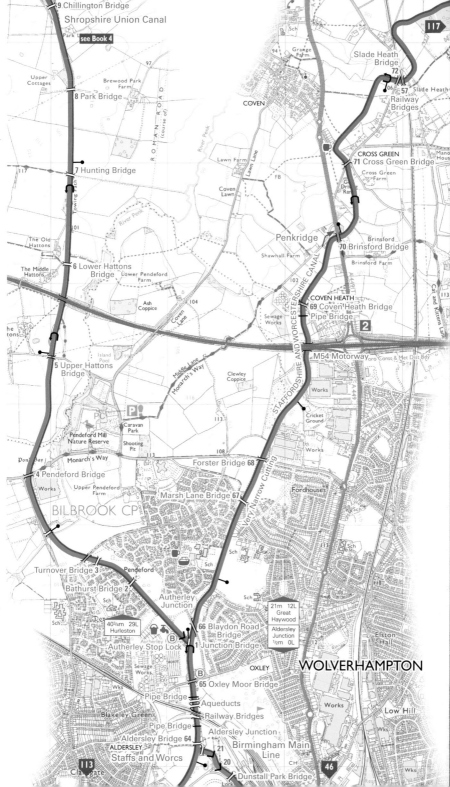

9 Chillington Bridge

Shropshire Union Canal

see Book 4

117

Slade Heath Bridge

72
06
57 Slade Heath
Railway Bridges

Upper Cottages

Brewood Park Farm

8 Park Bridge

COVEN

CROSS GREEN
71 Cross Green Bridge

Cross Green Farm

Lawn Farm

Lawn Lane

7 Hunting Bridge

Coven Lawn

FB

Penkridge

70 Brinsford Bridge

Brinsford

Brinsford Farm

The Old Hattons

6 Lower Hattons Bridge

Lower Pendeford Farm

Shawhall Farm

COVEN HEATH
69 Coven Heath Bridge
Pipe Bridge

The Middle Hattons

Ash Coppice

Coven Lane

Sewage Works

2

5 Upper Hattons Bridge

Island Pool

Middle Lane

Monarch's Way

Clewley Coppice

M54 Motorway

Works

Cricket Ground

PC

P

Caravan Park

Shooting Pit

Works

Pendeford Mill Nature Reserve

Monarch's Way

Forster Bridge **68**

Very Narrow Cutting

Fordhouses

4 Pendeford Bridge

Works

Upper Pendeford Farm

Marsh Lane Bridge **67**

BILBROOK CP

Turnover Bridge **3**

Pendeford

Bathurst Bridge **2**

Autherley Junction

21m 12L
Great Haywood

Aldersley Junction ½m 0L

40¾m 29L
Hurleston

66 Blaydon Road Bridge

B

1 Junction Bridge

Autherley Stop Lock

OXLEY

WOLVERHAMPTON

Elston Hall

Sewage Works

Wks

B

65 Oxley Moor Bridge

Works

Low Hill

Pipe Bridge

Aqueducts

Railway Bridges

Pipe Bridge

Aldersley Junction

Birmingham Main Line

Aldersley Bridge **64**

ALDERSLEY

21

Staffs and Worcs

20

46

Claregate

113

Dunstall Park Bridge

Gailey Wharf

The considerable age of this canal is shown by its extremely twisting course, revealed after passing the railway bridge. There are few real centres of population along this stretch, which comprises largely former heathland. The canal widens just before bridge 74, where Brindley incorporated part of a medieval moat into the canal. Hatherton Junction marks the entrance of the former Hatherton Branch of the Staffordshire & Worcestershire Canal into the main line. This branch used to connect with the Birmingham Canal Navigations. It is closed above the derelict second lock, although the channel remains as a feeder for the Staffordshire & Worcestershire Canal. There is a campaign for its restoration. There is a marina at the junction. A little further along, a chemical works is encountered, astride the canal in what used to be woodlands. This was once called the 'Black Works', as lamp black was produced here. Gailey Wharf is about a mile further north: it is a small canal settlement that includes a boatyard and a large, round, toll keeper's watch-tower, containing a useful canal shop. The picturesque Wharf Cottage opposite has been restored as a bijou residence. The canal itself disappears under Watling Street and then falls rapidly through five locks towards Penkridge. These locks are very attractive, and some are accompanied by little brick bridges. The M6 motorway comes alongside for 1/2 mile, screening the reservoirs which feed the canal.

Pillaton Old Hall South east of bridge 85. Only the gate house and stone-built chapel remain of this late 15th-C brick mansion built by the Littleton family, although there are still traces of the hall and courtyard. The chapel contains a 13th-C wooden carving of a saint. Visiting is by appointment only: telephone (01785) 712200. The modest charge is donated to charity.
Gailey and Calf Heath reservoirs 1/2 mile east of Gailey Wharf, either side of the M6. These are feeder reservoirs for the canal, though rarely drawn on. The public has access to them as nature reserves to study the wide variety of natural life, especially the long-established heronry which is thriving on an island in Gailey Lower Reservoir. In Gailey Upper, fishing is available to the public from the riparian owner. In Gailey Lower a limited number of angling tickets are available on a season ticket basis each year from BW. There is club sailing on two of the reservoirs.

Boatyards

Ⓑ **Otherton Boat Haven** Otherton Hall Farm, Offerton (01785 712515; mobile 07966 184182; pdorrington@bun.com). 🛊 🛊 🎣 D Pump out, gas, overnight and long-term mooring, boat and engine sales and repairs, toilets.
Ⓑ **J D Boat Services** The Wharf, Watling Street, Standeford (01902 790811, www.jdboats.co.uk). Pump out, gas, boat and engine repairs, engine sales, boat building. Gifts and provisions opposite in the Roundhouse.
Ⓑ **Viking Afloat** At J B Boat Services (01905 610660, www.viking-afloat.com). Narrowboat hire.
Ⓑ **Calf Heath Marina** King's Road, Calf Heath (01902 790570, info@calf-heath-marina.co.uk). 🎣 D Pump out, gas, overnight and long-term moorings, telephone, toilet.

Pubs and Restaurants

✕ ♀ **Misty's Bar & Restaurant** Calf Heath Marina, King's Road, Calf Heath (01902 790570, info@calf-heath-marina.co.uk). Restaurant serving excellent and reasonably priced home-cooked food (V) *L and E*. Children welcome, garden.
🍺 **Spread Eagle** Watling Street, Gailey (01902 790212). About 1/2 mile west of Gailey Wharf. Large road house serving real ale and food (V) *all day*. Children welcome, and there is a spacious garden.
🍺 **Cross Keys** Filance Lane (01785 712826). Canalside, at Filance Bridge (84). Once a lonely canal pub, now it is modernised and surrounded by housing estates. Family orientated, it serves real ale and food (V) *L and E*. Garden, with *summer* barbecues. 🎣 There is a useful Spar shop 100yds north, on the estate.

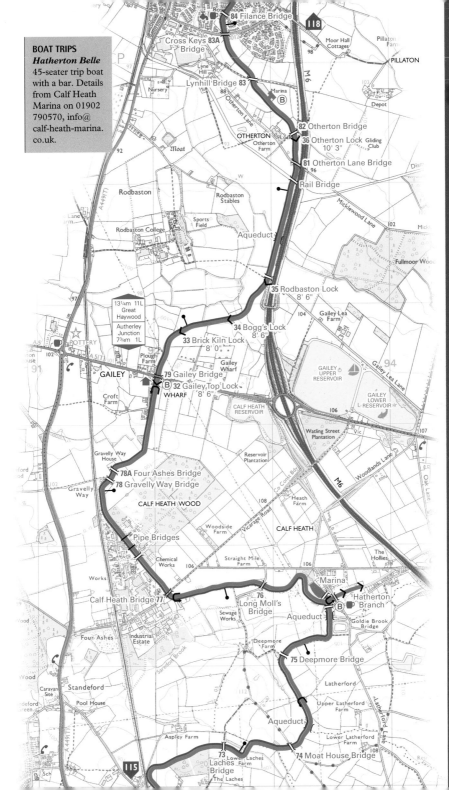

BOAT TRIPS
Hatherton Belle
45-seater trip boat with a bar. Details from Calf Heath Marina on 01902 790570, info@ calf-heath-marina. co.uk.

84 Filance Bridge

118

Cross Keys 83A Bridge

Moor Hall Cottages

Pillaton Farm

PILLATON

Lynhill Bridge 83

Depot

Marina
B

82 Otherton Bridge

OTHERTON

36 Otherton Lock Gliding Club
10' 3"

Rodbaston

81 Otherton Lane Bridge

Rail Bridge

Rodbaston Stables

Micklewood Lane

Sports Field

Aqueduct

Fullmoor Wood

Rodbaston College

13¼ 11L
Great Haywood
Autherley Junction
7¾ 1L

35 Rodbaston Lock
8' 6"

Gailey Lea Farm

94

Gailey Lea Lane

34 Bogg's Lock
8' 6"

33 Brick Kiln Lock
8' 0"

Gailey Wharf

GAILEY UPPER RESERVOIR

GAILEY

79 Gailey Bridge
B 32 Gailey Top Lock
8' 6"

WHARF

Croft Farm

CALF HEATH RESERVOIR

GAILEY LOWER L. RESERVOIR

Watling Street Plantation

Gravelly Way House

Reservoir Plantation

Woodlands Lane

78A Four Ashes Bridge
78 Gravelly Way Bridge

Gravelly Way

CALF HEATH WOOD

Woodside Farm

Heath Farm

CALF HEATH

The Hollies

Pipe Bridges

Chemical Works

Straight Mile Farm

Works

Calf Heath Bridge 77

76 Long Moll's Bridge

Marina

Hatherton Branch
B

Sewage Works

Aqueduct

Goldie Brook Bridge

Four Ashes

Industrial Estate

Deepmore Farm

75 Deepmore Bridge

Caravan Site

Standeford

Pool House

Latherford

Upper Latherford Farm

Lower Latherford Farm

Aqueduct

Aspley Farm

73 Lower Laches Bridge

The Laches

74 Moat House Bridge

115

Penkridge

The navigation now passes through Penkridge and is soon approached by the little River Penk: the two water courses share the valley for the next few miles. Apart from the noise of the motorway this is a pleasant valley: there are plenty of trees, a handful of locks and the large Teddesley Park alongside the canal. At Acton Trussell the M6 roars off to the north west and once again peace returns to the waterway. Teddesley Park Bridge was at one time quite ornamental, and became known as 'Fancy Bridge'. It is less so now. At Shutt Hill an iron post at the bottom of the lock is the only reminder of a small wharf which once existed here. The post was used to turn the boats into the dock.

120

Farm
Wesleigh Farm
Brookflat
Barnhurst Farm
Roseford Farm
Roseford 94 Bridge
Acton Gate
Hotel
Ivy House Farm
M6
Actonmill Farm
Mill Lane
78
Wattles Lane

ACTON AND BE

Dunston Farm
School
Dunston
A449
93 Acton Bridge
ACTON TRUSSELL
Acton Trussell Farm
99
Rowley Moor

STAFFORDSHIRE AND WORCESTERSHIRE CANAL

8¼m 2L
Great Haywood
Autherley Junction 12¾m 10L

Meadow Lane
92 Acton Moat Bridge
82
Plashes Farm

91
Cockpit Plantation
91 Shutt Hill Bridge
Moat House Farm
Home Farm
Shutt Hill Lock 41 6' 0"
Wellington Belt
Adams Ba

Drayton Manor
River Penk
Acton Pasture Barn
M6
Staffordshire Way
117

Honey Pots
103
Sewage Works
TEDDESLEY PARK
The Beeches
102

Lower Drayton
90 Park Gate Bridge
Park Gate Lock 40 7' 6"
B
94
Lower Drayton Farm
Parkgate Farm
Lodgerail Pool

89 Teddesley Park Bridge
WOOD BANK
M6 Motorway Bridge
Wood Bank Farm

Chase View
Longford Bridge 88

Hayes Wood
Bangley Park
Hazel
Pond Bar

The Roller Mill
Sch
87 Broom Bridge
39 Longford Lock 10' 0"
Wolgarston
B5012
Quarry Heath

Viaduct
Market
Sch
86 Penkridge Bridge
38 Penkridge Lock 9' 3"
B
85 Princefield Bridge
Sch
103
Quarry Heath Farm

Pinfold Lane
Little Penkridge
FILANCE LOCK 37 10' 3"
PENKRIDGE

Cuttlestone Bridge
Nursery
The Deanery
84 Filance Bridge
83A Cross Keys Bridge
Moor Hall Cottages
Pillaton Hall Farm

117

● **Penkridge**
Staffs. PO, tel, stores, garage, bank, station.
Above Penkridge Lock is a good place to tie up in this relatively old village. It is bisected by a trunk road, but luckily most of the village lies to the east of it. The church of St Michael is tall and sombre, and is well-kept. A harmonious mixture of styles, the earliest part dates from the 11th C, but the whole was restored in 1881. There is a fine Dutch 18th-C wrought iron screen brought from Cape Town, and the tower is believed to date from about 1500. There are fine monuments of the Littletons of

Pillaton Hall (see the previous section), dating from 1558 and later.
Teddesley Park On the east bank of the canal. The Hall, once the family seat of the Littletons, was used during the last war as a prisoner-of-war camp, but has since been demolished. Its extensive wooded estate still remains.
● **Acton Trussell**
Staffs. Tel, stores. A village overwhelmed by modern housing: much the best way to see it is from the canal. The church stands to the south, overlooking the navigation. The west tower dates from the 13th C, topped by a spire built in 1562.

Boatyards

ⓑ **Teddesley Boat Company** Park Gate Lock, Teddesley Road, Penkridge (01785 714692, www.narrowboats.co.uk). **D** Pump out, gas, narrowboat hire, overnight and long-term mooring, winter storage, crane, boat and engine sales and repairs, boat building,

telephone, books and maps, café. *Closed Sun.* For chandlery telephone (01785) 712437.
ⓑ **Tom's Moorings** Cannock Road, Penkridge (01543 414808). Above Penkridge Lock.
⚓ Pump out, gas, overnight and long-term mooring.

Tixall Lock (see page 120)

Pubs and Restaurants

🍺 **The Boat** Cannock Road (01785 714178). Canalside, by Penkridge Lock. Mellow and friendly red-brick pub dating from 1779, with plenty of brass and other bits and pieces in the homely bars. Real ale is served, and food (V) is available *L and E (not Sun E).* Children welcome, garden.
🍺 **Star** Market Place, Penkridge (01785 712513). Fine old pub, tastefully renovated and serving real ale and bar meals (V) *12.00–17.00 in summer, reduced hours in winter.* Children welcome. Outside seating.

🍺 **White Hart** Stone Cross, Penkridge (01785 712242). This historic former coaching inn, visited by Mary, Queen of Scots, and Elizabeth I, has an impressive frontage, timber framed with three gables. It serves real ale, and meals (V) *at the usual times.* Outside seating.
🍺 **Railway** Wolverhampton Road, Penkridge (01785 712685). Real ale is available in this listed and historic main road pub, along with meals (V) *L and E.* Children welcome. Garden.

WALKING & CYCLING
The Staffordshire Way crosses the canal between bridges 89 and 90. This 90-mile path strtetches from Mow Cop in the north (near the Macclesfield Canal) to Kinver Edge in the south, using the Caldon Canal towpath on the way. It connects with the Gritstone Trail, the Hereford & Worcester Way and the Heart of England Way. A guide book is available from local Tourist Information Centres.

Tixall

Continuing north along the shallow Penk valley, the canal soon reaches Radford Bridge, the nearest point to Stafford. It is about 1¹/₂ miles to the centre of town: there is a frequent bus service. A mile further north the canal bends around to the south east and follows the pretty valley of the River Sow. At Milford the navigation crosses the Sow via an aqueduct – an early structure by James Brindley, carried heavily on low brick arches; there is a good farm shop south of bridge 105, through the railway bridge. Dredging around here revealed the presence of great numbers of freshwater mussels. Tixall Lock offers some interesting views in all directions: the castellated entrance to Shugborough Railway Tunnel at the foot of the thick woods of Cannock Chase and the distant outline of Tixall Gatehouse. The canal now completes its journey to the Trent & Mersey Canal at Great Haywood. It is a length of waterway quite unlike any other. Proceeding along this very charming valley, the navigation enters Tixall Wide – an amazing and delightful stretch of water more resembling a lake than a canal, and navigable to the edges. The Wide is noted for its kingfisher population. On the low hill to the north is the equally remarkable Tixall Gatehouse, while woods across the valley conceal Shugborough Hall. The River Trent is met, on its way south from Stoke-on-Trent, and crossed on an aqueduct. There is a wharf, and fresh produce can be purchased at the farm near here; gifts are sold in the old canal toll booth. The Trent & Mersey Canal is entered through an elegantly arched bridge, the subject of a very famous photograph taken by the canal historian Eric de Maré.

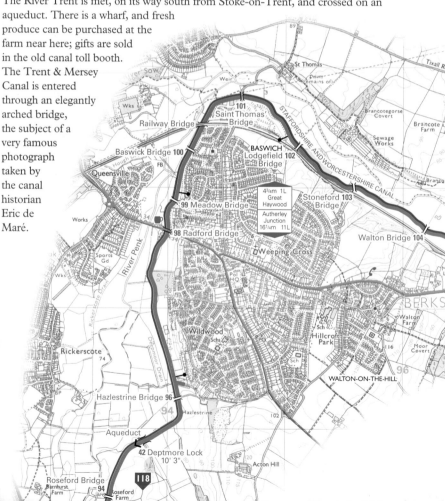

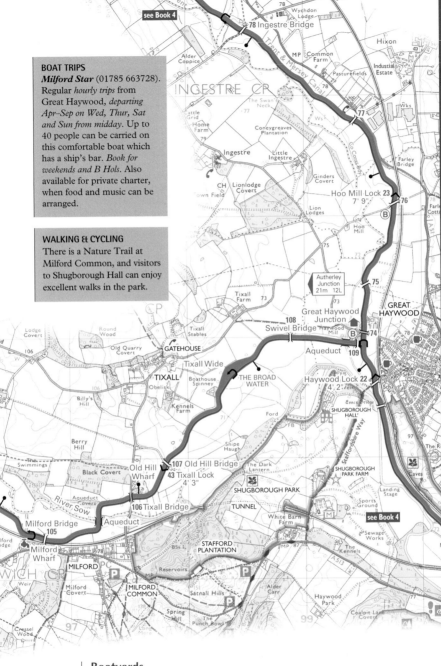

BOAT TRIPS

Milford Star (01785 663728). Regular *hourly trips* from Great Haywood, *departing Apr–Sep on Wed, Thur, Sat and Sun from midday*. Up to 40 people can be carried on this comfortable boat which has a ship's bar. *Book for weekends and B Hols*. Also available for private charter, when food and music can be arranged.

WALKING & CYCLING

There is a Nature Trail at Milford Common, and visitors to Shugborough Hall can enjoy excellent walks in the park.

Boatyards

Ⓑ **Anglo Welsh** The Canal Wharf, Mill Lane, Great Haywood (01889 881711, www.anglowelsh.co.uk). 🚽 🎁 ♿ D Pump out, gas, narrowboat hire, day-hire craft, overnight and long-term mooring, boat sales, engine repairs, chandlery, toilets, books, maps and gifts.

Stafford

Staffs. All services. This town is well worth visiting, since there is a remarkable wealth of fine old buildings. These include a handsome City Hall complex of ornamental Italianate buildings, c.1880. The robust-looking gaol is nearby; and the church of St Mary stands in very pleasing and spacious grounds. There are some pretty back alleys: Church Lane contains a splendid-looking eating house, and at the bottom of the lane a fruiterer's shop is in a thatched cottage built in 1610.

The Shire Hall Gallery Market Square, Stafford (01785 278345). A stimulating variety of work by local artists, craftsmen, printmakers, jewellers, photographers and others. *Open Mon–Sat 09.30–17.00.*

Tourist Information Centre Market Street, Stafford (01785 619619, tic@staffordbc.gov.uk).

The Stafford Branch

Just west of bridge 101 there was once a lock taking a branch of the Staffordshire & Worcestershire to Stafford. One mile long, it was unusual in that it was not a canal but the canalised course of the River Sow.

Milford

Staffs. PO, tel, stores, garage. Best reached from Tixall Bridge (106). Milford Hall is hidden by trees.

Tixall

Staffs. Tel, stores. Just to the east are the stables and the gatehouse of the long-vanished Tixall Hall. This massive square Elizabethan building dates from 1598 and is fully four storeys high. It stands alone in a field and is considered to be one of the most ambitious gatehouses in the country. The gatehouse is now available for holiday lets: telephone the Landmark Trust (01628 825925) for details.

Great Haywood

Staffs. PO, tel, stores. Centre of the Great Haywood and Shugborough Conservation Area, the village is not particularly beautiful, but it is closely connected in many ways to Shugborough Park, to which it is physically linked by the very old Essex Bridge, where the crystal clear waters of the River Sow join the Trent on its way down from Stoke.

Shugborough Hall *NT.* Walk south along the road from bridge 106 to the A513 at Milford Common. The main entrance is on your left. The present house dates from 1693, but was substantially altered by James Stuart around 1760 and by Samuel Wyatt around the turn of the 18th C. The Trust has leased the whole to Staffordshire County Council who now manage it. The house has been restored at great expense. There are some magnificent rooms and treasures inside.

Museum of Staffordshire Life This excellent establishment, Staffordshire's County Museum, is housed in the old stables adjacent to Shugborough Hall. Open since 1966, it is superbly laid out and contains all sorts of exhibits concerned with old country life in Staffordshire.

Shugborough Park There are some remarkable sights in the large park that encircles the Hall. Thomas Anson, who inherited the estate in 1720, enlisted in 1744 the help of his famous brother, Admiral George Anson, to beautify and improve the house and the park. In 1762 he commissioned James Stuart, a neo-Grecian architect, to embellish the grounds. 'Athenian' Stuart set to with a will, and the spectacular results of his work can be seen scattered round the park.

The Park Farm Designed by Samuel Wyatt, it contains an agricultural museum, a working mill and a rare breeds centre. Traditional country skills such as bread-making, butter-churning and cheese-making are demonstrated.

Shugborough Hall, Grounds, Museum and Farm (01889 881388; www.nationaltrust.org.uk). *Open Apr–Sep Tue–Sun 11.00–17.00 (also first 3 Suns Oct).* Charge. Parties must book. Tea rooms, shop.

Pubs and Restaurants

The Radford Bank Inn Canalside at bridge 98. (01785 2428250). Food (V) is served *all day, every day until 21.00,* along with real ale. Children are welcome *until 21.00,* and there is a garden.

The Clifford Arms Main Road, Great Haywood (01889 881321). There has apparently been a pub on this site for almost 1000 years. At one time it was a coaching inn. Now it is a friendly village local with an open fire, serving real ale and bar and restaurant meals (V) *L and E.* Small garden with yews.

Lockhouse Restaurant Trent Lane, Great Haywood (01889 881294). Personally run, very friendly and handy for Anglo-Welsh visitors, they offer morning and afternoon tea, coffee and cakes, hot and cold carvery *L daily* and home-cooked English food (V – but book for special dishes) *E Fri–Sat only (booking advisable).* Real ale is available for the thirsty. Canalside garden, and just a couple of minutes' walk from the village.

The Fox & Hounds Main Road, Great Haywood (01889 881252). Plush village pub with an open fire, serving a good selection of real ale. Home-made food (V) *L Thur–Sun and E Mon–Sat.* Children welcome, and there is a garden.

STOURBRIDGE & DUDLEY CANALS

MAXIMUM DIMENSIONS
Length: 70'
Beam: 6' 10"
Headroom: 6' 6"

MANAGER
Stourton Junction to the aqueduct at
Wordsley Junction: 01785 284253
enquiries.norbury@britishwaterways.co.uk

East of the aqueduct at Wordsley Junction:
0121 506 1300
enquiries.tipton@britishwaterways.co.uk

MILEAGE
Stourbridge Canal
STOURTON JUNCTION to:
Wordsley Junction: 2 miles
Stourbridge: 3¹/4 miles

BLACK DELPH bottom lock: 5¹/4 miles
Locks: 20

Dudley No. 1 and No. 2 Canals
Dudley No. 1 Canal
Delph Bottom Lock (Stourbridge Canal) *to:*
PARK HEAD JUNCTION: 2 miles
Dudley Tunnel (north end): 4 miles
TIPTON JUNCTION: 4¹/2 miles
Locks: 12

Dudley No. 2 Canal
PARK HEAD JUNCTION to:
WINDMILL END JUNCTION: 2⁵/8 miles
HAWNE BASIN: 5¹/2 miles
No locks

The Stourbridge and Dudley Canals are to some extent inseparable, being part of the same grand scheme to link the Dudley coal mines with the Stourbridge glass works, and with the Severn Navigation by means of the Staffordshire & Worcestershire Canal – indeed the Acts for the two canals were passed on the same day in 1776. Well supported by local glass masters, the Stourbridge Canal was soon under way, with Thomas Dadford as engineer. From a junction with the Staffordshire & Worcestershire at Stourton, the canal ran to Stourbridge. There was a 2-mile branch to the feeder reservoirs on Pensnett Chase, with 16 rising locks, and another level branch ran to Black Delph, where it met the Dudley Canal.

Combined with the Dudley Canal, the Stourbridge was soon profitable, and it was not long before the two companies were seeking to increase their revenue. They decided to try to capture some of the rich traffic on the Birmingham Canal. A joint proposal for a junction with the Birmingham Canal line via the Dudley Tunnel was authorised in 1785, and the through route was opened in 1792. Although the two companies worked closely together, they resisted the temptation to amalgamate, relying on their mutual dependence to sort out any problems. Although the Dudley Canal became part of the BCN system, the central position of the Stourbridge made it a very profitable undertaking, and throughout the early years of the 19th C the trade steadily increased. Even the opening of the rival Worcester & Birmingham Canal in 1815 did not affect the profits. Revenues were further increased in 1840 when the Stourbridge Extension Canal, later GWR owned, was opened to capture the coal trade from the Shut End collieries.

In the middle of the 19th C railway competition began to affect the canal, first from the Oxford, Worcester & Wolverhampton Railway, and later from the Great Western Railway. Revenues began their inevitable decline, but the Stourbridge was able to maintain its profits, and thus its independence, until nationalisation in 1948, although by then it was in the same run-down state as most canals in Britain. Commercial traffic died away, and by the 1950s the canal was no longer usable.

In 1964 the Staffordshire & Worcestershire Canal Society and the BWB (now BW) decided to restore the 16 locks and re-open the line between Birmingham and the Severn. Today these canals are both useful routes into the BCN and excellent cruising waterways in their own right, passing through a mixture of fine countryside, old industrial surroundings and extensive new development.

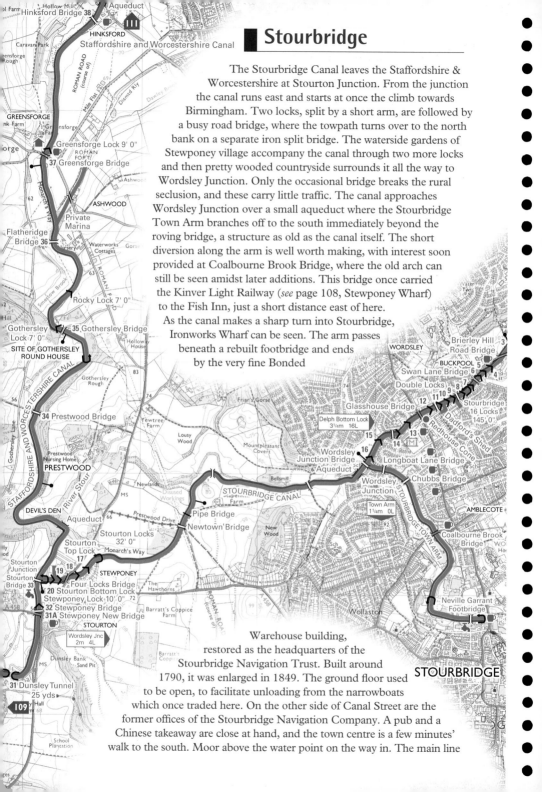

Stourbridge

The Stourbridge Canal leaves the Staffordshire & Worcestershire at Stourton Junction. From the junction the canal runs east and starts at once the climb towards Birmingham. Two locks, split by a short arm, are followed by a busy road bridge, where the towpath turns over to the north bank on a separate iron split bridge. The waterside gardens of Stewponey village accompany the canal through two more locks and then pretty wooded countryside surrounds it all the way to Wordsley Junction. Only the occasional bridge breaks the rural seclusion, and these carry little traffic. The canal approaches Wordsley Junction over a small aqueduct where the Stourbridge Town Arm branches off to the south immediately beyond the roving bridge, a structure as old as the canal itself. The short diversion along the arm is well worth making, with interest soon provided at Coalbourne Brook Bridge, where the old arch can still be seen amidst later additions. This bridge once carried the Kinver Light Railway (see page 108, Stewponey Wharf) to the Fish Inn, just a short distance east of here.

As the canal makes a sharp turn into Stourbridge, Ironworks Wharf can be seen. The arm passes beneath a rebuilt footbridge and ends by the very fine Bonded

Warehouse building, restored as the headquarters of the Stourbridge Navigation Trust. Built around 1790, it was enlarged in 1849. The ground floor used to be open, to facilitate unloading from the narrowboats which once traded here. On the other side of Canal Street are the former offices of the Stourbridge Navigation Company. A pub and a Chinese takeaway are close at hand, and the town centre is a few minutes' walk to the south. Moor above the water point on the way in. The main line

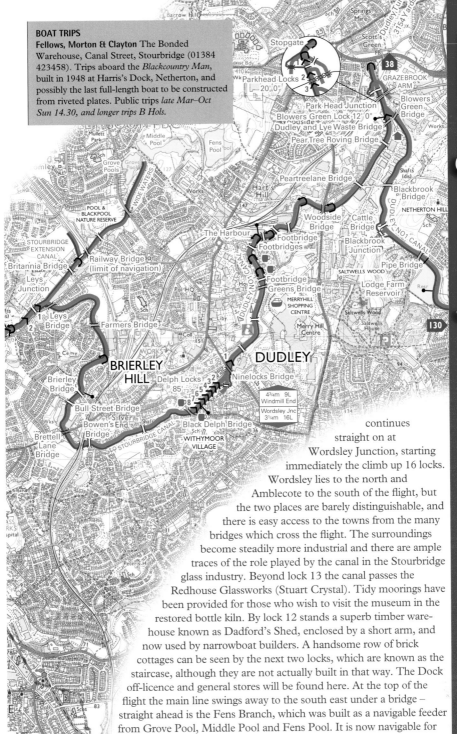

BOAT TRIPS
Fellows, Morton & Clayton The Bonded
Warehouse, Canal Street, Stourbridge (01384
423458). Trips aboard the *Blackcountry Man*,
built in 1948 at Harris's Dock, Netherton, and
possibly the last full-length boat to be constructed
from riveted plates. Public trips *late Mar–Oct
Sun 14.30, and longer trips B Hols.*

continues
straight on at
Wordsley Junction, starting
immediately the climb up 16 locks.
Wordsley lies to the north and
Amblecote to the south of the flight, but
the two places are barely distinguishable, and
there is easy access to the towns from the many
bridges which cross the flight. The surroundings
become steadily more industrial and there are ample
traces of the role played by the canal in the Stourbridge
glass industry. Beyond lock 13 the canal passes the
Redhouse Glassworks (Stuart Crystal). Tidy moorings have
been provided for those who wish to visit the museum in the
restored bottle kiln. By lock 12 stands a superb timber warehouse known as Dadford's Shed, enclosed by a short arm, and
now used by narrowboat builders. A handsome row of brick
cottages can be seen by the next two locks, which are known as the
staircase, although they are not actually built in that way. The Dock
off-licence and general stores will be found here. At the top of the
flight the main line swings away to the south east under a bridge –
straight ahead is the Fens Branch, which was built as a navigable feeder
from Grove Pool, Middle Pool and Fens Pool. It is now navigable for

about 300yds to the railway bridge (where you can wind), with 300yds of the Stourbridge Extension Canal, which branches off to the north west, also navigable (although there is now a very heavy growth of weed), making mooring possible, with shops nearby in Bromley. The reservoirs form the Fens Pools Nature Reserve, and are a pleasant place to walk. The towpath stays on the north for the branch, but turns over to the south bank on the main line which swings south round Brierley Hill, and then a more open landscape flanks the canal in the latter stages of its journey. After passing under the last bridge Delph Bottom Lock comes into sight, and here the Stourbridge Canal ends.

The Dudley No. 1 Canal joins the Stourbridge Canal at the bottom of Delph Locks. This flight, now designated a conservation area, is notable for its high waterfall overflows, which are very dramatic after a prolonged spell of wet weather. Known as the Nine Locks, seven of the original flight were rebuilt as six on the present line in 1858. Some remains of the old locks can still be seen to the east. Old stables by lock 3 have been well restored. Leaving the flight, the canal winds its way through what was once the site of Round Oak Steelworks, which ceased production in 1983 after almost two centuries of steelmaking, but is now the vast new Merryhill Shopping Centre. This massive and popular development transports those on the canal briefly into another dimension, with sparkling new buildings, restaurants and bars lining the towpath, and extensive car parks, seemingly full to the brim, leading shoppers into a vast modern world of retailing. There are good moorings and lots of restaurants here for those who wish to stop but, if you keep going, it all suddenly ends beyond Woodside Bridge, and you are immediately back in more familiar surroundings.

A cast iron bridge marked Horseley Co, Tipton 1858 carries the towpath over what was, until subsidence caused its closure in 1909, the old Two Lock Line – a short cut which avoided the longer route to the Dudley No. 2 Canal via Park Head Junction. Now the canal passes along a side cut embankment with good views towards Netherton Hill as it approaches Blowers Green Lock, the deepest on the BCN, built to replace two earlier locks which suffered from subsidence. Note the restored Blower's Green Pumphouse here, these days in the care of the Dudley Canal Trust. Park Head Junction immediately follows, where a sharp turn to the south east must be made to continue towards Windmill End. Straight ahead, the three Park Head Locks climb to the southern entrance of Dudley Tunnel (see note below), accompanied by a toll office and a fine lock house, and overlooked by a railway viaduct. At the top of the flight the entrance to the long-defunct Pensnett Canal can be seen on the west side, with the more substantial remains of the Grazebrook Arm, abandoned in 1953, to the east.

Leaving Park Head Junction towards Windmill End the canal skirts Netherton Hill, which is topped by St Andrew's Church, where cholera victims were buried in mass graves. High Bridge spans a cutting which was originally Brewins Tunnel, built in 1838 but opened out only 20 years later. However, the rural feel here soon disappears as houses appear and Lodge Farm Reservoir is passed.

Boatyards

Blackcountryman Canal Shop Opposite The Bonded Warehouse, Canal Street, Stourbridge (01384 423458). Gas, solid fuel, gifts.

Dadford's Wharf (Dadford's Shed), Mill Street, Wordsley (01384 485565/485554). Boat building, restoration and painting are now carried out on this historic site. Boat painter's supplies are also sold here, if you are working on your own craft. There are some fine ex-working boats moored in the basin, and you are welcome to stop and have a look around.

WALKING & CYCLING

The towpath is in excellent condition on both canals and as they, for the most part, wind through urban areas, it is relatively easy to devise circular walks, using a street atlas. For example, you can walk up the Stourbridge Sixteen and follow the canal to Delph. At the top of the locks turn left, and left again along the road to follow a fairly direct return route back to Brierley Hill Road Bridge. There are good short walks around the Pool & Blackpool Nature Reserve, to the west of the Fens Branch, and Saltwells Nature Reserve, to the west of the Dudley No. 2 Canal.

NAVIGATIONAL NOTES

1 Moorings at Merryhill are generally considered to be safe, but noisy (until midnight).

2 An anti-vandal key is required for Delph Locks.

3 An anti-vandal key is required for lock 1 of Parkhead Locks, and to access the facilities at Park Head Junction.

4 **Dudley Tunnel** Internal combustion engines must not be used in this tunnel, due to very limited ventilation. Passages through Dudley Tunnel may be subject to restrictions, *and headroom is limited (all boats are gauged)*. The Dudley Canal Trust operate an electric tug, the *John C Brown*, which can be made available to either tow, or escort those wishing to leg through. Please give *24 hours notice* if possible if you are approaching from the southern end – telephone (01384) 236275 – and a detailed leaflet is available from: The Dudley Canal Trust, Blowers Green Pump House, Peartree Lane, Dudley DY2 0XP, and local BW offices. Netherton Tunnel *is the most suitable route* through to the Birmingham Canal Main Line (*see* page 38).

● **Stourbridge**
Worcs. All services. Although the origins of Stourbridge go back to the Middle Ages, there is little trace of this today and it is almost entirely a 19th-C town, reflecting the great expansion of the glass industry during that period. The first glassmakers in Stourbridge were from Lorraine in eastern France, their presence being recorded in the Kingswinford Parish Register on 26 April 1612. Attracted by rich deposits of fireclay and coal, they originally established window glass production, and it was not until the discovery of lead glass in the 1700s that the manufacture of table glass became established here. Holloway End Glassworks, near the end of the Stourbridge Arm, is one of the surviving original factories, dating from the 17th C. *Each year, at the end of August*, the Dudley Glass Festival celebrates the area's long association with this craft with events at Broadfield House, Himley Hall and other venues. Information from the Tourist Information Centre *(below)*, who also produce a fascinating Crystal Trail leaflet.
Redhouse Glass Cone Wordsley, Stourbridge (01384 812750). By Glassworks Bridge on the Stourbridge Sixteen. The elegant brick cone, one of the few still surviving in the country, stands 100ft high and is right by the canal. Built 1788–94, it replaced earlier buildings on the same site, and housed a furnace around which the glass-making activities took place. Visitors can now see glassmaking, glass-blowing and cutting in progress, and visit the Stuart Crystal shop (01384 342701). *Open 09.00–17.00 (16.00 in winter) daily.* Charge. Tearoom. Good moorings for visits only.
Broadfield House Glass Museum Compton Drive, Kingswinford (01384 812745). 1 mile north of Glasshouse Bridge, this museum celebrates the history of British glassmaking, with a particular focus on the achievements of the local Stourbridge industry, where glass has been produced for over 400 years. The

entrance is through the largest all-glass structure in the world, and once inside you may watch glass blowing and decoration, explore the mythology and technology of glass, and view exhibits illustrating the history of glass. There is also a multi-screen presentation, a collection of British glass, and a kaleidoscope of glass objects. Look out for the small Pegasus on a plinth outside the museum: this is by Andrew Logan *(see Berriew, Book 4)*. *Open Tue–Sun 10.00–16.00.* Free. Shop.
Tourist Information Centre The Library, St James's Road, Dudley (01384 812830).
● **Brierley Hill**
West Midlands. All shops and services. A Black Country town founded on coal, iron and limestone, where no less than 12 pit pumping engines (known as whimseys) once kept the mines dry. Of course these mines are no more, and redevelopment has wrought extensive changes. There are a great many pubs, notwithstanding the decline since 1843, when it was recorded that there was one for every 143 head of population, who found refuge from their daily tasks in ale and good company. The Victorian church, when first built, had the poet Thomas Moss appointed as perpetual curate. His most notable work was a sentimental piece called *The Beggar*, which adorned many Victorian drawing rooms and was mentioned by Dickens in *Nicholas Nickleby*.
● **Dudley Tunnel**
Re-opened in 1973 with the rebuilding of Park Head Locks, Dudley Tunnel is one of the wonders of the BCN. This narrow bore, 3154yds long, was opened in 1792 after the usual delays and problems, to connect with the Birmingham Canal at Tipton. Inside there is a vast network of natural caverns, basins and branches serving old quarries and mines. In all there are over 5000yds of underground waterways, some cut off and abandoned, others still accessible. *Internal combustion*

engines must not be used – see Navigational Notes, page 127. There are trips into the tunnel from the Black Country Museum (*see* page 39).

Lodge Farm Reservoir This was built in 1838, and covers part of the old line of the canal. The new, more direct, line was instigated by Thomas Brewin, who built a new tunnel. Although still known as Brewin's Tunnel, it was opened in 1858. The reservoir is used now for sailing and fishing, and also supplies the canal.

Pubs and Restaurants

🍺 **The Vine** Vine Lane, Stourbridge (01562 882491). Food (V) is available *L and E*, along with real ale. Children welcome, and there is a garden.

🍺 **The Glassworks** Camp Hill, Stourbridge (01384 482699). Real ale is served here, along with food (V) *all day, every day*. Children welcome, and there is a garden.

🍺 **The Gladstone Arms** High Street, Audnam (01384 442703). Food (V) is served here *12.00–20.00*. Children welcome *until 19.00*. Large-screen TV for sport fans.

🍺 **The Old Dial** Audnam Street, Amblecote (01384 390218). To the east of Chubbs Bridge. Smart and traditional real ale pub, serving food (V) *L and E*. Children welcome. Live music *Sat*.

🍺 **The Little Pig** High Street, Amblecote (01384 394833). To the east of Coalbourne Brook Bridge. Good value food (V) *L and E (not Sun E)* in a cheerful pub, which serves real ale. Children welcome, and there are seats outside.

🍺 **The Moorings Tavern** At the end of the Stourbridge Town Arm, this welcoming pub, which dates from 1837 and was originally 'The Navigation', serves real ale. Children welcome, and there are seats outside. The Chinese takeaway next door is handy.

🍺 **Samson & Lion** (01384 77796). By lock 5 on the Stourbridge Sixteen. A fine old canal pub where the boatmen's horses were once stabled.

Real ale, and meals (V) are available *L and E (not Sun E)*. Children welcome, and there is a garden. Singer on *Sun afternoon*.

🍺 **The Bell** (01384 572376). Close by the canal, at the bottom of Delph Locks. A fine renovated Victorian local, with a real fire, serving a selection of real ales and meals (V) *L and E (not Sun or Mon)*. Children welcome to accompany you if you are eating, and there is also a garden. Quiz night *Wed*.

🍺 **The Tenth Lock** 154 Delph Road, Brierley Hill (01384 79041). Canalside at the bottom of Delph Locks. A homely-looking pub with an attractive canalside garden. Meals (V) are served *L*. Disco on *Fri*, karaoke *Sat*.

🍺 ✕ **The Brewer's Wharf** (01384 483522). By Greens Bridge, on the edge of the Merryhill Shopping Centre. A handsome and busy canalside pub, serving real ale, with bar meals (V) available *until 18.00 daily*, and restaurant meals *L and E daily*. Children welcome *until 18.00*. Pleasant outside seating on the patio, and moorings nearby. There are numerous restaurants and bars right by the canal, and close to moorings, in the Merryhill Shopping Centre.

🍺 ✕ **The Bar Edge** (01384 483756). On the edge of the Merryhill Shopping Centre, and by the canal. A Wetherspoon's pub, serving real ale (of course) and food (V) *all day, every day*. Children welcome at mealtimes.

Windmill End

Windmill End

Netherton was at one time a centre for the manufacture of chains and anchors, although there is little to be seen of this activity now, with the wharves covered in the spoils of late-20th-C preoccupations. Just after Bishtons Bridge a short arm full of moored narrowboats encloses pretty gardens cared for by the Withymoor Island Trust. Visitors are welcome to moor here, and pump out is sometimes available. Beyond Fox & Goose Bridge, the houses retreat and a fine green open space by a lake makes the perfect setting for Windmill End Junction, with cast iron canal bridges and the remains of Cobbs Engine House, its tall chimney still standing. The machine this building contained used to pump water from the local mines, to prevent flooding – it was said that if the engine ever missed a beat, a thousand women's hearts missed one also. The Bumblehole Branch, a lovely urban environment of canalside gardens and old and new houses looking out over landscaped workings, branches off to the west. This arm, which was once the main line of the canal prior to the building of Netherton Tunnel, terminates in a 'Y', overhung with willows. Straight on towards Windmill End Junction and the grand entrance to Netherton Tunnel, the canal sits high on an embankment in the midst of an area of reclaimed workings, now rich in bird and insect life. At a canal crossroads the short Boshboil Branch heads west, while to the east the Dudley No. 2 Canal continues on its way to Hawne Basin, at present a dead end, but one worthy of exploration. Straight ahead, through the tunnel, is the BCN. The Dudley No. 2 Canal once continued in a wide loop to join the Worcester & Birmingham Canal via the notorious and claustrophobic Lappal Tunnel, which closed in 1917 due to subsidence. Some 3795yds long, this rocky tunnel was the longest in the BCN network and one of the narrowest in the country. Leaving Windmill End, there is a toll island and a disused colliery basin, one of many which once fed traffic onto the canal here, and soon the waterway is passing through houses, factories and playing fields interspersed with newly landscaped areas, the tidy legacy of these once thriving industrial areas. At the entrance to the 577yd Gosty Hill Tunnel (no towpath) the lay-by once used by the tunnel tug can be seen – regrettably the tughouse is no more. If you are walking, look out for the tunnel ventilation shaft in the front garden of 171 Station Road as you pass over the hill. The waterway now passes through what was once a steelworks, recently demolished. Gradually it emerges from enclosing brick walls to pass a tidy trading estate and reach Hawne Basin, a canal/railway interchange until 1967 and now a friendly place full of moored narrowboats. You can moor here, but it is a bleak walk along Hereward Rise to the shops and pubs. The Lappal Tunnel Trust campaigns for the restoration of the rest of the canal between Hawne Basin and Selly Oak on the Worcester & Birmingham – the section to the south of the A458, by Leasowes Park, is currently receiving their attention.

● **Netherton Tunnel**
Opened in 1858, Netherton was the last major canal tunnel to be built in Britain and, as such, it is suitably grand. At 3027yds long, it was built with a bore sufficient to allow a towpath on both sides, and when opened was equipped with gas lighting, later converted to electricity. Although it passes deep underground, it is 453ft above sea level, and was built to relieve congestion in the Dudley Tunnel. It runs on a parallel course, joining the Birmingham Main Line at Dudley Port. **Tourist Information Centre** The Library, St James's Road, Dudley (01384 812830).

Stourbridge & Dudley Canals

Windmill End

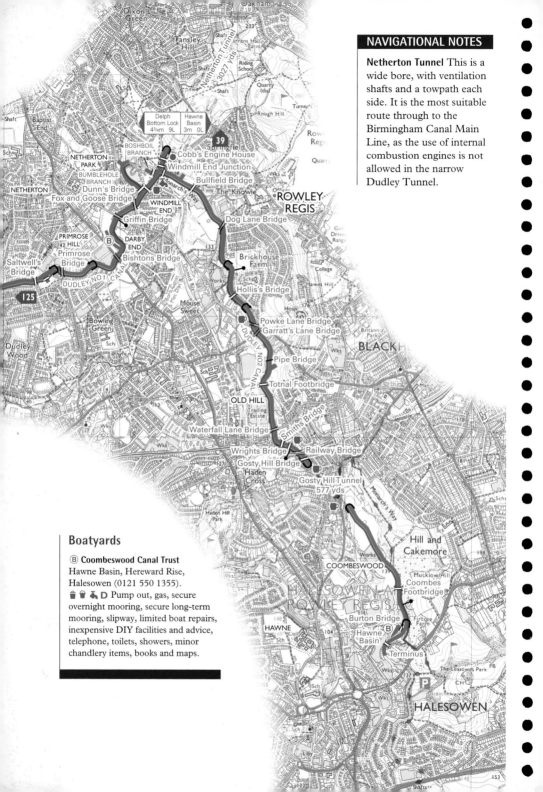

153

NAVIGATIONAL NOTES

Netherton Tunnel This is a wide bore, with ventilation shafts and a towpath each side. It is the most suitable route through to the Birmingham Canal Main Line, as the use of internal combustion engines is not allowed in the narrow Dudley Tunnel.

Boatyards

Ⓑ **Coombeswood Canal Trust**
Hawne Basin, Hereward Rise, Halesowen (0121 550 1355).
🚿 🚻 ⛽ 🔧 **D** Pump out, gas, secure overnight mooring, secure long-term mooring, slipway, limited boat repairs, inexpensive DIY facilities and advice, telephone, toilets, showers, minor chandlery items, books and maps.

	Delph Bottom Lock	Hawne Basin
	4¾m 9L	3m 0L

39

125

Pubs and Restaurants

☕ **The Dry Dock Inn** Windmill End (01384 235369). Opposite the Bumblehole Branch and Boshboil Arm and within sight of Cobb's Engine House and the west portal of Netherton Tunnel, this friendly pub is a remarkable renovation. Real ale is dispensed from a salvaged Runcorn six-plank hull set inside an imitation galleon. The walls are ornately tiled, and there is a bizarre assortment of Heath Robinson mechanical devices to be seen. An extensive range of food (V) is available, including Desperate Dan Cow Pies complete with horns (finish a pie and you will get a glutton's certificate) and faggots 'n' paes (peas), all served *L and E (not Mon)*. Children welcome *until 20.00*. There is a small, weedy, garden and a terrace. Occasional live Irish folk music.

☕ **The Wharf** 135 Station Road, Old Hill (0121 559 2323). Once the Sportsman & Railway, real ale is served in this attractively renovated canalside pub, with a large family room. Well known as being haunted, there have been many strange sightings. Meals (V) *L and E daily*. Garden.

☕ **The Neptune** Powke Lane, Rowley Regis (0121 559 9207). Renovated canalside pub serving real ale and snacks. Children welcome, and there are seats outside.

☕ **The Boat** Station Road, Old Hill (0121 559 3590). Up the steps from the northern portal of Gosty Hill Tunnel. An old-fashioned Black Country pub with a cosy bar and an open fire, serving real ale and snacks. There is a garden. Disco and karaoke once a month, on *Sat*.

☕ **The Lighthouse** 153 Coombs Road, Halesowen (0121 602 1620). Up the hill from the southern portal of Gosty Hill Tunnel. You surely can't miss this friendly pub, with its wonderfully painted outside wall by local artist Russell Lowe! Real ale is served, along with food (V) *L and E (not Sun or Mon E)*. Children welcome, and there is a garden. A singer performs *Wed and Sun*, and on the *first Sun in month* there is a blues night. Large-screen TV. Chinese takeaway nearby.

WALKING & CYCLING

There is a good towpath through Netherton Tunnel so, if you have a torch and are not bothered by the dark, you can enjoy a walk deep underground. You will need a street atlas. Start by walking over the hill from Windmill End. Cross Rough Hill, pass Oakham and descend to Tividale and Dudley Port. Then follow the long (3027yds), straight and very dark towpath back through the tunnel. There are excellent short rambles around Windmill End.

THE END OF WINDMILL END

Overlooking the southern portal of Netherton Tunnel stand the gaunt remains of what is known as Cobbs Engine House. Its actual name is the Windmill End Pumping Station. Sir Horace St Paul built it in 1831 to drain his mines where, as well as coal, iron stone and clay were extracted. Boilers, blast furnaces, open cooking hearths and brick kilns stood by the canal here, each contributing to the dirty and poisonous fumes which gave their name to the Black Country. Netherton Tunnel was opened in 1858 to ease the terrible delays caused by the claustrophobic Dudley and Lapal Tunnels, and soon the engine house stood witness to another scene of water-borne congestion, where horse-drawn boats vied with each other to enter the tunnel first. To the south east of Cobbs Engine House stood a second building housing a smaller engine, which operated a lift in a second shaft. The machinery here was dismantled in 1928 and shipped to the USA by Henry Ford, who erected it in his museum at Dearborn, Detroit. What happened to the Cobbs beam engine is not entirely clear: for some years it appears to have lain derelict before being broken up for scrap. The fate of the great beam, which had a stroke of 8ft and a rate of 6 or 8 strokes each minute to operate a pump some 7ft in diameter in a shaft 522ft deep, lifting about 400,000 gallons of water each day, remains a mystery. Many believe it broke free during removal and fell down the shaft, which was subsequently infilled.

STRATFORD-ON-AVON CANAL

MAXIMUM DIMENSIONS	MILEAGE
King's Norton to Kingswood	*KING'S NORTON JUNCTION to:*
Length: 70'	Hockley Heath: 9³/4 miles
Beam: 7'	*LAPWORTH* Junction with Grand Union
Headroom: 7' 3"	Canal: 12¹/2 miles
Kingswood to Stratford	Preston Bagot: 16¹/4 miles
Length: 70'	Wootton Wawen Basin: 18¹/2 miles
Beam: 6' 10"	Wilmcote: 22 miles
Headroom: 6'	*STRATFORD-ON-AVON* Junction with
MANAGER	River Avon: 25¹/2 miles
01564 784634;	Locks: 54
enquiries.lapworth@britishwaterways.co.uk	

The opening of the Oxford Canal in 1790 and of the Coventry Canal throughout shortly afterwards opened up a continuous waterway from London to the rapidly developing industrial area based on Birmingham. It also gave access, via the Trent & Mersey Canal, to the expanding pottery industry based upon Stoke-on-Trent, to the Mersey, and to the East Midlands coalfield. When the Warwick & Birmingham and Warwick & Napton canals were projected to pass within 8 miles of Stratford-upon-Avon, the business interests of that town realised that the prosperity being generated by these new trade arteries would pass them by unless Stratford acquired direct access to the network. And so, after the usual preliminaries, on 28 March 1793 an Act of Parliament was passed for the construction of the Stratford-on-Avon Canal, to start at King's Norton on the Worcester & Birmingham Canal (itself a long way from completion at that time). The junction was to be less than 3 miles from the junction of the Worcester & Birmingham with the Dudley Canal, and would thus provide a direct route to a major coal-producing area without passing through Birmingham.

Progress was rapid at first, but almost the total estimated cost of the complete canal was spent in the first three years, on cutting the 9³/4 lock-free miles to Hockley Heath. It took another four years, more negotiations, a revision of the route and another Act of Parliament to get things going again. By 1803 the canal was open from King's Norton Junction to its junction with the Warwick & Birmingham Canal (now part of the Grand Union main line) near Lapworth, with through traffic along the whole of this northern section. Even more delays then followed, with little enthusiasm on the part of private investors to put up more money. Cutting re-commenced in 1812, the route being revised yet again in 1815 to include the present junction with the River Avon at Stratford. From here, the Avon was navigable down to the Severn at Tewkesbury.

In its most prosperous period, the canal's annual traffic exceeded 180,000 tons, including 50,000 tons of coal through the complete canal, down to Stratford. By 1835 the canal was suffering from railway competition. This grew so rapidly that in 1845 the Canal Company decided to sell out to the Great Western Railway. There was opposition, however, and it was not until 1 January 1856 that the sale was considered complete. Thus the canal had been in full, independent operation for less than 40 years. Traffic was not immediately suppressed by the new owners, but long-distance haulage was the first to suffer as it was a more direct threat to the railway. In 1890 the tonnage carried was still a quarter of what it had been 50 years before, but the fall in ton-miles was much greater.

This pattern of decline continued in the 20th C, and by the 1950s only an occasional working boat was using the northern section; the southern section (Lapworth to Stratford) was badly silted, some locks were unusable and some of the short pounds below Wilmcote were dry. It is believed that the last boat to reach Stratford did so in the early 1930s, but there is evidence that a pleasure cruiser reached Wilmcote during the Easter holiday of 1947.

After World War II interest began to grow in boating as a recreation. In 1955 a Board of Survey had recommended sweeping canal closures, including the southern section of the Stratford-on-Avon Canal, but public protest was such that a Committee of Enquiry was set up in 1958, and this prompted the start of a massive campaign to save the canal. The campaign was successful: the decision not to abandon it was announced by the Ministry on 22 May 1959. On 16 October of the same year the National Trust announced that it had agreed a lease from the British Transport Commission under which the Trust would assume responsibility for restoring and maintaining the southern section. The transfer took place on 29 September 1960 and restoration work began in earnest in March of the following year. The terms of the arrangement included a contribution towards the cost of restoration but a very substantial sum was provided by the Trust, which maintained the southern section at its own expense.

The reopening ceremony was performed by Queen Elizabeth the Queen Mother on 11 July 1964, after more than 4 years of hard work by prison labourers, canal enthusiasts, army units and a handful of National Trust staff. On 1 April 1988 control of the southern section of the Stratford-on-Avon Canal was passed to the British Waterways Board (now British Waterways), finally relieving canal users of the necessity to purchase a separate licence, and the National Trust of a property which, with what was certainly the best will in the world, it was not qualified to care for.

Lock 21 at Kingswood Junction (see page 137)

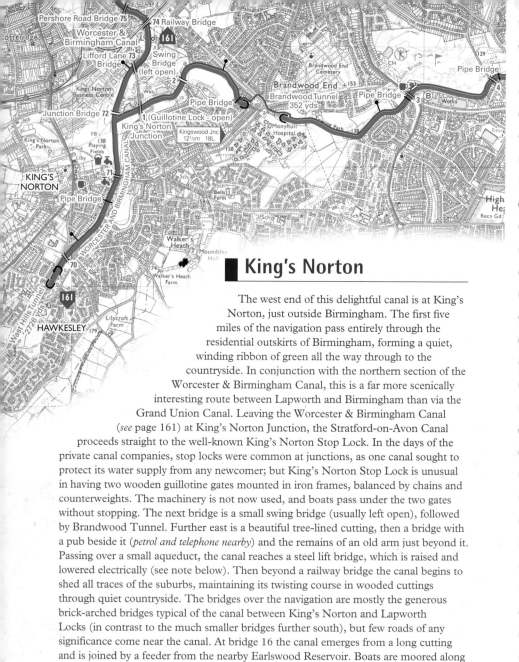

King's Norton

The west end of this delightful canal is at King's Norton, just outside Birmingham. The first five miles of the navigation pass entirely through the residential outskirts of Birmingham, forming a quiet, winding ribbon of green all the way through to the countryside. In conjunction with the northern section of the Worcester & Birmingham Canal, this is a far more scenically interesting route between Lapworth and Birmingham than via the Grand Union Canal. Leaving the Worcester & Birmingham Canal (*see* page 161) at King's Norton Junction, the Stratford-on-Avon Canal proceeds straight to the well-known King's Norton Stop Lock. In the days of the private canal companies, stop locks were common at junctions, as one canal sought to protect its water supply from any newcomer; but King's Norton Stop Lock is unusual in having two wooden guillotine gates mounted in iron frames, balanced by chains and counterweights. The machinery is not now used, and boats pass under the two gates without stopping. The next bridge is a small swing bridge (usually left open), followed by Brandwood Tunnel. Further east is a beautiful tree-lined cutting, then a bridge with a pub beside it (*petrol and telephone nearby*) and the remains of an old arm just beyond it. Passing over a small aqueduct, the canal reaches a steel lift bridge, which is raised and lowered electrically (see note below). Then beyond a railway bridge the canal begins to shed all traces of the suburbs, maintaining its twisting course in wooded cuttings through quiet countryside. The bridges over the navigation are mostly the generous brick-arched bridges typical of the canal between King's Norton and Lapworth Locks (in contrast to the much smaller bridges further south), but few roads of any significance come near the canal. At bridge 16 the canal emerges from a long cutting and is joined by a feeder from the nearby Earlswood Reservoir. Boats are moored along this, since it is the base of the Earlswood Motor Yacht Club. There are no villages along this rural stretch of canal, but at Salter Street there is a modern school and a strange Victorian church.

NAVIGATIONAL NOTES

You will need a BW key and a windlass to operate bridge 8.

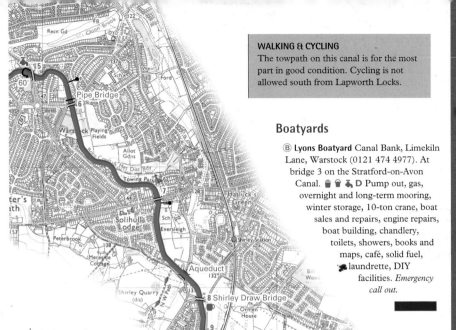

WALKING & CYCLING
The towpath on this canal is for the most part in good condition. Cycling is not allowed south from Lapworth Locks.

Boatyards

ⓑ **Lyons Boatyard** Canal Bank, Limekiln Lane, Warstock (0121 474 4977). At bridge 3 on the Stratford-on-Avon Canal. 🚽 🚿 ♨ D Pump out, gas, overnight and long-term mooring, winter storage, 10-ton crane, boat sales and repairs, engine repairs, boat building, chandlery, toilets, showers, books and maps, café, solid fuel, laundrette, DIY facilities. *Emergency call out.*

Pubs and Restaurants

🍺 **Drawbridge** Drawbridge Road, Shirley (0121 474 5904). By bridge 8, this friendly pub serves real ale, along with food (V) *all day, every day.* Children welcome. Canalside patio. Quiz on *Mon.*

🍺 **Red Lion Hotel** Lady Lane, Earlswood (01564 701911). 500yds south of bridge 16, near Earlswood Reservoir and ideal for walking. Real ale and bar meals (V) *all day, every day.* Children welcome, and there is a garden.

Yardley Wood, Earlswood and Warstock all have a *PO.*
Brandwood Tunnel 352yds long, this tunnel has no towpath. Horse-drawn boats had to be hauled through by means of an iron handrail on the side. Lengths of this rail can still be seen in the tunnel.
Earlswood Reservoir Half a mile south of bridge 16 is this canal-feeding reservoir, surrounded by trees and divided into three lakes: Windmill Pool, Engine Pool and Terry's Pool.

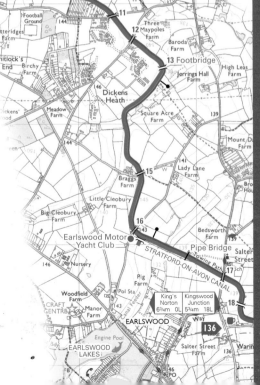

Lapworth Locks

The canal continues on its south easterly course, passing through quiet countryside interrupted only by the incessant roar of the M42 motorway, crossing overhead. There is a good bakery north of bridge 20. There are no locks, and the bridges – especially those in the cuttings – are still the big brick arches worthy of a broader canal. At Hockley Heath (bridge 25) there is a tiny arm that once served a coal wharf. Nearby the Wharf Inn overlooks the canal, and there is a useful petrol station here. East of here things change dramatically, for the first of the locks down to Kingswood Junction is reached. The top lock is numbered 2, as the old stop lock at King's Norton is number 1. The surroundings of the top lock are indeed pleasant: a white house enclosed by walls and hemmed in by trees stands beside the lock, while a cottage with a delightful garden faces the towpath just below. To the south west can be seen the spire of Lapworth church. After the first four locks, there is a 1/2-mile breathing space: then the Lapworth flight begins in earnest, with each of the next nine locks

Boatyards

B **Swallow Cruisers** Wharf Lane, Hockley Heath (01564 783442). 🛁 🛁 🔧 D Pump out, gas, overnight and long-term mooring, winter storage, slipway, groceries, chandlery, books and maps, boat sales, outboard engine sales and repairs, toilets, off-licence. *Emergency call out. Closed Mon except B Hols.*

B **Stephen Goldsbrough Boats** Warings Green Wharf, Lime Kiln Lane, Hockley Heath (01564 778210). 🛁 🛁 🔧 D Pump out, gas, overnight and long-term mooring. *24hr breakdown service.*

NAVIGATIONAL NOTES

1 Bank erosion is a serious problem on all canals, and especially so on this one. *Please go slowly* to minimise your wash.
2 Bridges 26 and 28 operate hydraulically, using a lock windlass.
3 Due to rebuilding, the chamber of lock 15 on the Lapworth flight is now over 2ft shorter than the other locks. Those in full-length boats should take extra care when descending.

Stratford-on-Avon Canal

Lapworth Locks

spaced only a few yards from its neighbour. There is a useful canal shop by lock 14 selling groceries, home-made bread and cakes, brassware and gifts. The short intervening pounds have been enlarged to provide a bigger working reservoir of water, so that one side of each lock is virtually an isthmus. The locks have double bottom gates and are not heavy going. They are interspersed with the old cast iron split bridges that are such a charming feature of the Stratford-on-Avon Canal. These bridges are built in two halves, separated by a one inch gap so that the towing line between a horse and a boat could be dropped through the gap without having to disconnect the horse. Below lock 19 is Kingswood Junction: boats heading for Stratford should keep right here. A short branch to the left leads under the railway line to the Grand Union Canal, or you can use the Lapworth Link after lock 22 if you are heading north to the GU, avoiding unnecessary lockage.

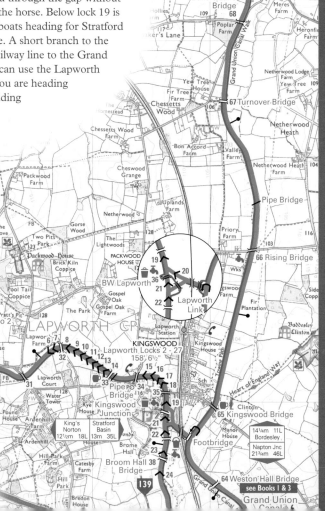

● **Hockley Heath**
Warwicks. PO, tel, stores, garage. A featureless place, but the several shops are conveniently close to the canal bridge, and the pub is pleasant.

● **Lapworth**
Warwicks. PO, tel, stores, garage, station. Indivisible from Kingswood, this is more a residential area than a village. Two canals pass through Lapworth: the heavily locked Stratford-on-Avon Canal and, to the east, the main line of the Grand Union Canal. These two waterways, and the short spur that connects them, are easily the most interesting aspect of Lapworth. The canalside buildings are attractive and there are two small reservoirs at the junction. The mostly 15th-C church is quite separate from the village and is 1¹/₂ miles west of the junction; it contains an interesting monument by Eric Gill, 1928.

Packwood House *NT* (01564 782024). Hockley Heath, 2 miles west of bridge 66. Timber-framed Tudor house, dating from the late 16th C and enlarged in the 17th C, where Cromwell's general, Henry Ireton, slept before the Battle of Edgehill in 1642. Owned by the Featherstones until 1869, it was eventually purchased by Alfred Ash, who repaired the house and reinstated the gardens. Collection of tapestry, needlework and furniture. Park with formal grounds and 17th-C yew garden possibly laid out to represent the Sermon on the Mount, the trees taking the place of Jesus and his followers. *House open Mar–Oct, Wed–Sun 12.00– 16.30.* Charge. Events are staged *during the summer.*

Pubs and Restaurants

🍺 **The Bull's Head** Lime Kiln Lane, Salter Street (01564 702335). ¹/₄ mile south of bridge 17. Pleasant, low-ceilinged country pub in converted cottages, serving traditional and continental food (V) *L and E Mon–Sat, and Sun 12.00–18.00.* Real ale. Garden with a water pump, and there is a resident ghost – a 17th-C limekiln worker who appears during *Jul and Aug.* Games in the cupboard, and dominoes are played *Thur and Sun.* Live music *middle Sat of month.*

🍺 **The Blue Bell Cider House** Warings Green Road, Hockley Heath (01564 702328). Canalside, at bridge 19. A pretty, traditional cider house serving real draught cider and a couple of guest real ales. It is a drinkers pub, but bar meals and snacks (V) are available *L and E (not Sun and Mon E)* with a children's menu. Garden with playground. *Wed* is quiz night. Good mooring jetty for patrons.

✗ ♀ **Kam-Shun** 2362 Stratford Road, Hockley Heath (01564 782782). Highly recommended Cantonese food *E Tue–Sun.* Children welcome.

🍺 ✗ **The Wharf Tavern** Stratford Road, Hockley Heath (01564 782075). Canalside, at bridge 25. A smart pub with a pleasant canalside garden and adventure playground, offering real ale and bar meals (V) (carvery) *L and E daily.* Children very welcome. *Thur* is quiz night. Moorings.

🍺 **The Boot Inn** Old Warwick Road, Lapworth (01564 782464). Near lock 14. Quaint cosmopolitan country pub serving real ale. Fashionable bar meals (V) from chargrill to oysters *L and E.* Garden with gas heaters for cooler nights!

🍺 **The Navigation** Old Warwick Road, canalside at Kingswood (01564 783337). By bridge 65 on the Grand Union. Real ale and real draught cider. Bar meals (V) *L and E.* Children welcome. Moorings.

Lapworth Locks (see page 137)

Lowsonford

The canal continues south, pursuing a fairly direct and wholly peaceful course. There is a barrel-roof cottage, typical of this part of the canal, by lock 28. At Yarningale, having followed a small stream for several miles, it crosses it on a tiny aqueduct adjoining lock 34. Preston Bagot Bottom Lock is squeezed in by the road – once this has been negotiated, the canal again resumes its peaceful course through rural Warwickshire. Good moorings are available by lock 25.

● **Preston Bagot**
Warwicks. The Church of All Saints has a pretty timber bell-turret and a spire, a Norman nave and a north wall with three Norman windows.

Pubs and Restaurants

◗ **The Fleur-de-Lys** Lowsonford (01564 782431). Canalside, just north of lock 31. Attractive 13th-C cottages, which once incorporated a bakehouse, converted into a beamy pub in the 15th C, with open fires and a large garden. The famous Fleur-de-Lys pies were once cooked here, but switched to mass production during the 1950s.

Real ale is served, along with bar meals (V) *L and E*. Children welcome, and a safe play area in the large canalside garden. and moorings (*but please ask first – don't tie-up to the trees*).

◗ **The Crab Mill Inn** Preston Bagot (01926 843342; www.thecrabmill.co.uk). An upmarket and recently refurbished country pub converted from a 300-year-old cider mill, with open fires. Real ale. Restaurant meals, specialising in modern Mediterranean cooking, (V) *L and E (not Sun E)*. Children welcome. Garden.

Edstone Aqueduct

The canal continues through delightfully quiet country as Austy Wood looms up on the hill to the east, with Austy Manor, a low stone hall, below. Beyond bridge 53 the canal widens into a basin – a craft centre, coffee shop and farm shop are just two minutes away to the west, and a basin and a pub are passed – then the canal immediately crosses the A34 road on a cast iron aqueduct. This is followed by a slight cutting – rare on the southern section of this canal – and then the waterway straightens out at Bearley Lock. Further south the canal rises on an embankment and is then carried across water meadows, a road and a railway by the splendid Edstone Aqueduct. At the southern end is a very pretty cottage and garden. The navigation now winds along a secluded section to Wilmcote. Just north of the village are the remains of a bridge – this used to carry a horse tramway that served nearby quarries. The winding hole and the cottages on the towpath at this point were built for the quarry trade. Wilmcote is close to the canal, and, if you wish to visit what we know as Mary Arden's House, you must moor north of bridge 59.

Wootton Wawen

Warwicks. PO, tel, stores, garage, station. This scattered but pretty village is a 1/2 mile west of the basin, and has been designated a conservation area. There are plenty of timbered houses and the late 17th-C Hall looks superb across the parkland and pond; but the chief glory is St Peter's Church on its rise overlooking the whole village.

St Peter's Church There was originally a wooden church on this site, built c.720–740 by Earl Aethelric, but the present structure dates from 1035, when it was erected by Wagen the Thane, a local landowner, as part of an early Saxon monastic complex. Most of the tower and parts of the walls survive from this time. Later additions include the barn-like Lady Chapel, added during the 14th C, the tower-top and clerestory added in the late 15th C, and various other additions since then. This has given it a pleasantly disorderly external appearance, but inside there are rare and fascinating things to see. The church is the only one in Warwickshire that derives from Saxon times, and the original sanctuary in the centre of the 11th-C church survives intact, still the focus of the building after over 900 years. The nave is conspicuously Norman, the chancel is bare but large, with a superb 14th-C east window. The Lady Chapel is probably the oddest part of the whole building – it is like a barn in more ways than one. It is enormous, with a primitive tiled roof and a completely irregular brick floor which still has traces of family pews and their fireplaces! All around the walls are a medley of monuments, together with fine 13th- and 17th-C oak parish chests.

Wootton Wawen Basin This wide, embanked basin was built when construction of the canal was halted here for a while. With a nearby pub and petrol station, the wharf is a popular halt with both boaters and motorists. A cast iron aqueduct carries the canal over the A34 by the basin. This aqueduct has often been damaged by lorries hitting the underside, so now a triangular road sign warning motorists of the headroom is mounted on the aqueduct. Unfortunately this sign has been positioned so that it almost completely obscures the original iron plaque that commemorates the opening of the aqueduct in 1813. Just down the hill is a fine brick watermill, built originally as a paper mill and still in good repair. This dates from the late 18th C.

Edstone (or Bearley) Aqueduct This major aqueduct, approaching 200yds in length, consists of a narrow cast iron trough carried on brick piers across a shallow valley. As with the two other – but much smaller – iron aqueducts on this canal (at Yarningale and Wootton Wawen), the towpath runs along the level of the bottom of the tank, so that towing horses and pedestrians get a duck's eye view of passing boats. This feature makes the aqueducts on this canal very unusual.

Wilmcote

Warwicks. PO, tel, stores, off-licence, garage. A small and attractive village, typical of this part of the country. A beautiful lime tree on the green is the centre of the village: nearby are a fine old pub and the most well-known building in the village – known as Mary Arden's House *(see below)*. The school and a vicarage by the church were built by William Butterfield in 1844 and 1845, and were his first non-religious buildings. The little railway station is to the east of the canal: with its trim roses and well-painted structures it is kept very much in the old tradition.

Mary Arden's House Wilmcote (01789 293455; www.shakespeare.org.uk). Thought for many years to be the home of Shakespeare's mother, it has now been discovered that she actually lived 30yds away at Glebe Farm. What we call Mary Arden's House was not actually built until 5 years after she had left the village. It incorporates a museum of agricultural implements and local rural bygones, and is furnished as the home of a yeoman farmer in Shakespeare's time. It is owned by the Shakespeare Birthplace Trust. *Open late Mar–May and Sep–Oct, Mon–Sat 10.00–17.00, Sun 13.00–17.00; Jun–Aug Mon–Sat 09.30–17.00, Sun 10.00–17.00; Jan–late Mar and Nov–Dec Mon–Sat 10.00–16.00, Sun 10.30–16.00. Closed Xmas. Entry fee. Refreshments room.*

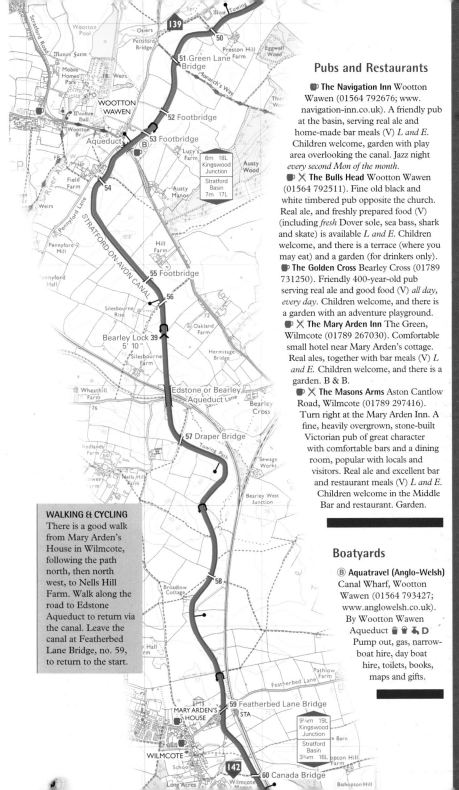

Pubs and Restaurants

🍺 **The Navigation Inn** Wootton Wawen (01564 792676; www.navigation-inn.co.uk). A friendly pub at the basin, serving real ale and home-made bar meals (V) *L and E*. Children welcome, garden with play area overlooking the canal. Jazz night *every second Mon of the month*.

🍺 ✕ **The Bulls Head** Wootton Wawen (01564 792511). Fine old black and white timbered pub opposite the church. Real ale, and freshly prepared food (V) (including *fresh* Dover sole, sea bass, shark and skate) is available *L and E*. Children welcome, and there is a terrace (where you may eat) and a garden (for drinkers only).

🍺 **The Golden Cross** Bearley Cross (01789 731250). Friendly 400-year-old pub serving real ale and good food (V) *all day, every day*. Children welcome, and there is a garden with an adventure playground.

🍺 ✕ **The Mary Arden Inn** The Green, Wilmcote (01789 267030). Comfortable small hotel near Mary Arden's cottage. Real ales, together with bar meals (V) *L and E*. Children welcome, and there is a garden. B & B.

🍺 ✕ **The Masons Arms** Aston Cantlow Road, Wilmcote (01789 297416). Turn right at the Mary Arden Inn. A fine, heavily overgrown, stone-built Victorian pub of great character with comfortable bars and a dining room, popular with locals and visitors. Real ale and excellent bar and restaurant meals (V) *L and E*. Children welcome in the Middle Bar and restaurant. Garden.

Boatyards

Ⓑ **Aquatravel (Anglo-Welsh)** Canal Wharf, Wootton Wawen (01564 793427; www.anglowelsh.co.uk). By Wootton Wawen Aqueduct 🚿 🛈 🔧 D Pump out, gas, narrowboat hire, day boat hire, toilets, books, maps and gifts.

WALKING & CYCLING

There is a good walk from Mary Arden's House in Wilmcote, following the path north, then north west, to Nells Hill Farm. Walk along the road to Edstone Aqueduct to return via the canal. Leave the canal at Featherbed Lane Bridge, no. 59, to return to the start.

Stratford-upon-Avon

South of Wilmcote, the two long pounds from
Preston Bagot are terminated by a dense flight of
locks – there are 11 in the Wilmcote flight, in groups
of 3, 5 and 3. They are, in the main, set in pleasant
open country, in which Stratford can occasionally be
seen to the east. Beyond a rather large road bridge the
canal descends another lock and reaches the nether regions
of Stratford. There is little yet, however, to suggest you are
entering one of Britain's premier tourist destinations as you
pass through the light industrial surroundings typical of a
Midlands town. The canal then enters a residential area as it
approaches the River Avon, dropping steeply through several locks,
number 54 being in a particularly pretty setting. It then ducks
through the lowest bridge since Lapworth and emerges at the splendid
great basin in the middle of the riverside parkland beside the Shakespeare Memorial Theatre, a flower-decked area frequented by hundreds
of tourists. Ice creams and baguettes are sold from moored narrowboats.
Amidst all the relics of Shakespeare's life, have a walk over Tramway
Bridge, passing the handsome timber shed of J. Cox, to stroll in parkland
alongside the River Avon. If all the moorings in the basin are taken, a
place can usually be found on the river above Colin P. Witter Lock.

BOAT TRIPS
Countess of Evesham Stratford Basin (07836 769499). Cruises for lunch and
dinner, *all year around*. Meals are freshly produced on board, and there is a bar.
Also available for private hire.

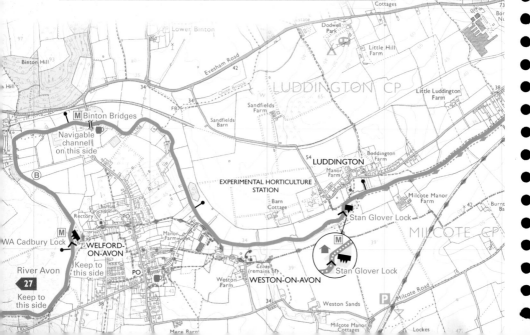

NAVIGATIONAL NOTES

Lock 47 is quite narrow – boats of over 6ft 10in beam should take extra care.

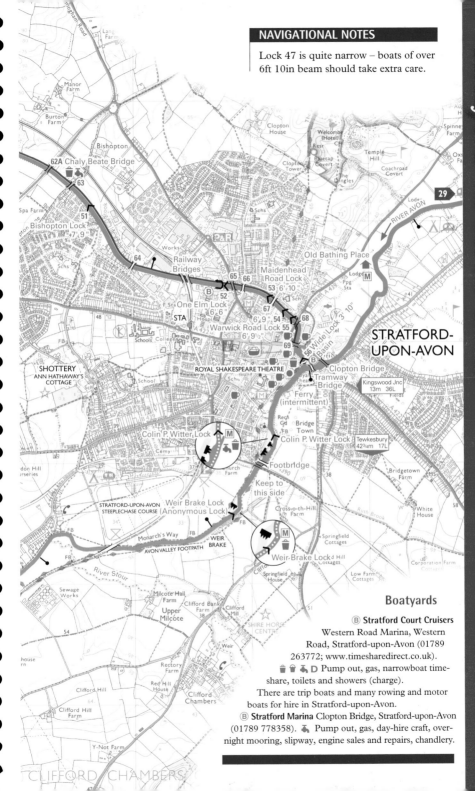

Boatyards

Ⓑ **Stratford Court Cruisers**
Western Road Marina, Western Road, Stratford-upon-Avon (01789 263772; www.timesharedirect.co.uk).
🚽 🚿 ♨ D Pump out, gas, narrowboat timeshare, toilets and showers (charge).

There are trip boats and many rowing and motor boats for hire in Stratford-upon-Avon.

Ⓑ **Stratford Marina** Clopton Bridge, Stratford-upon-Avon (01789 778358). ♨ Pump out, gas, day-hire craft, overnight mooring, slipway, engine sales and repairs, chandlery.

● Stratford-upon-Avon

Warwicks. All services. Tourism has been established for a very long time in Stratford. It was in 1789 that the first big celebrations in William Shakespeare's honour were organised by the actor David Garrick. They are now held annually on St George's Day (23 April), which is believed to have been Shakespeare's birthday. An annual Mop Fair on 12 October reminds the visitor that Stratford was already well-established as a market town long before Shakespeare's time. Indeed the first grant for a weekly market was given by King John in 1196. Today, Stratford is well used to the constant flow of charabancs and tourists, ancient charm vying with the expected commercialism that usually mars popular places like this. There are wide streets of endless low, timbered buildings that house dignified hotels and antique shops; plenty of these are also private houses. On the river, hired punts and rowing boats jostle each other while people picnic in the open parkland on the banks. The Royal Shakespeare Theatre, opened in 1932, is a splendid institution on an enviable site beside the Avon, but the aesthetic appeal of its massive industrial style is limited. It was designed by Elizabeth Scott to replace an earlier theatre, destroyed by fire in 1926. More in keeping with the historic Shakespearian tradition is the delightful Swan Theatre, risen phoenix-like from the ashes of the original building, thanks to the exceptional generosity of a single benefactor – for a long time anonymous. Attached to the main building, this theatre has a simple charm echoing the 16th-C Globe Playhouse and, in most part, presenting plays written by contemporaries of Shakespeare.

Shakespeare Birthplace Trust Stratford-upon-Avon (01789 204016; www.shakespeare.org.uk). This Trust was founded in 1847 to look after the five buildings most closely associated with Shakespeare; four of these are in Stratford (listed below) and the other is Mary Arden's House at Wilmcote (*see* page 140). Admission charge to each building. *The summer season is mid Mar–mid Oct. An all-inclusive ticket is available covering either the in-town properties, or all five Shakespeare Houses.*

Shakespeare's Birthplace Henley Street. An early 16th-C half-timbered building containing books, manuscripts and exhibits associated with Shakespeare and rooms furnished in period style. Gardens. Next door is the Shakespeare Exhibition. *Open late Mar–May and Sep–Oct, Mon–Sat 10.00–17.00, Sun 13.00–17.00; Jun–Aug Mon–Sat 09.00–17.00, Sun 09.30–17.00; Jan–late Mar and Nov–Dec Mon–Sat 10.00–16.00, Sun 10.30–16.00. Closed Xmas.*

Hall's Croft Old Town. A Tudor house complete with period furniture – the home of Shakespeare's daughter Susanna and her husband Dr John Hall, and . . .

New Place Chapel Street. The foundations of Shakespeare's last home set in a replica of an Elizabethan garden. *Open late Mar–May and Sep–Oct, Mon–Sat 11.00–17.00, Sun 11.00–17.00;* *Jun–Aug Mon–Sat 09.30–17.00, Sun 10.00–17.00; Jan–late Mar and Nov–Dec Mon–Sat 11.00–16.00, Sun 12.00–16.00. Closed Xmas.*

Anne Hathaway's Cottage Shottery, 1 mile west of Stratford (01789 292100). Dating from the 15th C this fine thatched farmhouse was once the home of Anne Hathaway before she married William Shakespeare in 1582. Her family, yeoman farmers, remained in occupation until 1892, when the cottage was purchased by the Shakespeare Birthplace Trust. The rooms retain their original features. The cottage was badly damaged by fire in 1969, but has since been completely restored. It has a mature, typically English garden, and long queues of visitors in the summer. *Open late Mar–May and Sep–Oct, Mon–Sat 10.00–17.00, Sun 13.00–17.00; Jun–Aug Mon–Sat 09.00–17.00, Sun 09.30–17.00; Jan–late Mar and Nov–Dec Mon–Sat 10.00–16.00, Sun 10.30–16.00. Closed Xmas.*

Royal Shakespeare Theatre (Tickets 01789 403403; www.stratford.co.uk/rsc/home). The home of the Royal Shakespeare Company, which produces Shakespeare plays to a very high standard *from Apr to Dec every year*. The building is a large, chunky red-brick affair, designed by Elizabeth Scott and completed in 1932. Radical at the time, it now appears quite dated. The first theatre in Stratford was a temporary octagon built for Garrick's festival in 1769. A permanent theatre was not erected until 1827, with a library and art gallery being added in 1881. These buildings survive, and are connected to the present theatre by a bridge.

The Ragdoll Shop 11 Chapel Street (01789 404111). An ideal place for those with young children, who will enjoy playing with the toys and speaking on the tots telephones. Toys and books for sale. They also work with British Waterways to produce water safety information for children. *Open Mon–Sat 09.30–17.30, Sun 12.00–16.00.*

Clopton Bridge A very fine stone bridge over the Avon, originally built by Sir Hugh Clopton c.1480–90 — he later became Lord Mayor of London. Tramway Bridge nearby was built in 1823 to carry a horse-drawn tramway connecting Stratford with Shipston-on-Stour. It is now a footbridge. One of the wagons, used for a while as a chicken coop before it was restored, stands beside the basin.

Stratford-upon-Avon Butterfly Farm Tramway Walk, Swan's Nest Lane (01789 299288; www.butterflyfarm.co.uk). Just south of the Tramway Bridge. Rainforest growth, fish pools and waterfalls, hundreds of butterflies and fascinating insects. For the not-so-squeamish there is Arachnoland, where you can view deadly insects (in perfect safety). Adventure playground, gift shop and refreshments. *Open 10.00–18.00 (dusk in winter).* Charge.

Tourist Information Centre Bridgefoot, Stratford-upon-Avon (01789 293127; stratfordtic@ shakespeare-country.co.uk). A mine of information, and lots of guide books and souvenirs for sale.

Stratford Lock

WALKING & CYCLING
The Stratford Greenway is a linear country park, almost 5 miles long, following the old Honeybourne Railway Line and providing a traffic-free walking and cycling route, together with two picnic sites. It starts immediately to the south of Colin P. Witter Lock, finishing in Long Marston, and interlinks with other riverside footpaths which can be used to form a number of circular walks. Visit the Country Parks Information Service at www.warwickshire.gov.uk.

Pubs and Restaurants

There are numerous restaurants, snack bars, fast food outlets and pubs in Stratford-upon-Avon:

The Pen & Parchment Bridgefoot (01789 297697). By bridge 69, at the entrance to the basin. Pleasant beamy pub in a listed building, where you can enjoy real ale in peace, without piped music. Good selection of Belgium beers. Wide range of food (V), including Balti and trout and tuna steaks, is available *L and E*. There are outside seats surrounded by tubs of flowers, where you can watch the tourist sightseeing buses depart. Quiz *weekly* and music *monthly*.

The Encore 1 Bridge Street (01789 269462). Town centre pub/restaurant, with a Shakespearean theme, serving real ale, and traditional British food (V) *all day, every day*. Children welcome.

The Old Tramway Inn 91 Shipston Road (01789 297593). Real ales in a recently refurbished pub, with a large garden. Meals (V) are served *L and E (not Sun E or Mon)*. Children welcome.

The Shakespeare Hotel Chapel Street (01789 294771). Beamy 17th-C hotel, with a black-and-white façade and huge fireplaces, in one of Stratford's most famous buildings. Meals (V) are served *L and E* in the restaurant and bar. Children welcome, and there is a garden. Themed breaks and events.

The Slug & Lettuce Guild Street (01789 299700). Friendly and cheerful pub serving real ale and food (V) *all day, every day*. Garden and roof terrace. Changing ownership as we go to press.

WORCESTER & BIRMINGHAM CANAL

MAXIMUM DIMENSIONS	MILEAGE
Length: 71' 6"	*WORCESTER, Diglis Basin to:*
Beam: 7'	Tibberton: 5³/4 miles
Headroom: 8'	Dunhampstead: 7¹/2 miles
	Hanbury Wharf: 9¹/4 miles
MANAGER	Stoke Wharf: 12³/4 miles
01564 784634	Tardebigge Top Lock: 15¹/2 miles
enquiries.lapworth@britishwaterways.co.uk	Bittell Reservoirs: 20¹/2 miles
	KING'S NORTON JUNCTION: 24¹/2 miles
	BIRMINGHAM Gas Street Basin: 30 miles
	Locks: 58

The Bill for the Worcester & Birmingham Canal was passed in 1791 in spite of fierce opposition from the Staffordshire & Worcestershire Canal proprietors, who saw trade on their route to the Severn threatened. The supporters of the Bill claimed that the route from Birmingham and the Black Country towns would be much shorter, enabling traffic to avoid the then-notorious shallows in the Severn below Stourport. The Birmingham Canal Company also opposed the Bill and succeeded in obtaining a clause preventing the new navigation from approaching within 7ft of their water. This resulted in the famous Worcester Bar separating the two canals in the centre of Birmingham. Construction of the canal began at the Birmingham end following the line originally surveyed by John Snape and Josiah Clowes. Even at this early stage difficulties with water supply were encountered. The company was obliged by the Act authorising the canal to safeguard water supplies to the mills on the streams south of Birmingham. To do this, and to supply water for the summit level, ten reservoirs were planned or constructed. The high cost of these engineering works led to a change of policy: instead of building a broad canal, the company decided to build it with narrow locks, in order to save money in construction and water in operation.

Work in Wast Hills Tunnel, described at the time as 'a stupendous undertaking', began in 1794; by 1807 boats could get from Birmingham to Tardebigge Wharf. Here work came to a standstill for several years while the company considered alternative cheaper ways of completing the line down to the Severn. Work eventually started again under a new engineer, John Woodhouse, a great exponent of boat lifts. He proposed reducing the number of locks down to Worcester from 76 to 12, using lifts to descend most of the fall. The company were less enthusiastic and limited his enterprises to one experimental lift at Tardebigge. This seems to have worked reasonably well but the company were still sceptical. They called in the famous canal engineer John Rennie, who decided that the mechanism would not withstand the rough treatment it would doubtless receive from the boatmen. Consequently locks were built but reduced in number to 58. The site of the lift became the top lock of the Tardebigge flight, reputedly the second deepest narrow lock in the country.

After this, work progressed steadily and the canal was completed in 1815. In the same year an agreement with the Birmingham Canal proprietors permitted the cutting of a stop lock through Worcester Bar. The canal had cost £610,000, exceeding its original estimate by many thousands of pounds. Industrial goods and coal were carried down to

Worcester, often for onward shipping to Bristol, while grain, timber and agricultural produce were returned to the growing towns of the Midlands. The canal basins in Worcester became important warehousing and transhipment points: Diglis Basin had warehousing for general merchandise, grain and wine, and Lowesmoor Basin specialised in coal and timber. Prosperous businesses were conducted from these wharves and they were an important port of call for the main canal carriers. However the opening of railways in the area in the 1840s and 1850s reduced this traffic considerably and had a profound effect on the fortunes of the canal.

In an attempt to win back salt carrying, the canal company cut the Droitwich Junction Canal in 1852 to connect the Droitwich Barge Canal and the town of Droitwich with their main line at Hanbury Wharf. Toll income and profits continued their relentless decline and, after 1864, the company was unable to pay a dividend. In 1874 the canal was bought by the Sharpness New Docks Company. The new management commenced a programme of works to improve the canal in the hope of attracting trade but, in effect, the canal was subsidised by the Gloucester & Berkeley Ship Canal for the rest of its working life.

The animals that used to draw the boats along the Worcester & Birmingham Canal were mainly donkeys worked in pairs, instead of the more usual horse – the donkeys could easily be carried on the boat while it was being towed by tug on the river. Both horse and donkey were unsatisfactory on the summit level with its four tunnels, for only the short Edgbaston Tunnel has a towpath through it. To overcome the delays caused by the need to leg boats through the other tunnels, steam tugs were introduced in the 1870s and successfully hauled trains of boats through the tunnels for many years.

By the early 1900s the commercial future of the canal was uncertain, although the works were in much better condition than on many other canals. Schemes to enlarge the navigation as part of a Bristol–Birmingham route came to nothing. Commercial carrying continued until about 1964, the traffic being mostly between the two Cadbury factories of Bournville and Blackpole (closed in the 1920s), to Frampton on the Gloucester & Sharpness Canal, and to Worcester Porcelain. After nationalisation, several proposals were made to abandon the canal, but the 1960s brought a dramatic increase in the number of pleasure boats using the waterway, thus securing its future.

THE EXTRA PADDLE

Sugar, cocoa beans, soap, tea, metal ingots and tinned food, unloaded at Avonmouth into barges and trans-shipped into narrowboats at Gloucester, were regular cargoes bound for the Midlands in the early years of the 20th C. Narrowboats, often in groups of 12, would lock down into the River Severn to be towed by one of the Severn & Canal Carrying Company's tugs as far as Worcester, and sometimes on to Stourport.

Those that had booked the tow were arranged in a double line behind the tug, perhaps it would be the *Alert*, with the tow ropes leading from one stern quarter of the boat ahead to the opposite forequarter of the boat following, thereby allowing each craft steerage.

The narrowboats, on arrival at Diglis, then locked up onto the Worcester & Birmingham Canal, collecting donkeys or mules from the stables to complete their journey to the Midlands.

Tardebigge Locks presented a formidable challenge to the crews, who would often urge the donkeys on at the locks, partially opening the gates while the water was still two foot off the level. A block of wood was then inserted between the gates to create an unofficial extra paddle – *a practice we would not even contemplate today*.

Worcester

The Worcester & Birmingham Canal begins at Diglis, on the south side of Worcester. It leaves the River Severn a few hundred yards north of Diglis Locks, climbs two wide (18ft) locks and opens out into one of the two Diglis Basins, where a large number of pleasure boats are moored, some of them seagoing. Lacking some of the style, but none of the charm, of Stourport, its counterpart further upstream, it has a less formal demeanour, perhaps echoing its position just a little closer to the sea. Beyond the basins the canal becomes hemmed in by the town as it enters the first of many deep,

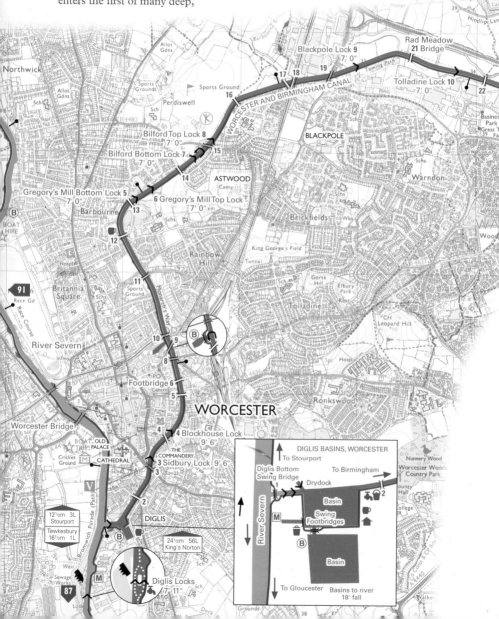

NAVIGATIONAL NOTES

The top gates of Offerton Locks can be difficult to open when the pounds above are full.

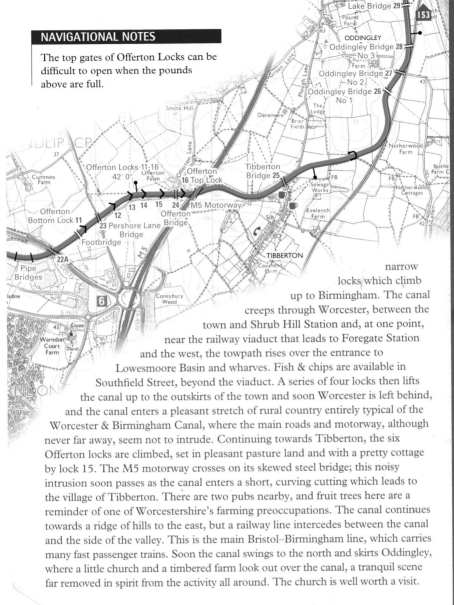

narrow locks which climb up to Birmingham. The canal creeps through Worcester, between the town and Shrub Hill Station and, at one point, near the railway viaduct that leads to Foregate Station and the west, the towpath rises over the entrance to Lowesmoore Basin and wharves. Fish & chips are available in Southfield Street, beyond the viaduct. A series of four locks then lifts the canal up to the outskirts of the town and soon Worcester is left behind, and the canal enters a pleasant stretch of rural country entirely typical of the Worcester & Birmingham Canal, where the main roads and motorway, although never far away, seem not to intrude. Continuing towards Tibberton, the six Offerton locks are climbed, set in pleasant pasture land and with a pretty cottage by lock 15. The M5 motorway crosses on its skewed steel bridge; this noisy intrusion soon passes as the canal enters a short, curving cutting which leads to the village of Tibberton. There are two pubs nearby, and fruit trees here are a reminder of one of Worcestershire's farming preoccupations. The canal continues towards a ridge of hills to the east, but a railway line intercedes between the canal and the side of the valley. This is the main Bristol–Birmingham line, which carries many fast passenger trains. Soon the canal swings to the north and skirts Oddingley, where a little church and a timbered farm look out over the canal, a tranquil scene far removed in spirit from the activity all around. The church is well worth a visit.

Boatyards

ⓑ **Worcester Dry Dock** John Pinder & Son, Diglis Basin (01527 876438).

ⓑ **M. W. Marine** Wharf Cottage, Diglis Basin (01905 763249 [*453479 after 17.00*]/mobile 07940 071416). Marine engineer carrying out all types of boat fitting and engine work.

ⓑ **Grist Mill Boatyard** Diglis Basin (01905 350814). Carpenters specialising in traditional craft, they also work on narrowboats, cruisers and commercial craft.

ⓑ **Viking Afloat** Lowesmoor Basin, Lowesmoor Terrace, Worcester (01905 612707; www.vikingafloat.com). 🚽 🚿 ⛽ D Pump out, gas, narrowboat hire, overnight and long-term mooring, boat sales, books, maps and gifts.

Worcester

Worcs. All services. A bishopric was founded in the Saxon town of Wigorna Ceaster around the year 680, and a castle was built here following the Norman conquest. During the Civil War the city was the first to declare for Charles I, and the last place where the Royalists rallied around Charles II. They were subsequently defeated in 1651 by Cromwell's army. These days Worcester has plenty to offer the visitor, although the enjoyment is lessened by the constant flow of heavy traffic through the city. A railway bridge at Foregate Street does not intrude, for the girders are suitably decorated and trains are infrequent. However the best area is around Friar Street, and of course the splendid cathedral.

Worcester Cathedral (01905 28854; info@worcestercathedral.org.uk). An imposing building which dates from 1074 (when Bishop Wulstan started to rebuild the Saxon church), but has work representative of the five subsequent centuries. There is a wealth of stained glass and monuments to see – including the tomb of King John, which lies in the chancel. Carved out of Purbeck marble in 1216, this is the oldest royal effigy in England. When he was dying at Newark, King John demanded to be buried at Worcester Cathedral between two saints, but the saints have gone now. The best way into the cathedral is from the Close with its immaculate lawns and houses, passing through the cloisters where one may inspect five of the cathedral's old bells, two of which were cast in 1374. The gardens at the west end of the building look out over the Severn and on to the Malvern Hills – a particularly fine sight at sunset. Gift shop and tearoom. *Open daily 07.30–18.00.* Donations. Disabled toilet. **The Three Choirs Festival** is held annually in rotation at the cathedrals of Worcester, Gloucester and Hereford, during the last week in *Aug.* This famous festival has inspired some fine music, one notable composer being Vaughan Williams. For further information about the festival, contact the Tourist Information Centre in any of the three cities.

City Museum and Art Gallery Foregate Street (01905 25371). Opened in 1896, it contains collections of folk life material and natural history illustrating man and his environment in the Severn valley. In the Art Gallery are a permanent collection and loan exhibitions. Children's activities. Also museum of the Worcestershire Regiment. Balcony Café. *Open Mon–Sat 09.30–17.30 (Sat 17.00), closed Xmas Day, Box. Day, New Year's Day and G Fri.* Free. Teas. Disabled access.

The Greyfriars *NT.* Friar Street, Worcester (01905 23571; greyfriars@ntrust.org.uk). Dating from 1480, this was once part of a Franciscan priory and is one of the finest half-timbered houses in the country. Charles II escaped from this house after the Battle of Worcester on 3 September

1651. It has a delightful walled garden. *Open Apr–Oct, Wed, Thur and B Hol Mon 14.00–17.00 and during the Three Choirs Festival.* Charge.

Museum of Local Life Tudor House, Friar Street, Worcester (01905 722349). A museum of local antiquities, furniture and porcelain housed in traditional Elizabethan buildings (the wattle and daub that make up the walls can be clearly seen in places). Amongst other exhibits are a modern copy of a traditional coracle, a tiny fishing craft used for thousands of years on the River Severn, and a painting of the Waterman's Church in Worcester – a chapel on a floating barge, last used in the 1870s, when it was taken ashore and set up on dry land. *Open Mon–Wed, Fri and Sat 10.00–17.00.* Free. Shop. Limited disabled access.

Royal Worcester & The Museum of Worcester Porcelain The Royal Porcelain Works, Severn Street, Worcester (01905 23221; www. royal-worcester.co.uk). Here, where it should be, is the most comprehensive collection of Worcester porcelain in the world, from 1751 to the present day. Visitor Centre. *Open Mon–Sat 09.00–17.30, Sun 11.00–17.00.* Tours of the porcelain works. Seconds, whiteware and clearance shop. Family restaurant.

Swan Theatre The Moors, Worcester (01905 27322; swan_theatre@lineone.net). Year-round drama, music and dance from local and national companies.

The Guildhall High Street, Worcester (01905 723471). Built in 1721–3 by a local architect, Thomas White, this building has a splendidly elaborate façade with statues of Charles I and Charles II on either side of the doorway and of Queen Anne on the pediment. It contains a fine assembly room and **The Assembly Rooms Restaurant** (01905 722033) which offers a tempting range of food (including appetising sweets made by their own patisseurs) and snacks *during Guildhall opening hours, Mon–Sat 09.00–16.30.* Free.

Tourist Information Centre Guildhall, High Street, Worcester (01905 726311; touristinfo@ cityofworcester.gov.uk). Enquire here about local guided walks.

Diglis Basin This is a fascinating terminus at the junction of the River Severn and the Worcester & Birmingham Canal. It consists of basins, old warehouses and a dry dock. Commercial craft have been entirely replaced by a mixture of pleasure boats designed for narrow canals, rivers and the sea. The locks will take boats up to 72ft by 18ft 6in, although obviously only narrowboats can proceed along the canal. The locks are under the supervision of the basin attendant, who is available *from 08.00–19.30 (16.00 winter) with breaks for meals.* Craft are not permitted to use the locks outside these times. The BW basin attendant can be contacted on (01905) 358758, or enquire through the Lapworth Office, (01564)

784634. Near the first lock is a small pump-house that raises water from the river to maintain the level in the basin.

The Commandery Civil War Centre Sidbury Lock (01905 361821; thecommandery@cityofworcester.gov.uk). Founded as a small hospital just outside the city walls by Bishop Wulstan in 1085: from the 13th C the masters of the hospital were referred to as commanders, hence the building's name. The present timbered structure dates from the reign of Henry VII in the 15th C, and served as Charles II's headquarters before the Battle of Worcester in 1651. The glory of the building is the superb galleried hall with its ancient windows and Elizabethan staircase. The museum is devoted entirely to the story of the Civil War, with recreations using life-size figures, sound systems and a video presentation of the Battle of Worcester, including Oliver Cromwell writing his dispatch before the battle. *Open all year Mon–Sat 10.00–17.00, Sun 13.30–17.00.* Charge.

● **Tibberton**
Worcs. PO, tel, stores (all to the south of the pubs). A small but expanding canalside village. There is a fine old rectory by the Victorian church.

● **Oddingley**
Worcs. The church and farm overlook the canal. The Church of St James was originally a dependent chapel of the church of St Helen, Worcester, and was first mentioned in 1288. The present building of lias limestone is mainly 15th-C, with 17th-C additions, and has been handsomely restored. There is some fine 15th-C stained glass, and a wooden arch of the same period in the south transept opening. Set into the floor of the sanctuary is a stone in memory of George Parker, a rector of St James who was murdered in his fields on 24 June 1806. He had demanded a rise in the church tithes from his parishioners, which were at that time paid in money, rather than in kind. When his parishioners refused, he built a barn with the intention of collecting the tithes in kind, but this was met with violent protest, and he was shot. His murderer fled into Trench Woods (east of bridge 29, over the railway). Some 24 years after the event, the remains of Richard Hemming, a carpenter from Droitwich, were found in a barn at Netherwood Farm (to the south east of Oddingley, over the railway). It transpired that he had been hired by Captain Samuel Evans, who lived in the farm by the church, to murder the rector. Hemmings in turn had been killed by Evans and 'old Taylor the farrier'. But they were both dead when Hemming's body was found, so no charges could be brought.

WALKING & CYCLING
The towpath is in a reasonable condition throughout for both walking and cycling. The Worcester Royal Connections Trail is a circular walking route around the city which details landmarks. Leaflet available from the Tourist Information Centre.

Pubs and Restaurants

🍺 **The Anchor Inn** Diglis Road (01905 351094). Right beside the basin. A friendly place, with a cosy bar, a nice fireplace and some canal pictures and models. You can enjoy real ale and bar meals (V) and snacks *L*. There is a canalside garden, skittle alley and function room. Children welcome. Live music and karaoke *Sat*.

🍺 **The Bridge Inn** Lowesmoor Wharf (01905 23980). A pleasant local serving real ale. Outside seating under a canopy. Live music *Sat*, quiz *Sun*.

🍺 **The Cavalier Tavern** Worcester (01905 25006). Canalside, at bridge 12. Comfortable and welcoming modern pub serving real ale and food (V) *all day until 20.30 (16.30 Sun)*. Children welcome, and there is a canalside garden. Skittle alley. Mooring.

🍺 **The Bridge Inn** Plough Road, Tibberton (01905 345874). Handsome traditional canalside village local serving real ale and home-made food *L and E (not Mon E or winter weekday afternoons)*. Children welcome away from the bar, and there is a secure canalside garden. Bread and milk are available *during opening times*.

🍺 **Speed the Plough** Plough Road, Tibberton (01905 345602). Up the road from bridge 25. An attractive 17th-C country pub named after the agricultural well-wishing 'God speed the plough', with a fine collection of clocks. No jukebox or gaming machines. Real ale and bar meals (V) *L and E (not Thur L)*. Children welcome *until 21.00* and there is a small garden with swings.

Hanbury Wharf

A wooded cutting beyond the crowded moorings at Dunhampstead leads to Dunhampstead Tunnel, the first of five between here and Birmingham. There is no towpath in the tunnel; horses used to walk over the hill while boatmen pulled the boats through by the handrail along each side. Leaving the tunnel, the canal enters flatter countryside as the hills recede to the east. The pretty, residential settlement of Shernal Green flanks the canal, while Hadzor Hall, built in the late 18th C in the classical tradition, is visible in the trees on the west side of the canal. This straight stretch is terminated by the very busy area of Hanbury Wharf, where an old arm encloses a busy boatyard, complete with gardens and a lighthouse.

There is a pub by the main road bridge, and the Droitwich Junction Canal (unnavigable here but undergoing restoration – *see* page 61) joins just to the north. Navigators should now cherish this 5½-mile level – it is easily the longest pound between Worcester and Tardebigge Top Lock. As the canal passes under the railway to take up position on its east side, the ridge of hills nears again, accompanied by attractive parkland around Hanbury Hall. Ahead are the six locks of the Astwood flight, set in pleasant open pastureland. A short walk from the top is a pub, beside the railway line.

Boatyards

ⓑ **Brook Line** Dunhampstead Wharf, Oddingley (01905 773889). (⚓ *opposite, charge*) Pump out, gas, narrowboat hire, boat and engine repairs. Gift shop opposite.

ⓑ **Hanbury Wharf** Hanbury Road, Droitwich (01905 771018; www.droitwichboats. co.uk). 🚽 🚿 ⚓ D Gas, long-term mooring, winter storage, crane, boat building, boat sales and repairs, engine repairs, chandlery, toilets, showers, books, maps and gifts, solid fuel.

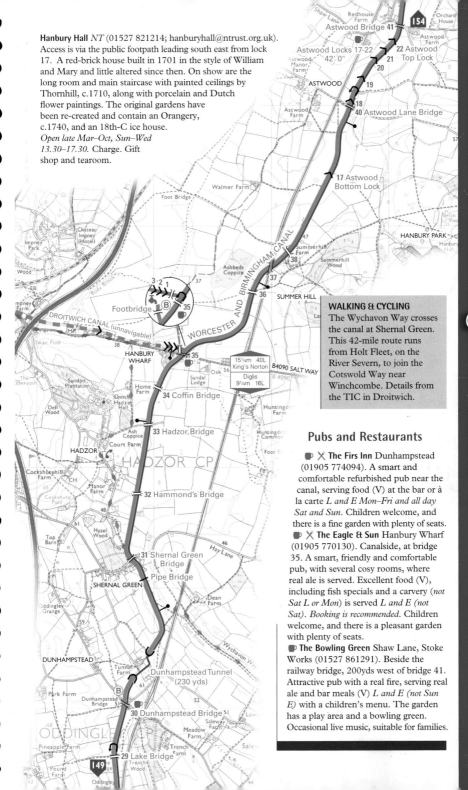

Hanbury Hall *NT* (01527 821214; hanburyhall@ntrust.org.uk). Access is via the public footpath leading south east from lock 17. A red-brick house built in 1701 in the style of William and Mary and little altered since then. On show are the long room and main staircase with painted ceilings by Thornhill, c.1710, along with porcelain and Dutch flower paintings. The original gardens have been re-created and contain an Orangery, c.1740, and an 18th-C ice house. *Open late Mar–Oct, Sun–Wed 13.30–17.30.* Charge. Gift shop and tearoom.

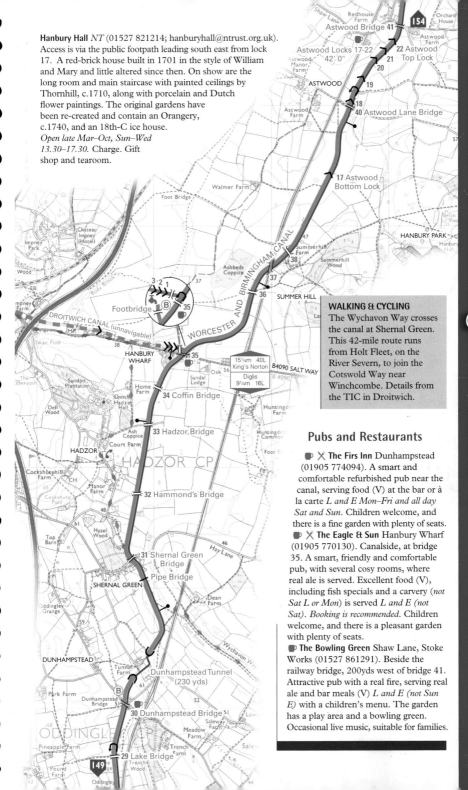

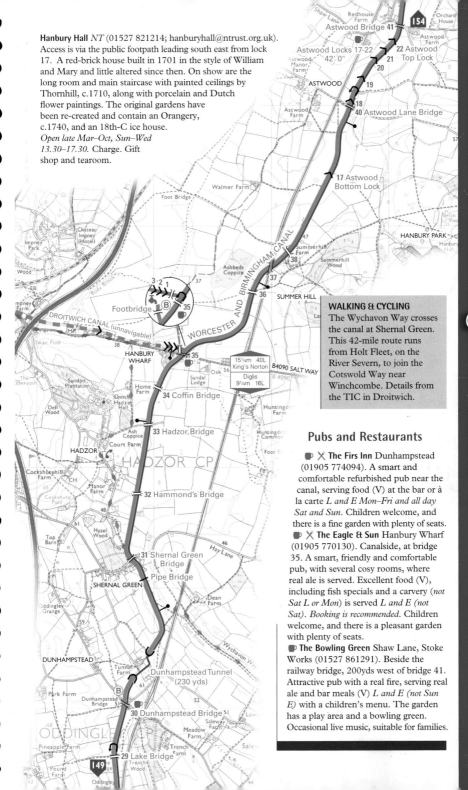

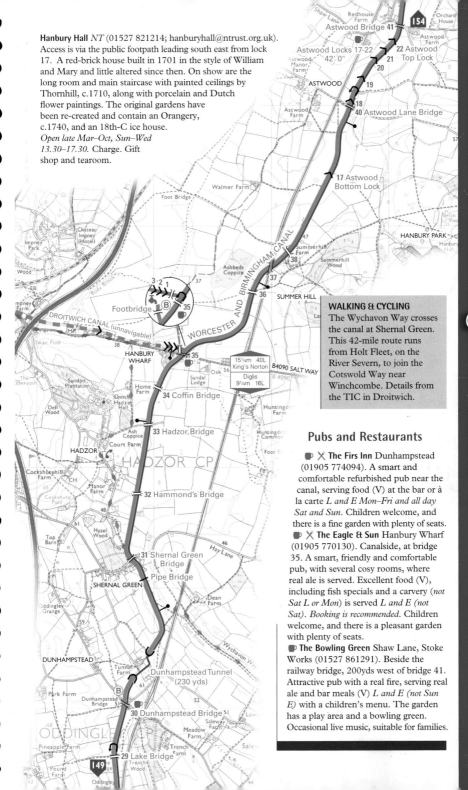

WALKING & CYCLING

The Wychavon Way crosses the canal at Shernal Green. This 42-mile route runs from Holt Fleet, on the River Severn, to join the Cotswold Way near Winchcombe. Details from the TIC in Droitwich.

Pubs and Restaurants

The Firs Inn Dunhampstead (01905 774094). A smart and comfortable refurbished pub near the canal, serving food (V) at the bar or à la carte *L and E Mon–Fri and all day Sat and Sun.* Children welcome, and there is a fine garden with plenty of seats.

The Eagle & Sun Hanbury Wharf (01905 770130). Canalside, at bridge 35. A smart, friendly and comfortable pub, with several cosy rooms, where real ale is served. Excellent food (V), including fish specials and a carvery (*not Sat L or Mon*) is served *L and E (not Sat). Booking is recommended.* Children welcome, and there is a pleasant garden with plenty of seats.

The Bowling Green Shaw Lane, Stoke Works (01527 861291). Beside the railway bridge, 200yds west of bridge 41. Attractive pub with a real fire, serving real ale and bar meals (V) *L and E (not Sun E)* with a children's menu. The garden has a play area and a bowling green. Occasional live music, suitable for families.

Map labels: Astwood Bridge 41, 154, Shaw Lane, Redhouse Farm, Orchard House, Astwood Farm, Astwood Locks 17-22 42' 0", 22 Astwood Top Lock, Astwood Manor Farm, 21, 20, 19, ASTWOOD, 18, 40 Astwood Lane Bridge, Astwood Farm, 17 Astwood Bottom Lock, HANBURY PARK, Hanbury Hall, Brick Kiln, Walmer Farm, Foot Bridge, Summerhill Wood, 38 Summerhill, 37, SUMMER HILL, 36, WORCESTER AND BIRMINGHAM CANAL, Château Impney (Hotel), Impney Park, Wood, EB, Ashbeds Coppice, 37, 3·2·1, Footbridge, 35, DROITWICH CANAL (unnavigable), MP, Swan Pool, 38, HANBURY WHARF, 35, 15¼m 40L King's Norton, 56, B4090 SALT WAY, Diglis 9¼m 16L, B 4090, Sandal Lodge, Oak, Sandpit Plantation, Home Farm, Church Hadzor, Hadzor Hall, Dell Pool, 34 Coffin Bridge, Huntingdon Farm, Dell Wood, Ash Coppice, 33 Hadzor Bridge, Huntingdon Common, Court Farm, HADZOR, HADZOR CP, Foot Br, Cockshutehill Farm, CH, 68, Manor Farm, Cockshute Pool, FB, 32 Hammond's Bridge, 48, Hazel Wood, 61, Top Barn, 46, Hay Lane, 31 Shernal Green Bridge, Pipe Bridge, SHERNAL GREEN, Oddingley Grange, Dean Farm, 59, Wychavon Way, DUNHAMPSTEAD, Tunnel Farm, Dunhampstead Tunnel (230 yds), Park Farm, 61, Dunhampstead Farm, 52, 30 Dunhampstead Bridge, 51, Meadow Farm, Saleway Farm, Pineapple Farm, ODDINGLEY CP, Trench Wood, Trench Farm, 29 Lake Bridge, 149, Pound Farm, Oddingley, 44

Tardebigge Locks

The canal now passes quietly through Stoke Works and approaches Stoke Wharf, from where the hills to the north east can be seen. Just through the bridge is the first lock for over a mile, and beyond it is a crowded mooring site, and then more locks, flanked by trees and pastureland. These locks, numbers 23–28, form the Stoke flight, but in fact there is only a breathing space of a few hundred yards, with a well-placed pub, before the first of the 30 Tardebigge Locks is reached just after Stoke Pound. Forward progress becomes a crawl as this great flight is climbed, but the pleasures of the surroundings make the effort worthwhile. The locks wind up through pretty, folding countryside, leaving the busy railway behind in the west. There are attractive, well-cared-for cottages scattered along the flight, generally near the bridges; their gardens overlook the canal. One of these cottages, between locks 31 and 32, by bridge 49, is available for holiday lets from the Landmark Trust (01628 825925), an organisation which was founded as a result of the demolition of Telford's handsome Junction House at Hurleston, on the Shropshire Union Canal. The locks themselves have great charm, being equipped throughout with traditional wooden gates and balance beams. Large paddles speed up locking, and so a reasonably well-co-ordinated crew of two can work through each lock quite quickly. The remote rural course of the canal takes it well wide of Bromsgrove, but Bromsgrove station is only 1 mile north west of bridge 51. Between locks 50 and 54 Tardebigge Reservoir can be seen behind an embankment on the east bank. This feeder reservoir is particularly popular with fishermen. As the reservoir is about 50ft below the summit level, a steam engine was installed to pump water up the hill. The engine house still stands near the canal. Tardebigge Top Lock, with a rise of 11ft, marks the end of the hard work. When the canal was built, there was a vertical boat lift here, but technical problems caused it to be replaced by the lock, and there is no trace of it now. Above the lock is Tardebigge Wharf, overlooked by the elegant spire of Tardebigge church, up on the hill to the east. At the wharf is an attractive BW maintenance yard, and a large mooring site. Leaving the wharf and its cottages behind, the canal vanishes into Tardebigge Tunnel, passing under a main road at the tunnel mouth. There now follows a most delightful stretch of canal, which winds through the hilly Worcestershire countryside: the flat Severn Valley now seems very distant as the canal plunges into Shortwood Tunnel.

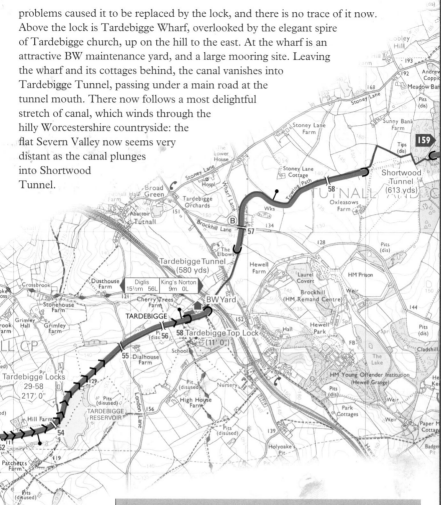

THOMAS' LAST WORKING DAYS

It was in May 1955 that the last load of coal was carried from the mines at Anglesey Basin to Townsends Flour Mill at Diglis Basin in Worcester in the *nb Thomas*, skippered by Ray White and pulled by Bob, the horse. The round trip of 103 miles was via Tardebigge, the New Main Line to Pudding Green and onto the Wednesbury Old Canal, then through Ryders Green Junction and down the eight locks to make a right turn at Doebank onto the Tame Valley Canal. A left turn at Rushall Junction brought the climb to Catshill, passing the Travellers Rest pub, once a popular overnight stop, but alas no longer there. After bearing right at Catshill Junction and left at Ogley a whole clutch of moored narrowboats, some full and some empty, would come into view at Anglesey Basin. Loading at the basin was swift and efficient (some remains of the chutes can still be seen today), with an average of a little under 30 boats being filled daily. *Thomas* carried 27 tons of coal back to Diglis, being towed through Wast Hills Tunnel by the tug, and worked through the Tardebigge flight 'like a bat out of hell'.

Stoke Works

Worcs. Now closed, this establishment was built in 1828 to pump brine (salt) from underground sources for industrial use, and provided much of the canal's trade (later gained by the railways). Now an industrial estate, where housing fronts the tree-lined canal.

Stoke Wharf

Worcs. A pretty canal settlement in the best tradition – a lock, a wharf, a boatyard and a warehouse – and a pleasant line of houses facing the canal. Stoke Wharf is the only compact element of Stoke Prior – perhaps the heart of the village was drawn to the canal when the latter was built, and has remained there ever since. Stoke Prior church, which is mainly of the 12th C, stands by itself a ¹/₂ mile north of the wharf, the other side of the busy railway junction. Stoke Prior is not a good place for shopping; it is better to obtain supplies at the settlement near bridge 42. There is a decent pub, however.

Avoncroft Museum of Buildings, Stoke Heath (01527 831363; www.avoncroft.org.uk). 1 mile north of Stoke Wharf, off the B4091. Old buildings rescued from demolition are re-erected and displayed here. Exhibits include an 18th-C post mill, a local nail and chain works, a 15th-C timber-framed house from Bromsgrove, a fully furnished post-war prefab and the 14th-C roof of Guesten Hall, Worcester. There is also a reconstruction of an Iron Age hut and the National Telephone Kiosk Collection, along with a three-seater earth closet from Leominster. *Open Mar and Nov, Tue–Thu, Sat and Sun 10.30–16.00; Apr–Jun and Sep–Oct, Tue–Sun 10.30–16.30 (17.00 weekends); Jul–Aug daily 10.30–17.00 (17.30 weekends).* Charge. Gift shop and café. Full programme of events.

Tardebigge

Worcs. (Stores at Aston Fields, about 1 mile north of bridge 51; PO at Finstall on the B4184, 1¼ miles north of the south portal of Tardebigge Tunnel). A small farming village flanking the main road. Apart from the settlement near the canal, the best part of the village is up on the 531ft hill, around the fine 18th-C church of St Bartholomew. Its delicate spire sits atop an airy Baroque bell-chamber and slender tower, designed by Frances Hiorn, who seemed not to bother with such inspirational ideas on the rest of the building. At the top of the locks a plaque commemorates the founding of the Inland Waterways Association in 1946 by L. T. C. Rolt and Robert Aickman, aboard the *nb Cressy*, which was moored here.

Tardebigge and Shortwood Tunnels 580yds and 613yds long respectively, these are two of the four tunnels on the 14-mile summit level of the Worcester & Birmingham Canal. Neither contains a towpath, and until the turn of the century a company tug used to pull all boats through Tardebigge, Shortwood and the great Wast Hills Tunnel. Navigators will find Shortwood Tunnel extremely wet and walkers will find the path diverted around the edge of a field.

WALKING & CYCLING
The Tourist Information Centre, Bromsgrove Museum, 26 Birmingham Road (01527 831809) has four leaflets giving details of 2-hour circular walks from Stoke Prior.

Pubs and Restaurants

Boat & Railway Shaw Lane, Stoke Works (01527 831065). Canalside, just south of bridge 42. Traditional pub with a fine terrace onto the canal. Real ale and bar meals (V) *L and E (not Sun)*. Skittle alley. The Worcestershire & Birmingham Canal Society have their headquarters here and meet on the *first Tue of the month, except Jul and Aug*. Between locks 22 and 23 opposite the pub there are handy ⚓ points.

✗ Navigation Behind Stoke Wharf on Hanbury Road, Stoke Prior (01527 870194). A fine spacious pub with a neat smoke room, serving real ale. Bar and restaurant meals (V) *L and E (not Sun E)*, with a paella evening on *Thur* (you must book for this). Children welcome in restaurant and lounge, and there is a garden. Live music *Wed*. Craft and garden centres nearby.

Queen's Head Sugarbrook Lane (01527 877777). Canalside at bridge 48. Popular and busy pub with good food and a carvery *L and E*, along with a large selection of real ales. Children welcome. Lovely waterside terrace, and fine floral displays. Large-screen TV. Handy for the Avoncroft Museum.

Boatyards

ⓑ **BW Tardebigge Yard** Tardebigge Top Lock (01564 784634). 🕯 🕯 🔧 Overnight mooring, long-term mooring, toilets.

ⓑ **Tardebigge Dry Dock** John Pinder & Son, Tardebigge (01527 876438).

ⓑ **Black Prince Holidays** Stoke Prior (01527 575115). 🕯 🔧 D Pump out, gas, narrowboat

hire, long-term mooring, boat building, boat sales, toilets, books, maps and gifts.

ⓑ **Anglo–Welsh Narrowboats** Wharf Lane, Tardebigge (01527 873898; www.anglowelsh. co.uk). 🕯 🔧 D Pump out, gas, narrowboat hire, day-hire craft, long-term mooring, books, maps and gifts.

Hanbury Junction (see page 153)

Alvechurch

East of Shortwood Tunnel and the surrounding fruit plantations, the canal emerges high up on the side of a low wooded hill, overlooking the modest valley of the River Arrow. The canal continues northward, winding steadily through this tranquil landscape until the small town of Alvechurch is reached. The town is set below the canal in a hollow, its church up on a hill; the canal winds tortuously along the steep hills round the outskirts, passing a boatyard and a canalside pub. Ahead, in the distance, is the ridge of hills that is pierced by Wast Hills Tunnel. To the north of Alvechurch the Crown Meadow Arm branches off to the east – *no boats are allowed to enter* and it remains a quiet haven for wildlife. A little further north an aqueduct carries the canal over a little lane that leads to Barnt Green. Beyond the aqueduct and through bridge 65, Lower Bittell Reservoir comes into view, beside and below the navigation. The canal crosses the valley on an embankment; at the north end of this is a pretty cottage, which stands at the point where the feeder from Upper Bittell Reservoir enters the canal. With these on two sides and an overflow weir and the lower reservoir on the third, the house seems to be virtually surrounded by water. Leaving the reservoirs, the canal curves through a slight cutting to Hopwood, where there is a pub and a busy main road crossing. To the north the canal enters a grander cutting, and, after passing under a fine, big, arched bridge, the mighty Wast Hills Tunnel beckons. The ridge of hills that this tunnel penetrates serves as an important geographical boundary: to the south of it is the rolling open countryside of rural Worcestershire, while to the north of the tunnel is Warwickshire, and the southernmost extremities of the Black Country.

● **Alvechurch**
Worcs. PO, tel, stores, garage, bank, station. A pleasant little town with some fine half-timbered houses, Alvechurch is situated at the bottom of a hollow and surrounded by folds of green hills. The church stands alone on a hill; it is of Norman origin but was largely rebuilt by Butterfield in 1861. There are some interesting monuments inside.

● **Bittell reservoirs**
These two reservoirs were built by the canal company, the upper to feed the canal, the lower being a compensation to local mill owners for the loss of water resulting from construction of the canal. The reservoirs are now popular with both anglers and bird watchers.

● **Hopwood**
West Midlands. Provisions are available at the mobile home site, 200yds north west of bridge 67. More a name than a village, Hopwood is merely a small settlement. A fast main road bisects the area.

Pubs and Restaurants

● ✕ **The Weighbridge** Alvechurch Boat Centre, Scarfield Wharf, Alvechurch (0121 445 5111; www.the-weighbridge.co.uk). Traditional style pub, built around part of an old weighbridge. Food (V) is served at *breakfast (book), L and E (book Sun L)*, and takeaways and sandwiches can be prepared, *as long as you give prior notice.* Children welcome, and there is a garden. *Closed Tue and Wed.*

● **Crown** Withybed Green, Alvechurch (0121 445 2300). Canalside, at bridge 61. Pleasant country pub serving real ale. Bar meals (V) are available *L and E (not Sun).* Children

welcome, and there are seats outside amongst the geraniums.

● **The Swan Hotel** Swan Street, Alvechurch (0121 445 5402). A fine large inn serving real ale, and bar snacks *L, and E (Thur–Sat).* Children welcome *until 20.00,* and there is outside seating. Quiz night *Thur.*

● **Hopwood House** Redditch Road, Hopwood (0121 445 1716). Canalside, at bridge 67. Spacious and tastefully refurbished pub with a large public bar, serving real ale. Bar meals (V) *all day, every day.* Children welcome *until 21.00.* Large grassy garden and an enclosed play area.

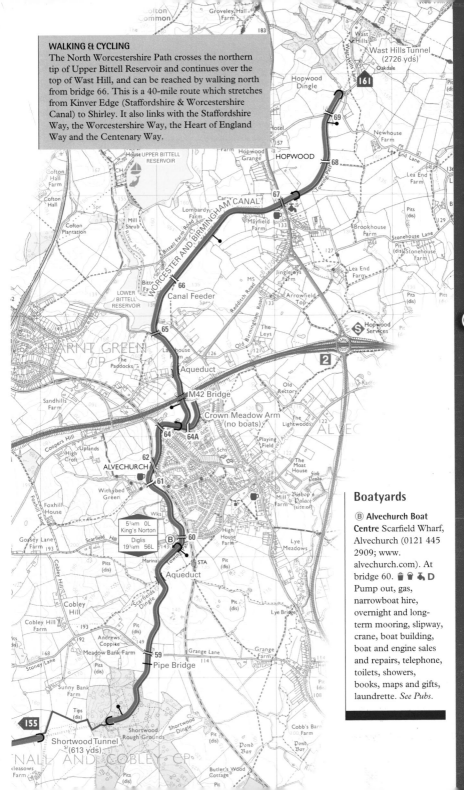

WALKING & CYCLING

The North Worcestershire Path crosses the northern tip of Upper Bittell Reservoir and continues over the top of Wast Hill, and can be reached by walking north from bridge 66. This is a 40-mile route which stretches from Kinver Edge (Staffordshire & Worcestershire Canal) to Shirley. It also links with the Staffordshire Way, the Worcestershire Way, the Heart of England Way and the Centenary Way.

Boatyards

Ⓑ **Alvechurch Boat Centre** Scarfield Wharf, Alvechurch (0121 445 2909; www. alvechurch.com). At bridge 60. Pump out, gas, narrowboat hire, overnight and long-term mooring, slipway, crane, boat building, boat and engine sales and repairs, telephone, toilets, showers, books, maps and gifts, laundrette. *See Pubs.*

Wast Hills Tunnel

The built-up area is revealed as soon as the canal leaves the cutting at the north end of Wast Hills Tunnel: to the west is King's Norton, while all around are new houses and light industry. Bridge 71 is the best access point for the village and its shops; just past it is the old canal house at King's Norton Junction. Here the Stratford-on-Avon Canal joins at right angles – the disused guillotine mechanism of the celebrated King's Norton Stop Lock can be seen a short way along it. Boats heading south east should turn off along the Stratford-on-Avon Canal here (*see* page 134). To the north of the junction, the Worcester & Birmingham passes through an industrial area, but thankfully seems to hold the factories at bay on one side, while a railway, the main line from Worcester and the south west to Birmingham, draws alongside on its west flank. Canal and railway together drive through the middle of Cadbury's Bournville works, which is interesting rather than oppressive. Beyond it is Bournville station, followed by a cutting. It is inadvisable to leave your boat unattended in this area.

WALKING & CYCLING
There is no direct route for walkers and cyclists over Wast Hill Tunnel. Heading north, follow Wast Hills Lane, and turn right at Redhill Road. Take the first left into Bracken Way, and then turn right at Longdales Road. Follow this road for almost 1 mile as it bends to the left, then turn left at Primrose Hill and continue down to rejoin the canal at bridge 70.

King's Norton
West Midlands. Tel, stores, garage, bank, station.
The village still survives as a recognisable entity, for the suburbs of Birmingham have now extended all around it, and the small village green, the old grammar school buildings and the soaring spire of the church ensure that it will remain so. The church is set back a little from the green in an attractive churchyard, and is mainly of the 14th C, although two Norman windows can still be seen. The grammar school is even older – it was probably founded by King Edward III in 1344. An interesting puzzle is that the upper storey is apparently older than the ground floor... The school declined during the last century and was closed in 1875. Now restored, it is an ancient monument.
Wast Hills Tunnel Sometimes referred to as King's Norton Tunnel, this 2726yd bore is one of the longest in the country. It is usually difficult to see right through, and there are plenty of drips from the roof in even the driest weather. A steam-powered – and later a diesel-powered – tunnel tug service used to operate in the days of horse-drawn boats, as there is no towpath. The old iron brackets and insulators that still line the roof were installed to carry telegraph lines through the tunnel. Grandiose bridges (nos. 69 and 70) span the cuttings at either end.
Bournville Garden Factory The creation of the Cadbury family, who moved their cocoa and chocolate manufacturing business south from the centre of Birmingham. The Bournville estate was begun in the late 1800s and is an interesting example of controlled suburban development. There were once old canal wharves here, which became disused when most of the ingredients travelled by rail – but the sidings closed in the late 1960s and now regrettably everything comes by road.
Cadbury World Linden Road (Information line 0121 451 4180). It is by the factory and signposted from the canal, where there are moorings. An exhibition dedicated to the history and the love of chocolate. Audio-visual displays, a jungle to explore, and Victorian Birmingham. *Open Mon–Fri 10.00–15.00, Sat and Sun 09.30–16.30 (restricted in winter – please telephone). Reservation for admission is advised, telephone 0121 451 4159.* Charge.
Selly Manor and Minworth Greaves Sycamore Road, Bournville (0121 472 0199). Two half-timbered Birmingham houses of the 13th- and early 14th-C re-erected in the 1920s and 1930s in Bournville. They contain a collection of old furniture and domestic equipment. *Open all year Tue–Fri 10.00–17.00, also Apr–Oct, Sat and Sun 14.00–17.00; closed Nov–Mar, Sat–Mon.* Charge. The nearest point of access from the canal is at Bournville station: walk west to the Cadbury's entrance. There is a public right of way (Birdcage Walk) through the works: bear right at the fork, then turn right at the village green. The two houses are close by, on the left. Selly Oak and Bournville both have a *PO*.

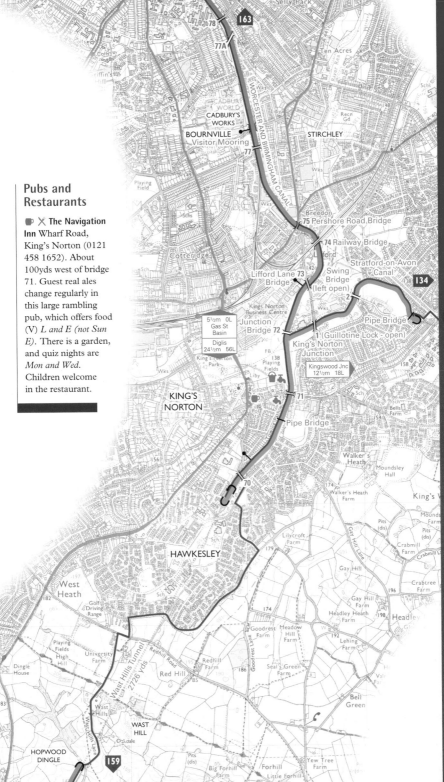

Pubs and Restaurants

🍺 ✕ **The Navigation Inn** Wharf Road, King's Norton (0121 458 1652). About 100yds west of bridge 71. Guest real ales change regularly in this large rambling pub, which offers food (V) *L and E (not Sun E)*. There is a garden, and quiz nights are *Mon and Wed.* Children welcome in the restaurant.

SELLY PARK

163

78

77A

77

CADBURY WORLD

CADBURY'S WORKS

BOURNVILLE
Visitor Mooring

STIRCHLEY

WORCESTER AND BIRMINGHAM CANAL

Breedon
75 Pershore Road Bridge

74 Railway Bridge

Stratford-on-Avon Canal

134

Swing Bridge
(left open)

2

Pipe Bridge

Lifford Lane **73** Bridge

Kings Norton
Business Centre

Junction
Bridge **72**

1 (Guillotine Lock - open)

5½m 0L
Gas St
Basin

Diglis
24½m 56L

King's Norton
Junction

King's Norton
Park

138
Playing Fields

Kingswood Jnc
12½m 18L

KING'S NORTON

71

Pipe Bridge

Walker's Heath

Moundsley Hall

King's

70

HAWKESLEY

179

Lilycroft
Farm

Gay Hill

Crabmill
Farm

West Heath

Golf
Driving
Range

156

182

HAWKESLEY

174

Goodrest
Farm

Meadow
Hill
Farm

Gay Hill
Farm

Headley Heath
Farm

196

Crabtree
Farm

198

Headley

Playing Fields
High Hill

University
Farm

Dingle
House

197

183

Wast Hills Tunnel
2726 yds

Redhill Road

Red Hill

Redhill
Farm

186

192

Seal's Green
Farm

Lehing
Farm

Wast
Hills

WAST
HILL

Oakdale

Bell
Green

HOPWOOD
DINGLE

159

Big Forhill
Farm

Forhill

Little Forhill
Farm

Yew Tree
Farm

Soon the railway vanishes briefly behind the buildings of Selly Oak. Between bridge 80 and the next, skewed, railway bridge is the site of the junction with the Dudley Canal, but no trace remains here now of either the junction or the canal itself. North of here the canal and railway together shrug off industry and town, and head north on an embankment towards Birmingham in splendid isolation and attractive surroundings. Below on either side is the green spaciousness of residential Edgbaston, its botanical gardens and woods. A hospital is on the west side. The University of Birmingham is on the east side; among its many large buildings the most conspicuous is the Chamberlain Campanile Tower, which was erected in 1900. At one of the bridges near the University, two Roman forts used to stand; but most evidence of them was obliterated by the building of the canal and railway. Only a reconstructed part of the larger fort now exists. There is a useful Sainsbury's just south of bridge 80. Past the University's moorings, canal and railway enter a cutting, in which their enjoyable seclusion from the neighbourhood is complete; the charming old bridges are high, while the cutting is steep and always lined by overhanging foliage. It is a remarkable approach to Birmingham. The railway is the canal's almost constant companion, dipping away here and there to reappear a short distance further on; but trains are not too frequent, and in a way their occasional appearance heightens the remoteness that attaches to this length of canal. At one stage the two routes pass through short tunnels side by side: the canal's tunnel, Edgbaston, is the northernmost of the five on this canal and the only one with a towpath through it. It is a mere 105yds long. The Worcester & Birmingham Canal now completes its delightful approach to Birmingham. The railway disappears underneath in a tunnel to New Street station, while the canal passes Holiday Wharf and makes a sharp left turn to the basin. The terminus of the Worcester & Birmingham Canal is the former stop lock at Gas Street Basin; this is known as Worcester Bar, for originally there was a physical barrier here between the Worcester & Birmingham Canal and the much older Birmingham Canal. The latter refused to allow a junction, and for several years goods had to be transhipped at this point from one canal to the other. This absurd situation was remedied by an Act of Parliament in 1815, by which a stop lock was allowed to be inserted to connect the two canals. Nowadays the stop gates are kept open and one can pass straight through, on to the Birmingham Canal (*see* page 35). Don't leave your boat unattended in this area, although Gas Street Basin should be OK.

The Dudley Canal This canal used to join the Worcester & Birmingham Canal at Selly Oak, thus providing a southern bypass round Birmingham. The eastern end of the canal has been closed for many years, and will certainly remain so. The tremendously long (3795yd) Lappal Tunnel, now collapsed, emerged 2 miles from Selly Oak. This bore was more like a drainpipe than a navigable tunnel – it was only 7ft 9in wide, a few inches wider than the boats that used it, and headroom was limited to a scant 6ft. Boats were assisted through by a pumping engine flushing water along the tunnel, but it must still have been a nightmarishly claustrophobic trip for the boatmen.

● **Edgbaston**
West Midlands. A desirable residential suburb of Birmingham, Edgbaston is bisected by the canal.
Botanical Gardens Edgbaston. Founded over 100

years ago. Alpine Garden, lily pond and a collection of tropical birds. *Open daily.*
Perrott's Folly Waterworks Road, off Monument Road, Edgbaston. About ¾ mile west of bridge 86, not far from the Plough & Harrow Hotel. This seven-storey tower was built in 1758 by John Perrott and claims to be Birmingham's most eccentric building. One theory as to its origin is that Mr Perrott could, from its height, gaze upon his late wife's grave 10 miles away. One of the Two Towers of Gondor, featured in J.R.R. Tolkien's *Lord of the Rings*, is thought to have been based upon this building. Tolkien's last address in Birmingham was at 4 Highfield Road, opposite the Plough & Harrow. From 1884–1984 the folly was used as a weather station and was subsequently renovated. *Open Easter–Sep, Sun and B Hols 14.00–17.00.* Modest charge. Tearoom.

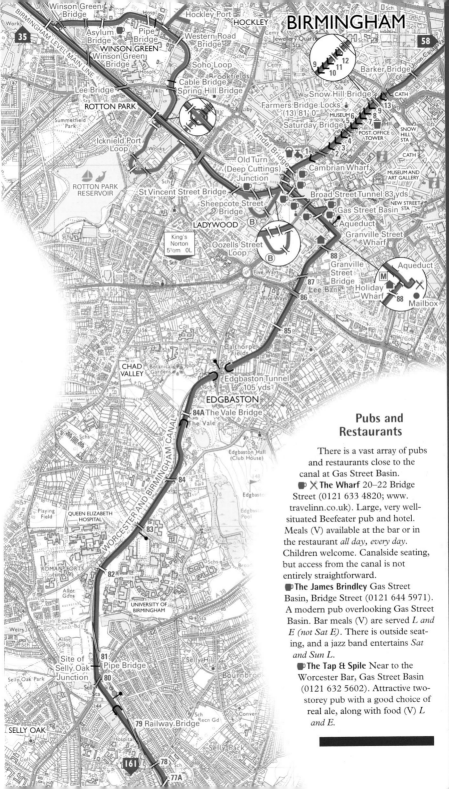

Pubs and Restaurants

There is a vast array of pubs and restaurants close to the canal at Gas Street Basin.

The Wharf 20–22 Bridge Street (0121 633 4820; www.travelinn.co.uk). Large, very well-situated Beefeater pub and hotel. Meals (V) available at the bar or in the restaurant *all day, every day*. Children welcome. Canalside seating, but access from the canal is not entirely straightforward.

The James Brindley Gas Street Basin, Bridge Street (0121 644 5971). A modern pub overlooking Gas Street Basin. Bar meals (V) are served *L and E (not Sat E)*. There is outside seating, and a jazz band entertains *Sat and Sun L*.

The Tap & Spile Near to the Worcester Bar, Gas Street Basin (0121 632 5602). Attractive two-storey pub with a good choice of real ale, along with food (V) *L and E*.

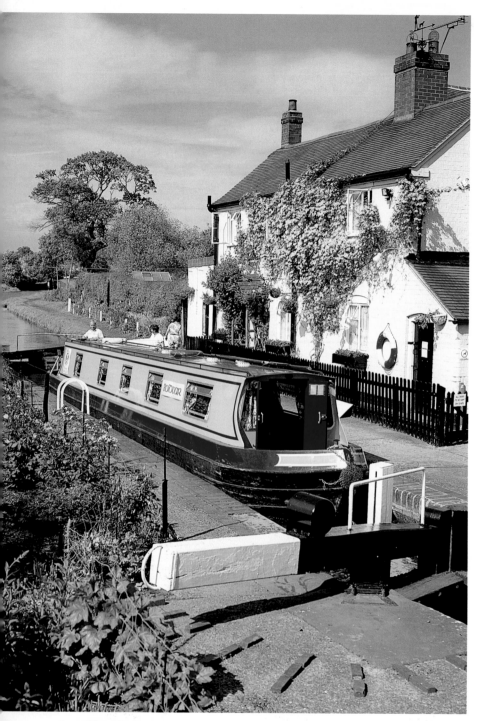

Astwood Bottom Lock (see page 153)

INDEX